The SCHMUCK
in My Office

The SCHMUCK
in My Office

HOW TO DEAL EFFECTIVELY WITH
DIFFICULT PEOPLE AT WORK

JODY FOSTER, M.D.,
with MICHELLE JOY, M.D.

ST. MARTIN'S PRESS ≈ NEW YORK

To my dearest Rafael, who brought light back to my life

www.stmartins.com

The Library of Congress Cataloging-in-Publication Data is available upon request.

ISBN 978-1-2500-7567-3 (hardcover)
ISBN 978-1-4668-8711-4 (e-book)

Our books may be purchased in bulk for promotional, educational, or business use. Please contact your local bookseller or the Macmillan Corporate and Premium Sales Department at 1-800-221-7945, extension 5442, or by e-mail at MacmillanSpecial Markets@macmillan.com.

First Edition: April 2017

10 9 8 7 6 5 4 3 2 1

CONTENTS

PART I

Meet the Schmuck

Introduction

When I was in business school, a classmate came to me with a disturbing story about his office. "Some guy, we think we know who it is," he said, "goes to the bathroom every day, takes a dump, and after he's done, smears his dirty toilet paper on the door of the stall. A little z pattern. What IS that?"

I received questions about behavior all the time in business school, though I'll admit this was an unusual one. In a class full of aspiring bankers and hedge funders, I was the psychiatrist. I became the person whom everyone came to with questions . . . questions about fights between coworkers, about intolerable bosses, about relationships, and, yes, about bizarre behavior. I enjoyed answering them, offering my insight about potential causes, possible solutions, interesting explanations. I looked forward to hearing what anecdotes my classmates would bring me and how my explanations and recommendations were received.

As a psychiatrist, you quickly get used to witnessing all sorts of seemingly extraordinary behavior. You work in psychiatric hospitals, in emergency rooms, in clinics, on the medical floors. You grow accustomed to interacting with people who think they're immortal, with people who think the devil is after them. Your days are filled with people who try to cut themselves, hang themselves, suffocate themselves. You hear horrendous stories of abuse—sexual and physical—some beyond your wildest imagination of what a person could do. Or endure.

I once had a patient who believed he had a bionic ear implanted by the government, in order to transmit classified information about impeding intergalactic war. Another one who tried to shoot an airplane out of the sky. But, believe it or not, what seems unbelievable can almost become expected. The atypical becomes typical; the horrific can seem routine. Your friends and colleagues are other psychiatrists and psychologists, and everyone has stories like this that fill their days.

Already a psychiatrist when I started business school, I was suddenly surrounded by people who found even commonplace interactions compelling. They were fascinated by their coworkers, and it was fun for me to explain the various permutations of office drama. I loved seeing how bent out of shape they got about people—their bosses, their coworkers, their direct reports— even their spouses. They came to me with tales of people they called *real schmucks*: those they neither liked nor understood. A quick explanation from me, and they were suddenly very relieved, very grateful. I realized how little people knew about why people acted the way they did and how seemingly simple insights could be extremely effective. Sometimes people wanted to know what to do about a coworker, but at other times they seemed to want to know *why* the coworker acted a certain way. More than anything, I realized that just a little bit of understanding goes a long way in helping someone empathize and even deal with the schmuck in their office. Going to business school provided an avenue for me to really see what other people said and thought about their work environments. Instead of being surrounded by people who were trained in, worked in, and inundated with understanding and analyzing behavior, I was now the one and only one with that skill set. And I liked it. It was from this experience that I realized just how much I wanted to use those abilities to help others in their workplace environments.

From those classroom discussions came a career of helping others understand individual and group dynamics at work. While I continued in more typical areas of psychiatry—running locked adult inpatient units and eventually becoming chair of the department of psychiatry at the nation's oldest hospital—I also combined my mental health experience with business training and those eye-opening classroom discussions. I worked as a consultant assessing entrepreneurial teams for venture capital companies. While in this role, I helped investors make backing decisions by allowing them to better understand the people in the company they were about to invest in and how they functioned together. Ultimately, I offered investment advice that was based on understanding personalities and relationships. In the morning I would see people suffering from schizophrenia, and in the afternoon I would help instruct and manage business, financial, and employment decisions using the same, albeit adapted, skill set of observing, asking, and figuring out what makes people tick.

I also developed a publicly offered "professionalism program" and, in that role, continue to help health care organizations create and maintain professional working environments. I began by consulting within my hospital system but now see individual consultations from all over and make recommendations to others on how to set up similar programs. Much like my function in those early business school conversations, I analyze how workers can better function alongside one another. In efforts to preserve safe and satisfying workplace environments, I assess problematic situations and develop plans to improve their functioning.

In these roles, I aim to figure out how difficult people and disruptive workplace behavior can be best addressed. No matter where people work, they bring their personalities with them, and oftentimes those personalities seriously, negatively affect the workplace environment. Bullying, micromanaging, and being entitled are all common problems at work, but thankfully they are all troubles that can be successfully addressed. Solutions can include everything from coaching to talk therapy for disruptive individuals to structural changes within the workplace environment itself.

As we will see, early and direct intervention really does work best. By the time I see referrals for troublesome behavior, the disruption has progressed pretty far. The smearer, for example, might have found new and even more disturbing uses for his evacuations. No one wants behaviors to get to this point. Instead, his coworkers could have learned to recognize his passive aggressive remarks and figured out what was bothering him before he started smearing feces. And by writing this book, I hope to show readers how to take the important steps toward identifying and rectifying disruptive behaviors before they get too unprofessional, uncomfortable, unsafe, or, in the case of this poor fellow, unsanitary.

And that idea is where the title of the book comes from. So many calls to me quite literally begin with, "I've got this schmuck in my office, and I should've called you about him ten years ago." The supervisor often had the unrealistic hope that the bad actor would simply stop causing trouble. But as the problems worsened over time, the supervisor felt increasingly ineffectual and avoidant, and the referral arrived laden with anger and resentment. The individual in question is most often not a schmuck at all. She's just being herself and no one ever really told her that her ways were causing problems.

The title thus refers to the frustration and annoyance that so many of us feel when we just don't understand someone or why that person is behaving in a way that doesn't make sense to us. It's easy to get angry and label someone a jerk or a schmuck. It's much harder to try to understand the underpinnings of why he or she approaches the situation that way. But we must try, and in so doing we will learn about our colleagues and ourselves and create a safer, healthier, better-functioning workplace.

Realizing what people do and don't know about how people function, I realized that I could yet again bring my psychiatric expertise into the workplace. In particular, I began to understand the power that being able to identify types of dysfunction can have in emboldening us to make better workplaces. From those business school discussions to my consulting experience and frequent conversations with friends and family members, I decided to help people understand workplace problems. I want people to know why the workplace can become disruptive and what can be done about it.

Just as disruptive behavior can and does show up anywhere and everywhere, this book can and should be read by anyone who works with other people. I will explain how interactions among coworkers can become maladaptive by examining the basics of personality traits, their development, and how they contribute to impaired performance and overall stress in the workplace. I will explain how to identify problematic behavior, how to explain it by understanding the personality traits behind it, and how to remedy it. Sometimes this can mean taking a look at ourselves and understanding our own role in creating or maintaining the behaviors.

And at times it may mean getting someone help either within or outside the organization.

This approach, however, requires a change in the way we approach disruptions around us. People are uncomfortable with things that are unpleasant—whether fear, sadness, anxiety, or illness—and try to avoid them. That evasion takes many forms. People avoid confronting those who upset them. People avoid bringing up their feelings or stay away from people that make them uncomfortable altogether. People think that systems can't change, that coworkers won't listen. People are afraid that they will get in trouble. People feel that they should be expected to endure things that are making them uneasy in the workplace. People think that certain positions of authority allow people to behave inappropriately.

People are wrong.

I'm writing this book to start a conversation. I'm on a personal crusade to get people to talk to one another, directly and honestly. Miraculous advances in technology have improved communication and efficiency tremendously, and yet they have added layers of separation between us. It's even easier now to avoid things, since there's a mode of communication customized to everyone's level of tolerance for intimacy. In many ways, this is great because most people can find a way to comfortably communicate. But we still have conflicts, and they still upset us, and we still need to address them. Oftentimes, conflicts cannot be avoided. Understanding when and how to handle them appropriately is the key to a better workplace for everyone.

In the following chapters, I will make broad generalizations about people and group them accordingly. I will describe anecdotes that you will recognize, because they are ubiquitous. My goal is for you to understand that the associated behaviors are of a type and are usually not driven by malice. There is great benefit in categorizing, because by understanding types, what drives them, and what works best to manage them, you will develop the skills to work well with anyone. This book is not intended to diagnose and no reader will become an expert in psychiatry, but it will give people a way to figure out the people and behaviors around them.

We will cover arrogance, distraction, social inadequacy, obsessiveness, manipulation, and simply weird people. I will suggest strategies for interaction and, if necessary, interventions to improve relationships. Know, however, that people are by no means one-dimensional. We each display many, many types of personality traits, and they all come together to make each of us who we are. These descriptions are not meant to lead you to overdefine or pigeonhole the people around you—they are simply presented to guide you in understanding and handling aspects of your relationships with them. Perhaps most important, in beginning to understand people, you can feel more empathy for their situations and why they may act as they do.

What Is Disruptive Behavior?

Disruptive behavior can take many forms. Yelling, throwing things, and assaulting people are pretty obvious ways to be disruptive. Making comments designed to condescend, belittle, intimidate, undermine confidence, or imply inadequacy or incompetence is common. Using one's authority, be it one's leadership role or even one's physical size, to take interpersonal liberties is yet another way to be difficult in the office. Choosing to "do your own thing" and not engage with your team can even be a problem for others. Being afraid to complete a task and taking steps to avoid it can cause trouble. The potential for difficult behavior is everywhere.

Sometimes difficult behavior is easy to spot. It's hard to miss people yelling obscenities or throwing things around the office. Sometimes, however, difficult behavior can be more insidious or passive. An employee who fails to give appropriate credit or withholds needed information, for example, may be disruptive, and so can forgetting how to do tasks or constantly misplacing needed materials. On the other hand, an individual who repeatedly speaks up about ways to improve the workplace or gives constructive negative feedback may be viewed as disruptive, when she actually is not. In some ways, the more egregious behavior is easiest to deal with because it is the simplest to spot and often has a straightforward solution through the reporting or management process. However, it is the more insidious behavior that creeps along, ruining hours or days of others' time, seemingly without recourse.

So how do we define this behavior that so easily throws off the workplace? Often, describing it is the hardest part. We bring our own experiences and biases to the table, and they affect us each differently. What totally irritates someone might be valued by someone else. The situation might be so subtle that we feel that something is wrong, but we don't know what it is. We need to examine the potential for difficult behavior anytime we walk away from an interaction feeling unexpectedly confused or negative. We might feel embarrassed, angry, sad, or frustrated. These emotions all have various causes, but in the workplace, they are flags for potential interpersonal problems. If the interaction continues to bother us, keeps popping up in our mind, comes up in our dreams, or interferes with other parts of our day, we should investigate further.

In some sense, I have to say that you'll know disruptive behavior when you see it. You'll know when it happens to you. How? You'll feel it. The feeling will be idiosyncratic: clear or confusing, but catered exactly to you and the type of person you are. Its level of importance to you, the extent to which it affects you, the intensity with which you'll feel something must be done about it all come later. Step 1 is having the confidence to recognize it and know that it's wrong. Step 2 is recognizing that change may involve some dedication to understanding and accommodating the situation, even if you find it largely located in another person.

But you may not want to simply take my word for it. So I'll do my best to give you a little more information on just what exactly this disruptive behavior is. In the end, though, I trust you may only truly understand it when you have experienced it. And chances are, you already have.

It is also important to note that many companies have their own definitions of and policies about difficult behavior, so it might be interesting to look at how they are defined in your workplace setting. This is particularly true when deciding when to refer up for additional help, as will be discussed in future chapters.

Much of the professional understanding of so-called *disruptive behavior* originated from scholarship on how children act. This parallel serves as a historical point of comparison on understanding the schmuck in the office. It is also a way to introduce thinking about the behavior of others from a more empathic place of understanding.

The literature on disruptive behavior in children is straightforward about what is considered a problem. The behavior of children is said to be disruptive when it violates the rights of others or major societal norms. We can similarly apply this standard to working adults.

Another important point is that problematic behavior is significant in children when it is observed in multiple settings. The *Diagnostic and Statistical Manual of Mental Disorders* advises clinicians that the behaviors will be witnessed by parents, teachers, peers, coaches, and others. The same is true for adults. When someone is being disruptive in the workplace, they are likely to be disruptive in other settings, as well. By looking at workplace interactions, we can often see patterns of how individuals will interact with their significant others, with their family members, and with their friends. If it's only happening with you, pardon, but it may have more to do with you than with the other person. Any information on how an individual interacts with others—from their coworkers to their grandparents—is data to better help us understand what the problem might be and how to address it.

The very same behaviors that are a problem to the workplace can be easily observed in children: disrespectful language, name calling, throwing objects, refusing to complete tasks, interrupting meetings, and bullying, to name a few. Looking at patterns of behavior in children also points out important approaches to help. For one, early intervention is key. Delays in addressing any form of problematic behavior allow it to crystallize, which decreases the chances for a successful intervention. Strategies that may have worked at an earlier stage may no longer be effective after the pattern has been allowed to continue unobstructed—and perhaps at times even rewarded. The child who gets an ice cream cone for a tantrum can easily be the employee that gets promoted after bullying someone.

Thinking similarly about children and adults who are having problems interacting with others can help remove some of the anger from the interaction. Though we may be frustrated by the child who throws a tantrum in the shopping mall, by stepping outside the situation we can also see that the child does not intend to cause a headache. It is often difficult to appreciate this fact, but neither, for the most part, does the coworker set a goal of being difficult to work with. By better understanding the development of personality styles and character types, we are able to have more empathy and appreciation for why people act the way they do. Even when it's hard to work with them.

Another interesting parallel exists between the interventions for children and those for working adults. Addressing disruptive behavior follows many of the principles of effective parenting and may involve changing the behavior of multiple individuals. To change the child's behavior, the parent often needs to change his or hers. To change a coworker's behavior, you may need to change yours. Limits often need to be set and reinforced. Communication needs to be clear and understandable. And no change happens quickly.

Why Do We Care About Difficult Behavior?

While the early scholarly literature on disruptive behavior tended to focus on children, attention quickly expanded to include understanding problems in the workplace. Perhaps psychiatrists started with children because of the universal experience of having been a child and having been around children. But as the global economy changed the types and settings of available employment, workplace culture and its difficulties became an increasingly important area of study.

As small businesses grew into corporations and people began to work in increasingly complex settings alongside more and more strangers, the potential for disruptive behaviors also grew.

A lot of the literature on disruptive workplace behavior concerns medical settings. This academic trend likely occurred for multiple reasons. For one, the people conducting the research had probably experienced a lot of disruptive behavior during their training—whether in college, medical school, graduate school, research labs, or residency—as well as during their subsequent employment as doctors. They were, therefore, motivated to investigate it. However, an interesting historical anecdote relates to something called the Joint Commission. The Joint Commission is the U.S. organization that accredits hospitals; its goal is improving health care quality and value. Hospitals seek such accreditation in order to receive approval for certain types of federal funding. Part of the contemporary accreditation process is to demonstrate a policy for addressing disruptive behavior because of its potential to destabilize hospital safety.

In July 2008, a Sentinel Event Alert was sent to participating health care organizations. A *Sentinel Event* is defined by the Joint Commission as "an unexpected occurrence involving death or serious physical or psychological injury or risk thereof." Such events "signal the need for immediate investigation and response." Sentinel Event Alert 40 was an atypical alert, a report entitled "Behaviors That Undermine a Culture of Safety." The opening paragraph read:

> *Intimidating and disruptive behaviors can foster medical errors, . . . contribute to poor patient satisfaction and to preventable adverse outcomes, . . . increase the cost of care . . . and cause qualified clinicians, administrators and managers to seek new positions in more professional environments. . . . Safety and quality of patient care is dependent on teamwork, communication, and a collaborative work environment. To assure quality and to promote a culture of safety, health care organizations must address the problem of behaviors that threaten the performance of the health care team.*

This announcement created new responsibilities for health care organizations. Now, hospitals were required to have processes for reporting and investigating disruptive behavior. They were also required to document outcomes of such investigations and to have adequate staff training on these issues.

In truth, this is how my position as the head of a professionalism program came about. This federal requirement was largely an impetus for my consulting role in maintaining professional workplace environments in hospitals. At the same time, the requirement had other important effects, including encouraging organizations to improve how they defined, described, and addressed disruptive behaviors.

Difficult behavior can appear anywhere, and different fields tend to attract certain kinds of disruptive behaviors. In corporations, ruthlessness can be perceived as a successful strategy for getting ahead. The actions are often rewarded despite making people feel uncomfortable, or worse. This pattern is common in Narcissus, for example, as we will see in a later chapter. What is considered okay behavior for the CEO of an expanding business may be different from what is expected of someone in a seminary. That's an extreme comparison, of course, but it is true that the context of a workplace is its own culture that often determines what is considered acceptable behavior and what is not. But just because something is currently considered part of the workplace culture does not mean it is right. It is never right for someone to be discriminated against, harassed, belittled, or insulted, no matter the context.

Difficult people can be huge problems for an organization. In addition to single individuals feeling uncomfortable, angered, upset, or otherwise perturbed by someone's behavior, the company as a functional unit can experience profound difficulties. How employees treat one another affects their ability to work together but also their feeling toward the job and organization as a whole. And people don't like to put in the work at places they just don't like or like to be at. When they are surrounded by many difficult people or beleaguered by just one, employees can be less motivated and less committed to their jobs. This effect can begin to influence other workers until the productivity or creativity of an entire organization slows to a halt.

In one survey of fifty U.S. hospitals, results indicated that both nurses and doctors were considered offenders of difficult behavior. Such actions caused tension, irritation, and impaired relationships with others and as well as negative effects on relaying information, working in teams, and even sustained employment (Rosenstein and O'Daniel 2005; Martin 2008). Such disruption has been tied to serious downstream effects like decreased quality of work, safety problems, errors in patient care, and staffing shortages. These interactions may not represent particularly rare relationships, as a number of studies have shown that many—even a vast majority of—adverse clinical outcomes in hospitals are related to dysfunctional workplace behavior (Martin 2008). Unfortunately, but perhaps not surprisingly, patient satisfaction is often negatively affected, too. There have even been settlements awarded to the tune of hundreds of thousands of dollars for patients who have felt bullied by their physicians (Martin 2008).

Even when there is observation of dysfunctional behavior and its relation to undesirable outcomes, people don't speak up. The most common reasons cited for this lack of reporting include fear of punishment or retaliation, a feeling that the behavior will continue regardless of intervention, and perceived lack of assistance with taking needed steps (Rosenstein 2002). Nonetheless, even in workplaces populated with difficult interactions, members feel that they would benefit from increased time and space for discussion, clearer policies to define acceptable and unacceptable behavior, and more educational opportunities about how to address work-place disruption.

The studies of medical settings are likely applicable to most or all organizations. If any one of us reflects on our careers working with people, it would be the exception rather than the rule were we truly unable to recall some disruptive behavior. The complex interplay of situations, events, and personal traits that we bring into an office setting makes occasional struggle and conflict inevitable. This difficult behavior is important to understand and manage because of its multiplicity of negative effects on the affected individual, on coworkers, and on the success of a business, let alone on the person who may be seen as perpetrating the problems.

Difficult Personalities

Okay, so what do we have so far? Disruptive behavior is everywhere. It has a preponderance of negative effects. No one wants to experience it, and, apparently, no one wants to cause it. So why does it happen?

When thinking about why disruptive behavior occurs, it's best to regard the behavior as the product of interaction between two or more people. One person by himself does not create a disruption. The trouble happens because his behavior negatively affects those around him.

In this book, when I describe dysfunctional behavior, we will think about how one person interacts with all the people around her. As we look at different difficult behaviors, we will consider how the individual characters, like Narcissus and Lost, affect others in the workplace from thinking about flavors of personality.

What, then, is a personality? In the simplest of terms, a *personality* is a set of behaviors, thoughts, and emotions typical for an individual. It includes how a person relates to others, how he or she behaves, and what his or her morals and values are. Some aspects of a person's personality are inherited while others are the result of familial, cultural, educational, and other experiences; the biology and life events of a person will tend to produce specific kinds of behaviors, including particular kinds of disruption. By understanding certain personas, we can more easily understand behaviors and plan potential interventions.

I am not encouraging you to diagnose personality disorders in this book. Most of the people with whom you interact, as difficult as they may be for you, are not in any way disordered. There is an important distinction between personality *traits* (which we all have, or we'd all just be plain beige) and personality *disorders*. This is discussed in more depth at the introduction to part II: In the Spotlight, and is of key significance.

History sheds light on how we think about personalities today. In ancient Greek and Roman times, thinking about styles of interacting was related to what was called *the four humors* (Woo and Keatinge 2008). In this schematic, those who were "phlegmatic" were apathetic, those who were full of bile were the irritable "choleric" type, those with excess blood were the extroverted "sanguine" ones, and the ones who were pessimistic had excess "black bile." Thinking about individuals' personalities in a slightly more contemporary sense dates back to the writings of the Greek philosopher Aristotle. During the fourth century BCE, in a text entitled *Rhetoric*, he examined the characteristics of individual persons over time, an idea that was expanded on by his student Theophrastus (Corr and Matthews 2009). Theophrastus described thirty undesirable characters with such colorful titles as the "late learner," the "evil speaker," and the "patron of rascals." Since these early writings, interest in personality has been a centerpiece of inquiry into being human. Nearly two thousand years later, the founder of American psychology, William James, wrote his foundational text *Principles of Psychology* (1890), which contained specific sections on the nature of personality.

Even at birth, infants are noted to have the building blocks of temperament, which later—through experiences—becomes personality. Newborns show different amounts of inhibition. Through interactions with the world and caregivers around them, they develop different patterns of behavior that become personalities. Perhaps the most common contemporary approach to thinking about personality is the five-factor trait model, developed in the 1960s. The five factors that contribute to a given personality are extraversion, neuroticism, openness to experience, conscientiousness, and agreeableness (Hilgard, Bem et al. 2000). Using this model, the personality of an individual is a combination of various degrees of these "Big Five" factors.

In this book I am not using strict psychological definitions of personalities but rather character types as broad classes of people—the Narcissus, Mr. Hyde, or the Eccentric—whose personas cause certain patterns of dysfunction in the workplace. I hope to offer familiar scenarios that describe an individual's personal conflicts, how they lead to certain behaviors, and how those behaviors can cause ripple effects around them. As an example, let's consider a builder. Let's say that this particular builder happens to walk through life imagining a "target on his back" and is chronically terrified of getting sued. Further, let's say that this terror leads this builder to be overcautious and controlling in his work and he sees apprentices as "loose cannons," always on the verge of making dangerous errors on his projects. He fears that, as the man in charge, he will be considered ultimately responsible for the trainee's mistake, and he will become known as a builder who makes mistakes, and he will lose business, and he will lose his livelihood and his identity, and so on and so on. This cascade of fears makes him unpleasant to work with, because in his need to try to control outcomes, he's unable to effectively teach or mentor; he's rude when others don't function exactly as he feels he needs them to; he's nervous at work and has trouble developing rapport with people; and when he comes home at night, he's so tense that he's not emotionally available to his wife and kids, and those relationships start to erode. This is the way in which I will describe and explain how one person's tendencies can affect so much of the workplace around him.

From the ancients through the modern age, I'll briefly explore the history of the study of personality in each chapter. The book will describe how specific behaviors that disrupt an environment may reflect how a given personality type interacts with those around it. It's absolutely critical to be able to recognize what types of people engage in what types of behaviors—when and where—if we're ever going to know what to do about it. The character-based approach is the essence of this book's view of disruptive behavior. Remember, however, that all categorization tends toward oversimplification. The point of thinking about character types is to gain traction on how to approach a difficult person, how to think about him, how to engage him. Techniques will require some flexibility and openness to trial and error.

Another reason why it is important to think about disruptive behavior in terms of types of people is to allow for empathy. Each person is a unique combination of biological factors and life experiences that set him up to act in a certain way. Having an appreciation for patterns of behavior should not be reserved only for conflict at work. Developing an empathic posture toward the people around you and helping people become more empathic toward you will help in all walks of life. Often, it's empathy alone that can make relationships more manageable.

It is also important to realize that factors beyond personality can contribute to disruptive behaviors. Some of these factors are related to the culture of a given workplace. As I mentioned, some workplaces are more welcoming to disruptive behavior, though this seems to be changing over time, and some of those cultures foster the flourishing of specific dysfunctional character types. I've frequently seen cases where an individual was labeled difficult or disruptive when she was simply misplaced in a particular work culture. And changing jobs solved the problem!

There may be other factors as well. For example, periods of stress for an individual or a workplace may increase incidents of disruptive behavior. When someone is ill or when a team is understaffed, for instance, there may be more dysfunction in the office. In addition, some lives are full of chronic stress beyond one's control, which can shade many of the person's interactions over time. In taking the character-based approach, these considerations are not comprehensively addressed in this book; however, it is important to understand that they may also contribute to troublesome behavior. Just because someone is acting a certain way does not mean that they always have or will.

Types of People, and What to Do About Them

Before I get into the nuances of how to address different personality types and distinct flavors of disruptive behavior, it's helpful to understand a more general approach to confronting disruptions. This includes considering both the severity of the disruption and the persistence of any trouble. Someone who has an isolated incident of inappropriateness may not need a referral for lengthy therapy, whereas someone who is continually, severely disruptive may not benefit from a simple conversation.

It is important to be aware of dysfunction and to *do something*, and, if that doesn't work, to be persistent and try something else. This book will serve as a guide for knowing what to do, for whom, and when to do it. Sometimes doing *something* will be having a simple, informal conversation, but sometimes it will mean getting management involved. Basically, the level of intervention depends on the situation and may intensify over time. For a single episode of behavior that makes you uncomfortable, maybe you just need to sit down with the person over a cup of coffee and privately discuss the incident, your reactions, and their thoughts about it.

If there is a pattern of difficult behavior, however, there may be a need for a more formal intervention. This approach will involve pointing out the pattern—often using data or other witnesses—and making the individual aware of its existence. This might mean reporting the number of absences in the last month, discussing complaints the individual has received, or acknowledging beer bottles found under the person's desk. Oftentimes, merely pointing out the repetition can help someone adjust their problematic behavior. Research on disruptive behavior in physicians, for example shows that about 60 percent of doctors will eliminate their pattern of disruptive behavior after it is simply pointed out to them (Hickson, Pichert et al. 2007).

People need to understand what is expected of them. Sometimes people act out because they don't fully understand the rules of engagement, or they may be in a situation where those rules change suddenly or without explicit instruction. It's imperative that we define the playing field and what is considered acceptable behavior within that field. It's essential to let people know when they've crossed lines.

Too many times, I've seen managers watch bad behavior occur and, frozen like deer in headlights, be unable to approach the offender and clarify that whatever happened was unacceptable. Time passes until the disturbing event becomes more of a memory than an emotionally charged experience. The manager's will to intervene lessens, other employees become disheartened, and the offender walks away assuming that whatever he did was just fine. Managers eventually call me and describe long-standing patterns of behavior. Had these managers communicated directly,

honestly, and in a timely manner, chances are they wouldn't have needed to call me at all. And you can imagine how coworkers often noticed the behaviors far before it came to the attention of the manager.

So step number 1 is to be clear about expectations; step 2 is to react with clarity and in a timely manner when there is a breach. If this is too difficult or the approach seems too confusing, get help. Avoiding a pattern of behavior will not cause it to magically disappear but will instead allow it to fester. And as a dysfunctional pattern persists and is resistant to change, interventions become increasingly specialized. But even when they become more formal, in many cases the approach does not need to be disciplinary and can still be supportive.

It's important to recognize, however, that once a manager gets involved, there are often only a limited number of interventions to make. Again, that's why it's usually better for the first person to witness or experience the behavior to act right away. A stern talking to by a manager or referral to a specialist who deals with disruptive behavior, however, may nonetheless allow for improved insight and better behavior with certain individuals. A bad actor may also need to make tangible adjustments, such as reducing his work hours, joining a different sector of the company, avoiding a particular type of situation, or even leaving an organization. There might be referrals to executive coaches or, always in concert with human resources or the legal department, to various therapeutic interventions, such as short-term, supportive therapy (to address a particular recent stressor), cognitive-behavioral therapy (to address, for example, anger or frustration management), or even longer-term dynamic therapy (to uncover and address long-standing personality issues). Occasionally, if illness is suspected, there may

be referrals for physical workup, neuropsychological testing, or medication management. The following chapters will detail these interventions—what they are, for whom they apply, and when to engage them.

How Do I Really Use This Book?

The book is divided into relatively neat categories. These are the ten types of people who, from my experience, are more likely to be perceived as difficult and, yes, who are sometimes perceived as schmucks in your office. A particular person may not fit squarely into just any one of these categories. She may prove an unpleasant mélange of character types. Many people have similarities to more than one type.

Indeed, very few people fall neatly into a single category, and you may find yourself wondering how to actually use the information here. It's important not to use the book in order to diagnose anyone. Instead, we all have problematic characteristics, and we all evidence these characteristics with varying intensity. When thinking about the schmuck in the office, some of her characteristics may appear to stand out, and my suggestion is that you note them and attempt to use the associated strategies outlined in the book to mitigate whatever is bothering you. If more than one trait competes for center stage, use other strategies, too. In general, they can all work together. So try not to get caught up in the fact that your boss isn't quite Narcissus because there's a little Bean Counter in there. You can use both sets of skills—catering to her ego while also trying not to fight over details.

Don't just read the book "hunting" for your schmuck. I'm frequently approached by managers who express concern about someone who seemingly does only one notably difficult or annoying thing. They become so focused on this one issue that they don't stop to view the person's full picture and the other qualities she is bringing to the table. In reading this book, such managers will become frustrated if they can't find a similar character that does this thing. It would of course be impossible to catalog every single idiosyncrasy. So, again, try to step back and evaluate what type of person has this issue and not get stuck on the thing itself.

In fact, it's really common to have overlapping character types. Swindlers are often a bit Suspicious. Venus Flytraps are frequently Bean Counters. Narcissus and the Distracted can count quite a few beans, too. And anyone can become Mr. Hyde. Or become Lost. So don't get caught up in the fact that one chapter comes close to describing your schmuck but didn't quite cover it all. Take what you know about the individual—his or her life, background, struggles, goals—and craft a story to help you understand why the troublesome behavior might be occurring.

Maybe someone you work with is unpleasantly competitive and self-propagating, always trying to get ahead of you, always damning you by faint praise. Would it help to know that her sister is world famous, brilliant, and the apple of her parents' eyes? And that your coworker has spent a lifetime trying to get her parents' attention, to be recognized for some of her accomplishments without always feeling like second-best? Maybe she's playing that rivalry out at the office, with you and with others. And maybe—just maybe—you can see that even though the behavior is directed at you, it's not actually about you? Instead of competing with her, try complimenting her on her achievements and making her feel special. You may find it go a million miles to improve your relationship.

It's not that hard. It's just a matter of putting your frustration aside for a moment and trying to think through the dynamic at play. Of course, you may not know and are certainly not privileged to know someone's whole life history. However, people are generally pretty open, whether they realize it or not, and will generally tell you or at least give you hints about what's really on their minds. People want connection, we know that. We have only to look down at the device probably sitting nearby right now to realize how very much we want to be in touch with one another. So I'm going to suggest something old school and "retro." Talk directly to people, live and in person, particularly if you don't understand them and it's causing concern. Look into their eyes as they speak. Listen to their tone; get a sense of their physical energy. And hear what they are saying to you without jumping to conclusions, because those conclusions may very well be more about what you're bringing to the table than what they are.

Another thing that may strike you is why you have to do so much work to get along with these people. Why do *you* need to learn strategies? Aren't *they* the ones with the problems? You may feel like you're doing somersaults to accommodate them. Even reading this book is an investment you're making in them. It seems perverse, I know.

Try to think of relationships as fifty-fifty splits. The disruptive individual may seem to control 90 to 100 percent of the relationship at a given time, I understand. But all you need to do is mind your 50 percent and use the strategies in this book to make your half of the dyad as healthy as possible. That's really all you can do.

Important Disclaimers

A word of caution. This book provides guidance for understanding and interacting with difficult characters in general, but most particularly in the workplace. It should not, however, serve as a substitute for human resources practices that comply with applicable employment laws and regulations. Because many laws regulate the workplace, it is easy for the unwary to make decisions, engage in conduct with other employees, or say things that run afoul of these standards. For example, throughout this book, I discuss interventions with employees such as when and how therapy, discipline, or even discharge from employment may be appropriate for particular disruptive characters. The Americans with Disabilities Act and corresponding state and local laws protect employees with disabilities from discrimination. Among other things, such laws limit the times and manner in which an employer is permitted to ask questions about an employee's possible mental or medical condition or require an employee to undergo an examination by a health care provider. Such laws also require employers to provide reasonable accommodations to employees with disabilities to allow them to perform their essential job functions. Given the complexity of the legal framework in the employment setting, therefore, it is important for managers to educate themselves on the applicable laws and consult with human resources or legal professionals who can assist in providing guidance to help navigate decisions that affect employees.

So when I say someone was referred for therapy or suggest a variety of therapy interventions, please assume that they were referred through appropriate channels at work or referred from sources outside the workplace. Also—recall—I'm a psychiatrist! I think everyone should have some therapy, and almost all training psychiatrists enter therapy themselves! Many people without mental illnesses enter and benefit from therapy for better understanding of themselves, getting over the loss of a loved one, or figuring out how to be more successful at work. It would be remiss if not impossible for me to discuss these scenarios and not mention the various psychotherapy interventions. It is generally not appropriate for you to recommend this to colleagues, bosses, or subordinates in your work role (again, this is something to discuss with human resources or legal experts in this area), but since I'm trying to give you a broad sense of what *can* be done for the various people we discuss, the descriptions are in there.

While I don't address serious mental illness in this book, such as schizophrenia or bipolar disorder, I want to make a quick point about job opportunities for such populations. Even beyond the above legal requirements and protections, I also want to make the point that employment for individuals with mental illness can be very important. As a whole, I support the employment of people when they want to and are able to work. It can be an extremely important part of a recovery from mental health struggles and of having a fulfilling, meaningful life. With the proper skill set and in the appropriate setting, the opportunity to work should be supported for all desiring individuals, regardless of mental health problems.

And remember—the purpose of this book is NOT to help you decide on diagnoses for the problem people at your work! You must not attempt to use the book in this manner, and you must not imagine that the book will empower you to do so. Psychiatric diagnosis is complex, specific, and longitudinal. Psychiatrists go to school for at least twelve years of specialized training—from undergraduate education through medical school, residency, and sometimes fellowship—to develop the skill set, and even then it requires a process of getting to know people very personally over time. I'm not even technically "allowed" to diagnose a personality disorder, on the basis of one psychiatric evaluation or "permitted" to diagnose a celebrity without seeing that person in session. This book flatly excludes those with major, diagnosable mental illness. This is why the chapter labels are not medical and why distinction is made between the types we are discussing and psychiatric disorders. Instead, if there is a related diagnosis that I describe in a given chapter, a reader may want to think of this discussion as a way to gain further insight and understanding into how to thoughtfully help a colleague, rather than just labeling them with having a disorder.

The character and chapter names are not meant to disparage or insult anyone. They are simply mnemonic tools to help you remember and envision the various types and their behaviors. They also, once again, work to help distinguish these characters from diagnosable disorders. The point is for you to simply observe your coworker for themes and to use these themes to get a sense of the individual and why he or she might be acting in the ways that cause concern. When you have that basic framework, it becomes easier to step back and understand why he did this or said that. In understanding, it becomes a bit easier to find empathy, even for things that seem ugly or mean. Just slapping a label on someone and accusing her of being sick or disordered in some way would be an overt perversion of the book's intent.

You will also find that the interventions in this book are not miraculous, and in general they are not meant to cure. Many of the types described within these pages display patterns of behavior that are entrenched and long-standing. Even when we are motivated to change the fixed aspects of our personalities, we cannot do so quickly. Recall, most everyone described is not technically "ill," so curing isn't really the goal. We strive to improve a situation such that the parties in the office can work better together, when possible. We attempt to help people fully elucidate and understand the rules of engagement and the consequences of crossing defined boundaries. We seek to create settings that are manageable, workable, and respectful. In so doing, we attempt to make work relationships more comfortable. As you will see, sometimes even these goals are unachievable, and part of the solution is to realize when this is the case and remove another individual—or even ourselves— from the hostile environment.

Finally, there is not one single "real" person in any of these cases. Each description is a composite of many, many different people. I took pieces of the thousands of cases I have seen in my nearly thirty years of treating patients and consulting with organizations to sew together features that I believe to be most indicative of a type. So if you think you recognize a particular someone in any of these cases, you don't. That person you are reading about is composed of many people and hence is a Frankensteinian figment of my imagination.

PART II

In the Spotlight: Drama Kings and Queens

Dramatic, Emotional, and Erratic: Character Pathology

There are a lot of people—including coworkers—who are able to be diagnosed with what are called *personality disorders*. According to the *Diagnostic and Statistical Manual of Mental Disorders*, "when personality traits are inflexible and maladaptive and cause significant functional impairment or subjective distress . . . they constitute personality disorders" (American Psychiatric Association 2013). By definition, the behaviors of people with personality disorders interfere with their social and/or occupational functioning because they have difficulty responding fluidly and accommodatingly to different situations. Personalities are supposed to steer our social interactions; they determine with whom and how we interact. When this goes awry, as it can in many ways, relationships are primarily affected. Reportedly about 10 to 15 percent of Americans are able to be diagnosed with a personality disorder (Woo and Keatinge 2008).

People with personality disorders have ways of thinking, feeling, and perceiving that are rigid, maladaptive, and impair their functioning. Underlying this, there may be difficulty with self-esteem, with understanding social relationships, and with knowing just exactly how one fits into a social context (Stern, Rosenbaum et al. 2008). With a healthy personality, an individual is able to connect well with other people, experience a full range of emotions, have a sense of who they are and want to be, and tolerate some degree of stress (Force and Association 2006). The contrast, however, is fluid, and there is no clear demarcation between what is healthy and what is not, since much of the clinical thinking—and the character types in this book—exists on a spectrum.

People with a personality disorder, however, often require sustained therapeutic relationships over time to have lasting change. Nonetheless, even in these individuals, dysfunctional behavior can be managed, but interventions will likely be more structured and long-term. When people with personality disorders seek mental health treatment for themselves, it is exceedingly rare for it to be directly for their personality disorder. This is because our personalities really are the core of who we are and how we identify with ourselves and relate to the world. As stated in the *Psychodynamic Diagnostic Manual*, "Personality is what one *is* rather than what one *has*" (Force and Association 2006). In fact, they often think that the problems are with those around them. As such, people don't come seeking help with flaws within themselves; they usually come because of symptoms—feeling depressed or anxious or even because they can't get a relationship or a promotion. The work in therapy comes from realizing that the negative things we feel and the goals we can't achieve may be related to the way we think, feel, and act—and then from instilling a desire to change these components of ourselves. The therapist can be a guide in helping someone understand why and how they encounter patterns of distress in their life.

One set of these personality disorders are historically titled the "Cluster B" or "dramatic" personality disorders—let's call them "Drama Kings and Queens." The character types in the upcoming pages are similar to such individuals. These characters are likely to have the most overt difficulty in the office—to cause the biggest shows, to produce the most openly egregious hurt, and to be the first schmucks you think of in the office. One hint that we're dealing with the people in this section of the book is that they may seem overwhelmingly dramatic, emotional, or erratic to the people around them. They may appear abusive, insincere, entitled, and lacking in compassion. At the same time, they do require our own empathy, as difficult as they may be. They often develop these patterns of interactions based on some inherited features, other biological factors, difficult childhoods, and stormy, chaotic adolescences. In addition, as committed as they might seem to acting as they do, remember that it is frequently causing them distress. Themes of interpersonal discord, dissatisfaction, and emptiness often mark their lives.

The character types that fall into this section have their own spectrum of difficulties. For one, they are likely to have difficulties with impulse control, meaning that they have difficulty regulating their behavior. They may act suddenly, riskily, and seemingly without much consideration for consequences. They also likely have difficulties controlling their thoughts, which are often rigid and distorted, as well as their feelings. They are likely to have difficulty managing their emotional reactions to events and interactions. These patterns are enduring and likely cause a great deal of distress to the person and those around them. Their relationships are often very affected—both inside and outside the office. In fact, in some ways, the whole difficulty with these individuals is how hard it is for them to have stable, functional relationships because they so often appear demanding, intrusive, and rapidly shifting.

The individuals in this section are the ones likely to cause more theatrical and stirring disruptions than the individuals in subsequent chapters. The characters in the spotlight are Narcissus, the Swindler, and the Venus Flytrap—and they're likely to cause very significant disturbances when present in the workplace.

Narcissus

Western culture has forever been fascinated with the Greek myth of Narcissus. The story is about a beautiful, proud son of a nymph and a river God. His name was Narcissus, and in the story he sees his reflection in a pool of water and becomes absolutely enchanted with the image. He falls so deeply in love with the face floating on the water's surface that it becomes his downfall. Not recognizing that this image is his own, Narcissus eventually dies beside the pool, captivated and finally killed by an obsession with his own beauty.

The story was told and retold in various forms over time and throughout the world, cementing its place in history. Two thousand years ago, ancient poets like Ovid and Parthenius of Nicaea tell their own versions of the tale. We see Narcissus gazing at his reflection in works of famous painters like Caravaggio and Dali. But it wasn't just artists who found the story compelling. The medical field has also long been interested in the tendency to fixate on oneself and ended up using Narcissus's name to describe various forms of self-obsessed vanity. The psychological idea of *narcissism* was introduced by a British physician named Havelock Ellis around the beginning of the nineteenth century (Pincus and Lukowitsky 2010). A sexologist, Ellis used the term "narcissus-like" to describe excessive masturbation—a different take on "self-love," for sure (Millon, Millon et al. 2012). The famous neurologist Sigmund Freud described a preoccupation with the self in his game-changing psychoanalytic theory, and other big-name psychoanalysts like Otto Kernberg and Heinz Kohut refined the psychology of narcissism over the course of the twentieth century (Pincus and Lukowitsky 2010). First, Kohut developed a theory based on what it means to feel narcissistically isolated in a life without meaning versus living a fulfilled and creative life (Mitchell and Black 1995). Kernberg, on the other hand, focused on development of the ability to love and form relationships with others.

This myth of Narcissus is ridiculous—*how could he!*—and yet also familiar. While most of us don't have a friend killed by Narcissus's extremes of self-loving, we all know that person who seems to stare in the pool just a little too long . . .

NARCISSUS'S BASIC TRAITS

It isn't wrong to have some narcissism. In psychiatry, narcissism boils down to your ability to think highly about yourself. A similar concept is self-esteem. This trait is not bad. In fact, it is essential in order to try new things with any possibility of success. Narcissism itself is a basic psychological quality of the human experience. Of course, it can get excessive, as with Narcissus himself, which is why this can get confusing. But it is truly important for a person to be able to hold his head up, to have faith in himself and in his ability to succeed. Healthy narcissism is what allows someone to apply to law school, to sign up for guitar lessons, to ask someone on a first date. Without any trust in our ability to succeed, we would naysay ourselves to the point of not pursuing dreams or even plans. Without narcissism, we might say, "I'm not going to apply to law school; I'm too stupid" or "I could never learn to play guitar" or "She'll just turn me down." If we never thought about ourselves, we wouldn't be able to take care of our needs or fulfill our desires. Narcissism lets us do this, by allowing us to think about ourselves and what we want—to have some faith in our ability to accomplish.

But then there are extremes. In psychiatry, pathological—or problematic—narcissism is when one's tremendous ego gets in the way of, let's say, succeeding as an attorney, learning the guitar from a teacher, or conversing on a first date. Narcissism becomes unruly when entitlement, self-centeredness, condescension, and attention seeking prevail (Ronningstam 2013). In such a world, the ego takes over and demands to be fed only praise and vanity. Problematic narcissism means the person appears so arrogant that they can't ask others for help, dates don't come back for second rounds, and new guitars are smashed when chords don't fit neatly together during the first week of lessons.

Recent psychiatric studies estimate that around somewhere below 6.2 percent of the population has true narcissistic personality disorder (American Psychiatric Association 2013). In this research, about 50 to 75 percent of all individuals with narcissistic personality disorder are males.

Richard: Part One

Throughout my career, I have certainly seen Narcissus. In fact, he tends to be some of the most difficult character types. One such person was Richard, a successful executive chef whom I was asked to see after he threw a large knife at a sous chef in the kitchen. Richard's tale is typical of many of Narcissus—a story marked by vanity, the need for admiration, sensitivity to criticism, and a lack of understanding others' feelings. (American Psychiatric Association 2013). This makes him a good example of the typical or "Look at Me" Narcissus. Later on, we will see the ways in which he is similar and different to the "Woe Is Me" Narcissus and the "Impossible" Narcissus types.

When I was asked to see Richard, he was already a well-known chef at a trendy restaurant. During a seemingly uneventful food preparation demonstration, he asked his assistant for a particular knife, but was presented with a different one. Slightly larger or not serrated or something of the sort . . . In a dramatic episode of screaming and yelling, he threw the knife back toward the horrified chef and stormed out of the kitchen swearing about how incompetent she was.

This knife-throwing incident was definitely not the first time Richard had left his staff astonished and horrified. In fact, he had a pattern of being demanding and deeply condescending toward anyone who didn't meet his expectations. Whenever he felt someone wasn't helping him achieve his lofty goals, he turned against them, sometimes instantly. Richard often used techniques in his kitchen that were downright dangerous, insisting that his novel approaches were best and would one day become "the new standard." One time he insisted on using a liquor for flambéing that everyone knew was unsafe—of course, forcing someone else to ignite the sauce. When not only the food, but the staff member's outfit caught on fire, Richard shouted that the person was not "worthy" of working in *his* kitchen.

He belittled anyone he perceived to be getting in the way of his progress. He would insult them, loudly, in front of coworkers and other supervisors, demanding that they do the job "right" but not offering any constructive criticism. He would throw food and utensils around the kitchen during angry tirades. Everyone was left guessing what he might want at a given time, unable to read his mind but essentially expected to anticipate his every wish. No one wanted to work with him, and he had trouble keeping a stable staff. Everyone he worked with was on edge, waiting for the next perceived mistake and consequent explosion. He would often storm out of the kitchen, slamming the door behind him—loud enough to let everyone, including patrons, know that he was upset and that he felt he had a reason to be.

Richard's behavior extended beyond the kitchen into all of his other interactions. Socially, he might go out to the bar with fraternity brothers from college or to events with other people in the restaurant business, but he did not have many close friends. In the beginning of a night out, he would meet lots of new people. They were drawn to his confidence and captivating storytelling about his elaborate successes: awards, recipes, connections galore. As the night wore on, however, his companions would become irritated by his insistence about talking about himself. No one else would get an opportunity to speak. Every topic was somehow an opportunity for Richard to talk about a successful event or a great review he'd received—however long ago. And no one was able to point this out, despite grace or humor, without receiving a barrage of insults in return.

How Richard viewed his own behavior, however, was very different from how others viewed his actions. After angry incidents at work, he was usually left feeling indignant and self-righteous. Richard felt that *he* was wronged by his team, not the other way around. He would wonder why everyone held him back from accomplishing everything he knew he could. The tears of his coworkers, the tension in the kitchen, and the apparent fear he engendered didn't bother him at all. In fact, it indicated to him that he was an effective leader, letting his team know that nothing less than the best would be accepted.

In understanding all of his anger and ego, I began to see Richard's behavior through the lens of narcissism. In all of his interactions, we see Richard trying to inflate his sense of self-worth. Despite a successful career, Richard is not able to settle for these accomplishments. To his friends and romantic interests, he exaggerates his accomplishments. At work, he overestimates his abilities and blames others for shortcomings. He expects others to readily notice and appreciate his value and openly demands praise from those around him.

We can also see that Richard is focused on the limitless expanses of what he feels he can achieve. When frustrated by lack of progress, Richard blames others who are holding him back. It is inconceivable to Richard that there may be inherent limits to his own abilities and successes. This tendency is rooted in an underlying, deeply entrenched sense of insecurity.

HOW DID NARCISSUS GET THAT WAY?

The typical Narcissus at work may not be throwing knives, since such dangerous behavior represents a very extreme example of problematic behavior. In the average workplace, though, there are people with very low self-esteem who try desperately to have others see them as important and worthy of admiration.

They share a character type with Richard: the Look at Me Narcissus. If there is one thing to remember about any Narcissus, it is that what appears to be flagrant arrogance hides a very fragile person struggling to feel significant. Whereas someone with healthy self-esteem can feel good about himself, the Narcissus desperately tries to overcompensate. The healthy person is able to stand on her own two feet and occasionally pat herself on the back, while the Narcissus relies on constant reinforcement from others.

In everyday conversation, we tend to think of a narcissistic person as having too high of an opinion of himself, when in fact the Narcissus just *appears* to be self-absorbed in order to protect himself from low self-esteem. These distressed techniques end up being problematic in the workplace. If we revisit the Greek story of Narcissus, we would see that the contemporary Narcissus would actually die looking into the water, not because he is in love with himself but because he is searching and waiting for the compliment of another.

If we conceptualize such a person as a young boy who feels small, not the large man before us, and understand that the boy must inflate himself like a balloon to feel big, we might find an empathic spot. His life is a big effort to pump air in the balloon, to keep it taut, to stay big, to keep the rubber as far as possible from the tiny, frightened boy at the center. The small person who inflates himself in this way is inherently fragile—the balloon is filled with air, after all, not the substance of self that would feel secure, stable, and hearty. Everything he does is to appear big in order to hide feeling small. As easily as a balloon can burst, the Narcissus can be reduced to his true emotional size, and he will go to great lengths to avoid this eventuality.

For example, when the Narcissus has no friends, she is likely to think "that's because they're too jealous of me" or "I don't need other people" instead of ever thinking it could be because of her own attitude or behavior.

As with other problematic personalities, there is no straight-forward "cause" that is known to create such narcissism. There is no single experience to be avoided or type of parent to be blamed. However, the general nature of early life experiences among such persons tends to be somewhat similar.

Richard was born into a wealthy and successful family that had accumulated a small fortune and resided in the suburbs out-side Boston. His basic needs and material desires were always ac-counted for, but beneath the veneer of comfort, Richard's position was more delicate. His mother, Helena, sought to ensure Rich-ard's happiness as a measure of her own success. Her family was supposedly related to a royal line in Hungary, and she always told Richard that he was of "princely blood." She started him in pri-vate school at age four—younger than any of his siblings had begun—and pushed him to succeed from an early age. All the while, Richard's father maintained a backseat role in the upbring-ing of his youngest son and often criticized him for being a "mama's boy."

In Richard's story, we see a typical upbringing of a Narcissus in a home where status and success are valued above all else (Dimaggio 2013). These early concerns become the focus of later life. At the same time, we see a tendency for his father to humili-ate him, making Richard learn to inflate his self-worth to protect himself from criticism. Though Richard's material needs were out-wardly provided for, it is difficult to say that his basic emotional needs were consistently met by his parents. In order to develop self-esteem, a child needs caregivers to validate their emotions and needs. They need a secure sense that those who care for them understand and value them.

Underneath the grand displays of Narcissus's self-praise are, in fact, self-criticisms and judgments (Ronningstam 2013). In his most private moments, the Narcissus fears that he isn't all that great and that he'll never really measure up to his and others' expectations. This very thinking is what makes the Narcissus exquisitely sensitive to criticism, which he responds to by belittling others. When he does not feel appropriately admired, the Narcissus in fact experiences extremely negative emotions: humiliation, disgrace, and worthlessness (American Psychiatric Association 2013).

The "Look at Me" Narcissus

Keeping Richard in mind, we can now look at some of the different ways that a Look at Me Narcissus can behave in the office. A subtle narcissistic technique is to discreetly pander for the reinforcement of others by "compliment fishing." For example, the Narcissus might walk into the office looking put together, but say something along the lines of "Ugh, I woke up late and just threw on the first thing I saw. And my hair's a total mess!" Such a statement is made for the purpose of obtaining reinforcement— think *Look at Me!*—"Your hair looks great, and I love that shirt! You always look good, no matter what." Compliment fishing might not directly sound narcissistic, but it is a technique used by those with low self-esteem for feeling better about themselves by getting compliments from others.

We all talk about ourselves at times, but the Look at Me

Narcissus is inclined to talk about himself, ad nauseam: *I did this, I did that. I have this, I'm going to have that.* We find ourselves rolling our eyes. *Here he goes again . . .* Sideways glances and deep sighs mark these one-way conversations. You try to relate, but they swoop in and gather your remarks like prey to their own story. "Huh, well that reminds me that I . . ." Trying to get a word in about yourself can feel like taking a sip of water from a fire hose. This onslaught of information lets them feel important. Again: Look at Me! Look at Me! They feel that people are interested in them and want to hear them. They get to regale an audience with tales of their accomplishments.

The Narcissus is unlikely to ask about you, and, when he does, he's only looking for a short answer. At the same time, he may seem to forget things that you've told him about yourself. By controlling most of the conversation, the Narcissus doesn't let anyone say something that might hurt him. That is one reason why the Narcissus continues to talk: their own narrative is less risky than hearing others talk, even if they are rambling on about nothing. They don't want to take the chance of hearing about someone else's accomplishments or a potential insult. Everything is about attention and admiration with little concern (or at times understanding) for how others are feeling. This tendency might also display itself as excessive rambling during meetings and Q and A sessions of presentations; this is the person that "talks to hear himself talk." At the same time, she might be playing on her phone or painting her nails when anyone else speaks as a subtle jab and display of superiority. The message: "I don't have to listen to this. I don't need it. I'm above it."

If the Narcissus does let you get in more than a word about yourself, you are likely to be met with criticism and put-downs. "Oh, well, I guess that's good for you . . . If I wanted to, I could do that, but I don't really like that kind of thing . . ." Their accomplishments are all diamonds; yours are still coal. In a sense, this is the proverbial "one-upping." You say you do something; he says he's done something better. He might even go so far as to say, "Oh, you're just jealous" or something else to demean you while elevating himself. Another common technique is for the Narcissus to frame insults as jokes, "I was hoping they'd send me an attractive assistant [wink, laugh]." This technique leaves the co-worker feeling critiqued and without power. A more subtle technique may be to deftly change the topic so that the Narcissus didn't have to hear about your own accomplishments, which would be painful for him to listen to. A non sequitur from conversation about your recent award to "I heard they're going to update the elevators in this building" may seem benign, but it is also frustrating and can indicate the presence of a Narcissus.

If, on the other hand, you dare lend an opinion about the Narcissus: *abandon hope, all ye who enter!* While we often feel like giving feedback in order to have a voice, it can backfire. Without the right approach, it causes the Narcissus to ratchet up his attempts at self-importance. Such sensitivity to criticism is a hallmark of this personality type, often causing grand displays of anger, even throwing or breaking things, and slamming doors for certain. If anything is likely to get the Narcissus mad, it is criticism, whether actual or perceived. They switch rapidly from one superficial emotion to another. This person is likely to misinterpret words as attacks to their self-esteem, so that even somewhat neutral comments may be met with rage. As a type, they are very likely to criticize others in their anger. This tendency is a part of the big, puffy layer of insulation that the Narcissus wears to protect his fragile ego at the core. Remember that this type needs to seem superior to others to feel good at all.

A Narcissus may also react to perceived insult by simply ignoring you, giving a cold shoulder, or sulking. The anger may come out in more passive-aggressive ways by not answering e-mails or contributing to the next project. By stepping back in this way, the Narcissus is able to indirectly attack and make others angry in retaliation for somehow poking a hole in their ego bubble. Other ways that the anger of the Narcissus might come out, for example, would be in spreading rumors or lies about someone in order to cut them down. Let's say a person just got a promotion: the Narcissus might tell other people at work that she "knows he failed his business school exam the first three times he took it."

Funnily enough, the Narcissus may "talk the talk" better than they "walk the walk," spending lots of time talking about their skills without many accomplishments to show for them. For all of the energy they spend talking about themselves, this type may seem to avoid certain tasks. For example, they might talk about being the best skier but then have other plans when the rest of the workplace plans a weekend trip to the slopes. This happens because the Narcissus sometimes avoids overt competition. On the one hand, competition can mean winning, but it can also mean losing, failure, and embarrassment. Everything that the Narcissus does is to maintain a grand and positive image. Competition is sometimes avoided: better safe than sorry. Losing is a huge blow to the Narcissus, particularly in front of others. At the same time, the Narcissus may avoid even more subtle challenges out of fear of failure. They may not take on big projects or ask for promotions for fear of not living up to expectations. Better to bow out and tell himself he could have done it than to try to achieve yet fail. In this way, the Narcissus may at times appear aimless and seemingly without commitment to his job.

Often, the Narcissus will try to surround himself with people that he wants to be like. In conversations, he is likely to name drop, even when inappropriate. He might try to latch onto someone of higher status, going out of his way to try to get that person's attention and regard. And the Narcissus is often successful at this game of forging beneficial relationships because, despite his numerous difficulties, he can also be charming, and his confidence can seem infectious. In the same stroke, the Narcissus may ditch others if they end up climbing any positions or ranks. They avoid associations with people perceived to be of lower status and may even make fun of people or things that they truly like in order to look better. For example, after a promotion, the Narcissus may no longer eat lunch with people with whom he previously worked for fear of tainting his new image. On the other side of the coin, however, if a Narcissus feels threatened by your success, he may also stop associating with you. In the same way that he can't hear about your accomplishments, there may be so much anger associated with your doing well (that is, better than him) that it becomes difficult to be around you, or perhaps to hear others speak highly of your progress. Instead of tolerating this, they just cut themselves off from being around you; perhaps they conspicuously don't show up to an important presentation or even award ceremony.

Unfortunately, this desire to shine can also eek into even more troublesome territory. The Narcissus may take credit for the work of others, particularly if the work was collaborated on. This character type does not necessarily outright cheat or steal (though they may) but are more likely to bend the facts in order to fit the image of being accomplished. For example, when speaking of the outcome of a group presentation that was particularly well received, they might say, "*My* presentation went very well," despite the fact that effort was shared by others. Conversely, the

Narcissus is likely to blame others when things go wrong—yes, you guessed it, even if they were largely responsible for the problems.

The Narcissus can ascend organizational hierarchies when his effusive confidence makes people want to follow his visions for the company. Once in a position of leadership, however, a Narcissus is likely to have an "it's my way or the highway" style. The coworker wonders "Why is he acting like this? Why is he yelling at me? Why is he making me come in on the weekend at the last minute? Why is he trying to bully me into doing work?" At the same time, the Narcissus leader gives himself permission for the inappropriate behavior. She tells herself stories of accomplishment: "Because I'm the boss!" or "My net revenue last year was $$$, and that means I get to tell you to come in on the weekend!" Inside his own mind, Narcissus excuses his mistreatment of others by relating it to some propped-up sense of achievement that, in turn, gives him permission to act as he sees fit. These same lines of reasoning are also what let the Narcissus get away with other bends and breaks of rules. For example, when the Narcissus expects everyone to work on a given task except for himself, the monologue inside his head might be, "Well, of course I don't need to do this. I'm special and that's why I deserve to have the others fill in on this one." Such interpretation of the workplace leads to a pattern of the Narcissus expecting endless favors from everyone around him. Similarly, they often feel that rules don't apply to them and so do not adhere to them.

If you feel that you are trying very, very carefully not to insult someone, this person may be a Narcissus. Interestingly, this means that you are paying lots of attention to the person and figuring out what he or she likes, which is exactly how the Narcissus wants you to act. Though being extremely sensitive to the needs of the Narcissus may not be the ideal way to spend your office day, in the end it can also save you unnecessary headaches if you can think just one move ahead of their ego. It also goes to show that, other than trying to suck up to people in positions of status, the Narcissus may also spend time with people that are nice, compliant, self-deprecating, and good listeners.

Other signs that you may be dealing with a Narcissus are feeling angry and ignored. You may notice yourself wanting to compete or prove the person wrong. The person likely seems arrogant and confident, while she can likewise be distant, cold, insensitive, controlling, and exploitative. It is important to remember that the Narcissus can possess a well-oiled veneer of allure that makes one feel fascinated, entertained, and even inspired. The shattering of this façade is what can be so difficult in dealing with a Narcissus. The person that we wanted to believe in or have fun with, to trust in or to laugh with shows himself to be someone who only cares about his own success and has no concern for our well-being. Such rapid disappointment can be another sign that one is dealing with a Narcissus.

THE MANY SHADES OF NARCISSUS

The "Woe Is Me" and "Impossible" Variations You May Encounter in the Office

The number of ways Narcissus behavior can manifest itself in the office is practically endless. This makes it important to understand the general ways that a Narcissus interacts with coworkers to inflate his self-esteem so that you can keep an eye out for the behaviors, but it is worth pointing out two additional Narcissus subtypes: Woe Is Me and Impossible.

The Woe Is Me Narcissus

Though his behavior was extreme, Richard's story is pretty representative of the haughty, arrogant character of the Look at Me Narcissus. Another pervasive version of the Narcissus is the Woe Is Me type. As we will see in the following example, the presentation is quite different, but there still exists the underlying split between trying to appear confident and having low self-esteem. This Woe Is Me type, however, is more about pandering for reassurance than the Look at Me Narcissus's aggressive insistences on arrogance.

I evaluated a man named Joe who was deeply successful in the field of finance. He wrote a seminal text and became chief of his department in a large international firm at an unusually young age. Though he had all the trappings of a man who had "arrived" professionally, he was preoccupied with all he felt he did not have—a big enough office, a better view, the true affection of his boss, an even bigger job. He wanted to be loved by everyone and to be sure that he was popular. He called the bulk of his contact list with regularity "just to say hi," and was always first with new gossip. The problem was that he really annoyed people. Everyone wondered, Where does he find all this time?!?! Isn't he supposed to be a really busy guy? His excessive outreach was perceived as dependent and needy. The calls, initially welcome, quickly became too much, as the content was usually all about him, often with multiple requests for reassurance that he did the right thing, no, the *best possible thing* that anyone could have done. He was also both needy and special in the midst of illness. Every sniffle is "the worst cold strain" of the year, of course the doctor had *never* seen quite so severe a case of carpal tunnel syndrome. Even when he talked about something being wrong with him—his health—Joe was able to be egocentric and narcissistic.

This was a man who should have deserved tremendous professional respect from everyone. And yet when his name came up, everyone either rolled their eyes or said things like, "Oh, poor Joe. I thought our year of therapy riding the train together every morning was starting to help but, alas . . . I guess no one is able to give him what he needs." As such, it becomes easy to see that Joe was as self-focused and self-propagating as Richard but that his approach was diametrically opposed. Richard was feared and disliked; Joe was avoided and belittled. "How pathetic!" everyone thought. This Woe Is Me Narcissus seeks approval by building coalitions of supportive people so he can be popular and "in the know." It's all about wanting to be liked or even loved and revered, all to keep his self-esteem reinforced by support and encouragement.

The Impossible Narcissus

Then, too, there is the type of narcissist who is simply unable to receive help—what I call the Impossible Narcissus—because the methods of protecting his self-esteem are too rigid to be affected by any treatment. This type is one with a true pathologically disordered personality. A key component of effecting change for the Narcissus is to recognize the problem, accept responsibility for owning it (regardless of how it started), and genuinely wish to get rid of it. As we will see, even Richard the chef was eventually able to take responsibility and develop insight into the personal causes for his problems. The Impossible Narcissus, on the other hand, simply cannot think beyond himself, has little capacity for empathy, can only blame others for his woes, and uniformly sees himself as "right." No amount of intervention or reality testing has impact in helping the Impossible Narcissus see his patterns. While other Narcissuses might occasionally be aware of deep-rooted insecurities, the Impossible Narcissuses will keep them out of their minds as a form of self-protection. That is, they protect their self-esteem by avoiding negative thoughts about themselves. This shielding mechanism means that they can't hear criticism and they can't realize flaws enough to be motivated to change them. If you meet an Impossible Narcissus in the workplace, it's unlikely that he'll be around for long because the depth of his problem keeps him from keeping stable employment.

I only briefly met Ameet through a referral initiated by his parents, for Ameet is a man who has never been able to maintain employment. His occasional efforts to work have uniformly failed because, unfortunately, he always seems to land jobs where bosses, coworkers, or everybody around him happen to be "idiots," "incompetent," or "crazy." He is usually quickly fired from jobs when bosses find his behavior untenable. His father, a successful entrepreneur, sold the family business for millions though stayed on as a part-time advisor. Ameet believes that this wealth should naturally mean eternal financial support for him because he "deserves it." His father also appeared to be a deeply conceited man who frequently elected to discuss his own "incredible" accomplishments, even in our brief interactions. Ameet has always felt slighted by his father, as if he lives under his shadow. His mother seemed to overcompensate by attempting to convince Ameet of his brilliance, his special stature, and his entitlement to have just about anything he desires. His home in a wealthy suburb, his handmade suits and expensive meals, and his world travel were all supported by his parents. As the years have passed, however, they are becoming annoyed and angry that none of their support has ever translated into any personal initiative. His tale of being "a financial consultant" actually means, "I sometimes move around stocks that my family gave me." His father has historically been the only one who has directly pointed this out, and so, more than ever, Ameet *hates* him. But his mother is beginning to think she created a monster, too. Confrontation, intervention, and therapy have made no impact. Ameet simply doesn't understand why anything needs to change—this is what he is entitled to! Waiting for the next check from his aging parents, noticing (occasionally) the absence of friends or romantic partners, and feelings of constant indignation—these are simply the cost of doing business in his family.

Looking at the Woe Is Me Narcissus alongside the Impossible Narcissus shows us once again the vast range of narcissist behaviors. While we might be irritated and maybe a little nauseated by Joe, we're much more likely to be infuriated by Richard or Ameet. Ameet's example also shows how the context of one's life can affect one's narcissistic traits. His family initially provided the substrate in which his narcissism grew, until it overstepped its own image, and his parents could no longer control his entitlement, despite their best efforts at engaging him in change.

WHEN THE SCHMUCK IN THE OFFICE IS NARCISSUS

With a basic understanding of what lies behind a Narcissus, one can appreciate trends of such egoists in the office. Various studies show that egotism seems to be particularly linked with positions of leadership at work. Narcissus leaders often attain their elevated positions because their decisions and goals are driven by characteristic arrogance and self-interest (Rosenthal and Pittinsky 2006). However, their fulfillment of these roles is often marked by self-promotion at the expense of a shattered organizational system (Rosenthal and Pittinsky 2006). They clamor to get ahead, leaving destruction behind them. Often the Narcissus obtains positions of leadership by articulating expansive goals for themselves and their organizations while then using exploitative, risky, or unethical means to achieve these goals (Campbell, Hoffman, Campbell, and Marchisio 2011). Narcissists as leaders often impair the ability of others to work effectively and thus negatively affect overall functioning of the group (Nevicka, Ten Velden, De Hoogh, and Van Vianen. 2011).

Narcissism in the office tends to create a climate where politics is the predominant culture. Everyone is always trying to figure out where they are in the hierarchy—who is above and who is below them. The environment feels competitive rather than supportive, at least among the rank and file, whereas the leaders of such organizations tend to do what they can to eliminate competition, feedback, and responsibility for themselves. Communication between bosses and their employees is often lacking, and a great deal of decision making seems to go on behind closed doors. There tends to be an enforced "acceptance" of rule breaking from above, at times with regard to escapades involving sex, money, or status.

In the office, the problems of a Narcissus have a lot to do with the culture of the workplace and acceptance of narcissistic behaviors. In some groups, for example, the drive to be "best" can be a great motivator if the whole team drinks the same Kool-Aid. With appropriate checks in place, such as anonymous professionalism or safety reporting, ambition and competitiveness can be important and effective. In other contexts, however, the demand for ever greater accomplishments can lead to bullying and detrimental overestimation of a group's potential. It is thought that certain hierarchical jobs such as investment banking, corporate law, or medicine can promote and even reward narcissistic behaviors. However, it is also important to see how the employees who work with the Narcissus day to day may be adversely affected by their behaviors.

DEALING EFFECTIVELY WITH NARCISSUS

Once you have identified a potential Narcissus at work, there are strategies that you can employ to help soften their ego-driven blows. These approaches can depend on your relationship to the individual in the workplace; that is to say that one may not be able to employ the same techniques toward a Narcissus boss as a new Narcissus trainee. In general, if you are an underling to a Narcissus boss, be liberal with your compliments and step aside; if you are an employer of a Narcissus hire, draw limits and make referrals to appropriate treatment; if you are a colleague or otherwise fall somewhere in between, there are a number of other approaches worth trying out (which might also include sucking up or getting other leadership to see the importance of a referral).

On a day-to-day basis, appealing to this person's egocentricity can be very effective. The occasional recognition of the person's achievement, strengths, or values may go a long way in avoiding anger or demeaning comments; in some instances, you may simply want to remark upon a person's good efforts. Fanning the embers of narcissism is particularly effective in avoiding unwanted conflict. Particularly if the Narcissus is your boss, you have to let them think that you perceive them as important. No matter how difficult it may be to do this, the Narcissus boss can make the workplace a living hell for anyone who they think is not on board with their success. Give them compliments, and try to do so without mocking them.

When asking for a favor or for some type of change that could be perceived as an insult, definitely attempt the route of first praising him in some way. Indeed, the only commentary that the Narcissus will be able to actually hear will contain some degree of praise in it. Even a simple statement like a reminder about a deadline might need some positive reinforcement embedded in it: "I can't wait to see your draft of the proposal on Friday." Remember that the Narcissus has special techniques for avoiding hearing criticism and can interpret even a simple suggestion or reminder as an insult if it doesn't contain anything positive.

Another strategy is paying attention to the Narcissus. If enough attention is not paid, he will perceive criticism. Even simple moves, like stopping by to say, "Have a good weekend" on the way out the door, can have positive effects on your workplace relationship. By the same token, it is important to respond to the Narcissus when asked, if it is possible. When this person asks you to swing by his office, it is far better to do so immediately—and postpone listening to your last voice-mail message—than to even say, "Let me finish up what I'm doing and I'll be over when I can." The Narcissus might hear this benign statement as, "I'm doing something important right now and in fact it's more important than you are because I think you are worthless," and this will nourish his rage. By the time you get to his office five minutes later, he's boiling inside and about to assign you two extra tasks in retaliation for the perceived criticism. The same goes for replying to his text messages, e-mails, and other forms of communication. Quick responses let the Narcissus imagine that you respect him and think he is important.

Obviously, all of this can feel incredibly frustrating. No one wants to accommodate Narcissus—not only is it difficult, but it feels extremely unfair to have to do so. You might find yourself asking why you should leap at someone's beck and call, and that question certainly makes sense. At the same time, however, you want to recognize that you are doing this because it is what works best. The other options are to be berated, bullied, or otherwise taken down by their ego. As difficult as it feels to cater to Narcissus, remember that you do it because the other options are even worse.

At the same time, if you think you are dealing with a Narcissus, it is important to keep in mind the potential downfall of the relationship. You can pay them attention or recognize their strengths, but it is important to acknowledge the persistent potential for this individual to sacrifice you for the benefit of her own advancement or acknowledgment. Particularly if this Narcissus has charisma! You don't have to live in a constant state of anxiety or paranoia, but being aware of this potential can help you to avoid disappointment and even protect some of your work. You may, for example, want to make sure you clearly indicate your name on drafts of documents sent to a Narcissus for review— anticipating the potential for taking credit for your work—and maybe even copy a third party on the communication.

Resist the impulse to spontaneously react to your annoyance with a Narcissus. Risky, poorly timed confrontations may cause the individual to avoid your suggestions or go to extreme lengths to criticize your own person before you have a chance to challenge him again. The Narcissus avoids hearing anything that may injure his self-esteem. An effective strategy is to sandwich a critique between compliments and to offer alternative manners of acting in specific situations. For example, "I really like the presentation that you gave this morning and think I learned a lot from your extensive experience. I wanted to note, though, that next time everyone might learn even more if you can keep from calling some of our coworkers' questions 'stupid' because I think it hurts people's feelings and distracts them from all of the great information you had in the presentation. I know I wouldn't want to miss out on any of that." This approach is probably more likely to be effective coming from a boss, or possibly a colleague, and only if done sensitively.

Although the Narcissus is known for a relative inability to understand others' emotions, recent research has indicated that this trait may be more flexible than previously understood (Hepper, Hart, and Sedikides 2014). Though the Narcissus may not consider another's perspective on his own, he may be prompted to do so. In pointing out a behavior that offended someone, it may not be enough to simply say, "It was rude of you to insult Alex at the staff meeting." If said this way, the Narcissus may simply hear you insulting them. "You are rude!" However, compliment sandwiches can be helpful in getting the Narcissus to hear what is coming next. Then, stating something along the lines of, "Imagine how Alex felt when you called her *stupid*. Imagine if someone called *you* stupid." Although it may not come naturally, evidence shows that being instructed to consider something from another's perspective can actually influence the Narcissus's ability to do so.

Another technique is to reflect the person's underlying emotions back to them. Because we understand that beneath the arrogant exterior is someone who feels scared, insecure, and small, statements that let the Narcissus understand that he isn't expected to be perfect, or that undertaking large projects can be difficult, can be incredibly useful. The secret is to not single him out or make him feel undervalued in the process. For example, we might say something like, "We are all stressed about the upcoming deadline right now. I know I am a bit on edge about how I will do" can translate into "Hey, it's okay if you're scared right now because we all are. You don't have to puff up." Such a statement might take the person's defenses down a notch. They can let out a sigh and relax from self-protection mode a bit. On the other hand, it could be nearly disastrous to say something like, "You look really stressed right now. Are you worried you aren't going to do a good job or something?" which would translate into "insult insult insult, insult?"

When dealing with behaviors of the Narcissus, leadership in the workplace can sometimes make certain structural interventions like avoiding special treatment, assigning tasks to help Narcissus's subordinates, and rewarding effective teamwork. Focusing on strengths can help bolster respect for the person behind all the difficult interactions. The Narcissus may do well in positions with shorter-term relationships, like sales or consulting, where they meet new clients rather than have to maintain long-term relationships. The Narcissus may have a great vision for progress and can often use his own confidence to promote assurance in a company. He might be particularly good in careers where he can wow potential purchasers/clients with confidence in a time-limited relationship that entails a lot of "show" up front.

Leadership, HR, or legal can enforce more structured interventions for the Narcissus, such as engaging in various types of therapy. Short-term anger or behavioral management can teach alternatives to dramatic behavior. Narcissuses can also benefit from group therapies where they learn how to more appropriately interact with other individuals. And cognitive therapies can address anger, behavior, and interactions by directly focusing on related thoughts. Severe cases of narcissistic personality disorder are usually treated by long-term psychodynamic ("talk") therapy that teaches individuals to change their patterns of using superiority to increase self-esteem. It can be very hard for the Narcissus to agree to treatment; in a sense, being told that he needs help is the ultimate blow to his puffed-up ego, and avoiding therapy seems to protect him from having to look at personal flaws. In the face of an ultimatum from an employer, there is frequent denial of any problem, commonly alongside efforts to blame any office difficulties on coworkers (Gabbard 2007).

One route to getting the Narcissus onboard with formal treatment is to frame it as help with achieving leadership goals, or as targeting depressed moods and life dissatisfaction. The Narcissus often feels bad because he hasn't lived up to his egotistical dreams and may be interested in receiving treatment for feeling empty in this regard. However, initial suggestions at treatment may evoke fear of talking about emotions, being exposed, or experiencing accusations. We want him to buy into the treatment. The Narcissus is known for dropping out of therapy early and often. But the path to feeling better in the long term involves understanding that these desperate attempts to enhance self-esteem often have the opposite effect and that, therefore, facing fears and sticking with treatment is key.

Thus, in long-term therapy for pathological narcissism, there are often breaks in the relationship with the therapist. These breaks and repairs occur in a safe setting where the person can begin to feel that he can be valued and understood and won't be turned away. In a sense, the same behaviors that cause problems get used as fuel for the fire of treatment. The therapist calls the patient who last week stormed out of the room screaming about the therapist being "an ass" to invite them back to therapy this week. This process takes time—usually a long time—and in a sense serves to correct the underlying flaws in self-esteem. They slowly begin to feel accepted and can then begin to let down their guard, first in therapy and then in the world outside.

When behaviors get anywhere near the level of knife-throwing extremes and interventions are necessary, it is important for leadership to set limits and to stick to their consequences. For the Narcissus, the extreme behaviors that require forced intervention will usually be dramatic displays of anger or rule breaking, both of which can be potentially unsafe in the workplace. For the Narcissus, interventions must place self-interest on the other side of enforced limits. He must know that loss of money, power, or status is at risk if he messes up again. It is important to be direct. For example, the Narcissus must clearly hear from a boss, legal, or HR that if he does not attend therapy or if he becomes enraged at work again, he will be subject to a demotion, will be moved to a less desirable office space, will lose income, or will lose the respect of someone admired. If such methods fail, the Narcissus is likely Impossible and should be removed from the workplace if possible.

Richard: Part Two

Richard's behavior had escalated to the point of being persistent and even unsafe, and thus a formal intervention was mandated by his employer. Interventions can often be difficult to carry out, since narcissistic individuals don't feel that they need treatment and often criticize it as useless (Gabbard 2007).

Richard was required by the restaurant owners to "get help" and, after consultation with me, was referred to a cognitive therapist. He was told that if he did not attend treatment, he would be demoted from executive chef to sous chef with a corresponding decrease in pay grade and that they would begin taking applications for a new head chef immediately upon his breaking the terms of their agreement. In this conversation, they also let Richard know how important he was to their success and how much they hoped to keep him on; they also spoke about their future goals and projections for the restaurant itself as a way to keep him invested. There were hints of acknowledging connections with other restaurants and how his reputation would be affected. The owners had a meeting with the kitchen staff that welcomed feedback about behavior that they found difficult or threatening. Despite the fact that Richard was extremely talented and qualified and brought in significant business to the restaurant— meaning that the owners largely wanted to keep him on despite the day-to-day problems—they realized that limits and consequences were the way to promote improvement both in Richard and the kitchen overall. They acknowledged the important consequences that changing Richard's behavior might have on productivity, morale, and retention of the employees that had to work with him. Perhaps most important was that the liability of knife throwing was regarded as too extreme a risk to not do something about.

At first, Richard was resentful and unengaged in treatment, but he attended religiously under threat of the outlined consequences for his success. He initially undermined the process and suggested that therapy might be helpful for some but that he, of course, didn't need it, had nothing to discuss, was only there because he was misunderstood by the owners, and was just putting in his time. He did, however, manage to flirt with his female therapist at every opportunity until she eventually addressed it directly. She asked why he thought she would want to spend time with him if he acted in this way. And why would he want to spend money week after week just to flirt with her? What were his goals in doing so?

Richard's reply was that he had to be there anyway, had nothing to talk about, and that she was "just adorable . . . even if she believed this quack stuff." He hoped that perhaps after all the therapy was said and done they could meet for coffee? His therapist took the opportunity to reiterate the concept of therapist-patient boundaries: they were working together—not friends, not partners—and their interactions would be limited to professional interactions in the office. The therapist also suggested there was more to his flirtation than just boredom and attraction. She suggested some possibilities. In attempting to make her squirm with discomfort, was Richard attempting to establish dominance in the room, to make himself bigger, because in truth he felt embarrassed and exposed? Did he need to take charge and control the sessions before she turned the magnifying lens upon him? She explored whether his style of interacting in the room was intended to keep her from taking a close look at him and his possible flaws. She hypothesized that Richard was afraid of being vulnerable, that he wanted to stay in control rather than have therapy turn toward examining his potential weaknesses—because this would be very uncomfortable for him.

Defensive and condescending during the session, Richard left deflated and depressed. Though he continued to insist that she was wrong, her words gnawed at him and he realized she was probably right. In subsequent sessions he was more respectful. Once he stopped trying to direct the therapy, the work could finally begin.

In treatment, Richard and his therapist painstakingly reviewed incident after incident, and Richard was eventually able to see that his methods were not only failing in the moment but were also making it impossible for him to achieve his goals. Multiple exercises where Richard was placed in the role of being one of his own employees helped him begin—just a little—to see how difficult he might be. This process, combined with acknowledging his lack of close relationships, left him with no one else to blame but himself. He realized that as a consequence of his actions, frequent turnover in the kitchen affected the restaurant's functioning and his personal reputation in the culinary community. With support, Richard began to look inward and accept that his behaviors were engendering his distress. He finally grew to despise his prior habits, was embarrassed that he hadn't noted them himself, and began to think more empathically. Over time, his behavior changed dramatically. He began to hold himself in higher esteem and saw that he could have more positive relationships in place of the empty and distressing ones that he previously held. He continued to work in his same kitchen position. Not only was he happier, but so were his staff members, and the restaurant owners were more satisfied knowing they had a safer and more productive restaurant environment.

No matter what our position is, we must realize that having

empathy for the Narcissus in the workplace can also help to heal him and to make the environment more reasonable for everyone. In seeing a person's behaviors as stemming from a fragile ego, the relationship that develops can truly be the mechanism of change. The person can believe that despite flaws, they can be respected. They learn that they don't have to cover up potential weaknesses or put others down. Of course, empathy is only the starting point, and the working relationship is likely to be fraught with anger and discontent. But it is worth knowing that a little bit of true compassion—not bolstered by haughty claims and shiny objects—can go a long way in allowing the Narcissus to accept himself and his position to those around him.

A Checklist of Ways to Effectively Deal with Narcissus

- Flattering with praise and/or compliments can help Narcissus from feeling threatened and reduce angry outbursts.
- Sandwich a request, suggested change, or criticism between compliments to make sure they can hear it.
- Respond quickly to their requests or invitations and avoid ignoring them.
- If possible, avoid putting the Narcissus in positions where they may take credit for your work or disparage you for their own gain.
- Encouraging them to consider the perspective of others or even recognize their own underlying emotions may be helpful if you need to point out their disruptive behavior.
- Consider implementing structural interventions, such as rewarding teamwork over individual efforts, maintaining transparency in task assignments, and avoiding special treatment.

- In extreme cases, mandated therapies or separation may be indicated but only in concert with HR and/or legal.
- Framing intervention as a way for Narcissists to achieve leadership goals, as opposed to addressing flaws, may help Narcissus engage in it willingly.

The Venus Flytrap

When I talk about these people who are creators of chaos, I usually ask someone to think about the most dramatic relationship they've ever been in or witnessed a friend in. This pairing may be marked by breakups and makeups, frantic phone calls and slammed doors; in the most extreme cases, there are perhaps marriage proposals followed by threats of suicide. It likely caused friends and family to gasp and shake their heads. The bringer of such turmoil is the Venus Flytrap, who, much like its botanical namesake, we are drawn to for her sticky sweetness despite its aura of danger or desperation.

The partner in the early stages of such a relationship may say it's the most exciting relationship he's ever experienced. Later, he may label it "unhealthy" or "infuriating." And a person may frequently alternate between thinking it is the very best or very worst. But that's part of the difficulty with the Venus Flytrap; this type ensnares you with an allure that is very hard to escape.

The Flytrap seeks you out and draws you in. You have something she feels she doesn't, and she wants it, or at least to be near it. She believes you will fill a void and complete her. She wants affection and caring. But—*buyer beware!*—even if you're showing your interest in her, she's preparing for something else. She's certain your interest can't last, and it makes her so anxious that she'll push and push and push until you prove her right. She's so worried that you *can't possibly stay* that her actions serve to prove her deepest insecurities correct. And all of this might happen right in the office and does not even have to involve romance or sex.

Flytraps are incredibly appealing and seductive—initially. They tend to be really interested in you—and, hey, who doesn't want to feel interesting? And whatever it is that you are seeking in this relationship, be it a friendship, a romance, or a trusted office colleague, at the beginning you'll get just that. It'll feel great, "intense," maybe the best of this type of relationship you've ever had, and you'll want the Flytrap to keep it up.

But she won't keep it up. She'll turn. She may come back, but she'll turn again and again, until the turning comes to define the relationship and replace the wonderful, positive intensity of what the beginning had to offer. And like a moth to a flame, until you realize that the Flytrap is just being a Flytrap and running through her requisite cycles, you may keep coming back after these turns, hoping against hope that this was the last round. You become dizzy from expectations falling short and the lightning-fast turns that you make to stay on your toes. You stand, hoping she will return to being the person you first met, who was so fun, so attractive, so supportive, so interested, so whatever it was . . . and that she'll stay that way. But the way of the Flytrap is not to be any one thing; it is, instead, to shift and slide, embodying all possibilities and living different extremes of identity. She is not only fun but also horrible—not only exciting but also devastating. There is little stability in who she is or the relationships she maintains.

I recall the story of an emergency room physician who was having real trouble in his nearly twenty-year marriage. As the kids were moving their way through high school, his wife became more and more erratic. She worked part-time at a local paint store, advising customers about home decoration. While at the shop, she frequently lamented how empty the house would feel once they had all moved on. And in private conversation with her husband, she began to accuse him of already cheating on her or of planning to walk out on her once the kids were away. She seemed to have an uncanny number of accidents in the kitchen, never enough for medical attention, but enough to come into work with an odd variety of cuts and bruises. Coworkers wondered what was happening, and more than one thought about domestic abuse given her increasing tendency to bemoan how her husband didn't value her. The various cuts, on the other hand, made her husband recall the woman's stories that she used to superficially cut her arms and legs with razors as a teenager. She had told him that she was so lost as a teenager, so devoid of feeling or direction, that the act of cutting and the vision of her own blood actually made her feel calmer and more alive. He always felt that his wife was dramatic, but the intermittent intense fighting over the years was tempered by her energy and charm. She was fun. His friends thought she was "hot" and that always pleased him. And she loved that her husband was a big, strong doctor. The strength of his persona seemed to fill her up inside.

But as the last child applied to college, she became more and more unraveled. At work, she became irritable and argumentative, messy with the paint without bothering to clean it up. She'd un-expectedly leave the office midday after yelling on the phone. The accusations and fighting at home were almost constant. She kept challenging him to leave her, and yet when he could no longer stand it and would walk toward the door, she would dramatically hold on to his legs, sobbing, begging him to stay. Then she would apologize, announce that she was "damaged" and needed him, and would inevitably seduce him. The seas would calm until the next episode. It's just that the episodes were now almost daily, and sometimes he would walk out, sleep in his car, or stay in a call room at the hospital. And all the while she would accuse him of leaving her, of hating her, of using her, but insist that she needed him and loved him? She made his head spin with confusion and chaos. When he thought about her, he only felt burden and dread. He could not continue to live this way. Where had the woman he loved gone?

As his loving feelings diminished over the months and eventually years of this bedlam, real hatred took hold. As his wife saw his love disappear, the inevitable outcome that she had both expected and catalyzed, she desperately needed to know he still cared in some way. So she'd fight and fight and fight, because as long as she could really upset him, she knew he still had feelings for her, for better or worse. And the underbelly of his love was better than no feelings at all. As he began to develop immunity to her antics, her desperation to get a rise out of him became all-consuming. "Without him I am nothing," she would tell herself, as she spiraled out of control with actions meant to prove that he couldn't possibly stay. She started to be even more erratic at work and was fired for showing up intoxicated and screaming pro-fanities at a customer who asked for assistance.

This all culminated when he was out shopping and received

a call from his own emergency room, stating that his wife was there with a blowout fracture of her eye socket. But his ER was forty-five minutes away—his daily commute—and there was a local ER right in their town. She'd told the doctors there, his colleagues, that her husband had beaten her, that he beat her frequently, and that she needed to safely get away from him. In reality, though, she had calmly taken a soup can from her cupboard and smashed it into her own face—a fact that she later admitted as a source of bizarre pride: "He was so horrible he made me act that way . . ."

This public humiliation led to his divorce decision (after he'd handled the assault complaint), and a fierce legal battle with impossible negotiations. Many years later, the divorce was finalized, and he hobbled away from his marriage feeling utterly broken.

THE FLYTRAP'S BASIC TRAITS

In psychiatry, we call the functioning of this type of personality *borderline*. This term has historically signified the "border" between neurosis and psychosis. Such individuals have been characterized as living between anxious distress (*neurosis*, think Freud, think neurotic) and lack of contact with reality (*psychosis*). The person's all-consuming anxiety revolves around the question of who they are in relation to the people around them. These individuals become nearly psychotic when they go to such extreme lengths to figure out their identities that they cause shocking disruption and conflict that seem truly incomprehensible to onlookers. Psychoanalyst Otto Kernberg is credited with most fully describing the theory of this personality type involving a nonpsychotic but unstable sense of identity (Stone 1993).

Adolf Stern, however, is the psychoanalyst first credited with introducing the term *borderline* in 1938. Unfortunately, part of the drive to define this group of patients stemmed from a perception that they were "extremely difficult to handle effectively by any psychotherapeutic method" (Stern 1938). This hasty portrayal has continued in part with the undue perception that individuals cannot get better and by the unfortunate usage of the term "borderline" to describe disliked patients (Garfinkel 1989). However, recent research indicates that many individuals with a diagnosis of borderline personality disorder can and do get better and live life as they would like to (Zanarini, Frankenburg, et al. 2003; Zanarini, Frankenburg, et al. 2010). As difficult as these patients can be for psychiatrists, the Flytrap is also difficult for colleagues in the workplace.

Marsha Linehan is considered perhaps the most influential mental health professional who has written on and researched borderline personality disorder in recent years. In 2011, she publicly disclosed that she herself struggled with having a borderline personality (Carey 2011). She describes the core of this condition as not being able to regulate one's emotions. Individuals are more sensitive, have more intense emotions, and take longer to recover from their emotional experiences (Linehan 1993).

Jane: Part One

There was a woman named Jane, a junior faculty member in a university English department. I was asked to see her by the legal department because Jane was demanding a promotion that she didn't deserve . . . by blackmailing a tenured professor. Jane had been sleeping with her boss, that professor, a married man with a wife and children. From what I learned of the affair, it had been passionate—marked by lavish vacations and secretive visits in the office. Eventually, the flames began to cool, and the boss chose his wife over Jane. This decision erupted into chaos in the workplace: she began publishing literary critiques based on notes found in his office and eventually taking the department hostage for promotions and book deals. Around the time I was consulted, she had cut her wrists with a box cutter in her office before she was scheduled to teach class that day, instead being rushed off to the hospital.

While everyone was astounded by the degree of chaos that had overtaken the department, such pandemonium was only the pinnacle of a pattern that had taken place in Jane's several years at the university. People saw her as fickle, irresponsible, and egotistical. She was easily offended and moved to angry sarcasm, and people felt uncomfortable around her. Even before the affair, she had been a force that created drama in the halls—quickly making friends only to sever ties between coworkers by spreading rumors, giving backhanded compliments, smoking indoors during faculty meetings.

Even as a consultant on the periphery of this chaos, you could feel the palpable anxiety and tension of the department. No one knew what to do or how to handle her. I, however, viewed her behaviors as related to being a Flytrap, which helps to make sense of all of the diverse behaviors that she showed over time.

The Flytrap has a pattern of intense and stormy relationships that tend to move from idealization of an individual to frank devaluation of that same person, even showing hatred and rage. When she feels someone might be leaving her, her emotions become intense. She might show these intense emotions by acting out dramatically. Behavior in general tends to be impulsive and frequently dangerous (unprotected promiscuity, addiction, spending beyond one's means, etc.) and often includes threatened or actual self-harm. Anger, and difficulty controlling it, is very common. Moods, though frequently shifting in response to immediate circumstances, are deeply felt, but Flytraps also tend to complain of feeling empty inside and of lives characterized by boredom and dissatisfaction. The Flytrap's sense of herself is unstable, distorted, and superficial. In times of extreme stress, she is susceptible to alterations in her perception of reality itself.

In the above example, Jane idealized the professor. She was interested in him from afar while she was in graduate school and preoccupied with him once hired. She was fascinated by his literary voice and extrapolated that he had incredible strength of character. She took every opportunity to hear him speak and was always at his door seeking supervision on her academic pursuits. Her dewy-eyed stares and words of adoration combined with her seductive nature made it difficult for the professor to resist her, and soon their wild affair began.

At first, the intensity of their sexual connection and Jane's heartfelt self-disclosures brought them close, and fast. The way Jane held the professor on such a high pedestal and always wanted to be near him—actually looked pained when they needed to separate—made him feel powerful like never before. Theirs was an intoxicating union . . . until he briefly left for an academic conference.

Jane became infuriated that the professor took his wife and kids to this conference, an annual event for their family. She couldn't quite decide what was worse: that he took them instead of her or that he had left her alone for the week. Both decisions devastated and enraged her. Before he left, she began to fight with the professor at work, yelling so loudly in his office that members of the department began to wonder about the nature of their involvement. His efforts to quiet her were met with bolder efforts to "go public" as she insisted that he must be ashamed or disgusted by her to treat her so badly. And also, she said that he was losing his edge in the literary world, that he was getting old and was not the man he once was. She would devolve into wrenching sobs, asking how he could leave her and why she wasn't good enough to choose over his wife. At this point, the professor knew he was in deep trouble.

Upon return from the conference, Jane came back full force, apologized for her behavior, and assuaged the professor enough to allow him to dive right back in. He was a tad gun-shy now, but being with her when all was good felt *so* good that it overrode any of his misgivings. Until the next time, and the time after that, and the next one. He began to fear her as much as he wanted her. His tipping point came when she began to call his house, appear at parties he attended with his wife, and even went as far as chatting with his wife at one of these events. It was clear that she was violating the boundaries they had set for their affair, and he was at risk of losing everything he'd built in his life. He began to despise her. *How could I have been so stupid as to give her this much power*, he thought to himself.

So he decided to end the relationship, and that's when it all broke loose. Jane was shameless in her efforts to destroy his reputation and his marriage and to negotiate leverage for herself. Whenever he confronted her, she reminded him that he was her senior, that he had exploited a junior faculty member, that she had loved him but that she must be bad or ugly or awful because it was clear he had never loved her. Couldn't he just come back to her and make it all right? It was after one of these confrontations that she slit her wrists in his office.

With Jane, we see her intense, almost contradictory efforts to avoid the professor's rejection, the cardinal sign of the Flytrap. Even before he truly tried to break it off, she saw the conference trip as a potential sign of their ending. Her experience of this trip was that it must be because she herself was a bad person. Because she had idealized the professor, the only possible reason for why he would leave her, even for a trip, was that she was not worthy of him. Jane started to hate him for how he made her feel. She took her anger out on him, making the relationship more unstable. With the Flytrap, these behaviors become cycles that are difficult for either partner to escape.

She is asking over and over again, through all of her actions, Can I be loved, and can this love be sustained? Her neurotic anxiety is scrambling to figure out, Who am I? What am I? What do I like? Whom do I like? As she nears losing touch with reality in her attempts to answer these questions, she becomes erratic or suspicious or, in this case, cuts her wrists. This pairing of opposites can be difficult to understand but is the core of the behaviors. The Flytrap is going to do everything possible to be revolting and repel those around her when all she wants to do is figure out if she is lovable enough to be kept. She thinks she is bad inside, if she is anything at all, and hopes against hope that someone will fill the abysmal pit of emptiness that defines her. This person is utterly afraid of being abandoned and will do anything possible to be held on to.

HOW DID THE FLYTRAP GET THAT WAY?

Research indicates that about 1 to 2 percent of individuals display these behaviors to the extent that they feel unable to be content or successful, and within psychiatry such people are said to have borderline personality disorder. Of note, the research also demonstrates that about three-quarters of diagnosed individuals are female. As with any disorder that is disproportionately diagnosed in one gender, it is worth thinking about the factors that may contribute to the slant. For example, there is the possibility that in a given society, females may express more emotion, which may then get diagnosed with a disorder such as borderline personality (Zlotnick, Rothschild, et al. 2002). At the same time, it has been stated that various forms of sexism, even including sexual abuse, may also contribute to females being diagnosed more frequently than males (Linehan 1993). But in order to understand some of these complicated factors, it is crucial to understand the basics of how any Flytrap gets to be the way he or she is.

How does someone become the Flytrap? It's easiest to think of in terms of parenting, though it's often not so simple. A child already predisposed to strong emotions, perhaps by her genetic background, is raised in an environment that is somehow not supportive (Linehan 1993). People around her show unpredictable responses and are insensitive to her experiences, at times both over- and under-reacting to how the child feels. Marsha Linehan contends that, in such environments, children are taught not to trust themselves or their emotions because there is no consistent outcome to their feelings. When Jane said she was upset, sometimes she was given candy and held, told she was "the best little girl in the world" and that she should "never ever have to feel sad." At other times when she was upset, she was told "no you're not—just get over it!" and ignored while her mother went back to talking on the phone.

Such mixed messages were a hallmark of Jane's mother's parenting, and as a child she didn't develop a clear sense of herself or others. For example, Jane's mom would say, "I'm going out for a minute," then she would go out to the store and come right back. On another occasion, she might again say, "I'm going out for a minute," go out, and come back. But the next time she said, "I'm going out for a minute," she was gone for three days. Jane was left wondering, What happened? Why? Did I do something? The behaviors her mother once called "cute" suddenly became "revolting." Or—even earlier in life—cries for food were first met with instant bottles but later neglected for hours. The child worries, Is Mom here or not here? Is she coming back? Am I bad? Does she love me? Later in life this translates into, Does my boss want me? Do my colleagues really value my work? Does my coworker care about me? Did I upset my employee? Will my supervisor check in on me? So what appears to be anger and drama in the workplace is really about a grown child figuring out who she is and whether she's worthy.

For the Flytrap, this early insecurity and inconsistency spurs the development of unstable relationships later in life. Feeling fear about who she is and if she is loved is so uncomfortable that she compels herself toward the perceived worst possible outcome, just to get it over with. If I'm afraid that, ultimately, I am bad and that you can't really appreciate me—that your support is ephemeral or that you're just mentoring me while you wait for a better employee—I may need to test your feelings to see if they are true. The uncertainty is too excruciating to tolerate.

As a child, Jane wasn't taught to manage her emotions. She didn't learn how to hold back inappropriate behavior when she felt strong emotions. Her mother did not demonstrate how to be organized and systematic about achieving her goals so that they were not so strongly dependent on her emotions. As a child, Jane wasn't taught to soothe herself, to calm herself, to let things wash over her without totally upsetting everything. Strong emotions became the driver of her behaviors and relationships (Linehan 1993).

Another factor in about 75 percent of people diagnosed with borderline personality disorder is a history of sexual abuse or sexual trauma (Linehan 1993). Such experiences can further teach an individual not to trust herself, her emotions, or those around her. They can cause confusion about what love and positive emotions are and how they are supposed to feel, in addition to feelings of guilt and shame (Linehan 1993). In this way, early groundwork for problems with emotional regulation and interpersonal relationships can be perpetuated by these violating experiences.

Of course, it is not recommended to inquire about a history of sexual abuse when in a workplace setting. In most cases, it would be inappropriate to ask about someone's personal sexual history outside of a doctor's or therapist's office, where confidentiality, important motivation, and proper support can be in place. Also, it should not be assumed that an employee who acts like a Flytrap does have a history of sexual trauma.

SPECIES OF FLYTRAP

As we saw with Narcissus, the difficulty one has at work related to being a Flytrap falls along a spectrum. The "border" between being neurotic and psychotic is a broad one. Some Flytraps have consistent, significant problems, while others simply evidence some of the traits in certain situations.

Even among individuals who psychiatrists would say have a borderline personality disorder, we see that a spectrum exists.

People with the most severe difficulties chronically struggle with the inability to control acting out behaviors like unsafe driving, unprotected sex, or excessive drug use and have increasingly dangerous self-mutilation and suicide attempts. They may have visits to psychiatric emergency rooms or inpatient hospital stays. More intense breaks with reality, such as paranoid or dissociated states, may be prominent and might further place these individuals in harm's way. Flytraps may briefly hallucinate, have out-of-body experiences, perceive their body to be severely distorted, feel others are talking about them, or have other experiences that appear psychotic (American Psychiatric Association 2013). However, these experiences usually occur in response to feeling as if they are going to be left alone, often last only minutes, and generally resolve when someone goes to lengths to comfort them. In contrast, someone with another psychotic disorder (like schizophrenia) is more likely to have these experiences at length and more consistently.

Then there are the Flytraps who maintain reasonable stability until they experience some intolerable stress in the world, at which point they display some of the common behaviors. At other points, they may be working without difficulty, seemingly getting along with others in and outside the office. The underlying difficulties—fear of being alone, intense interpersonal relations, and so on—may simmer along undetected. But without acute stimulation, Flytraps' behavior may stay under control. Even without significant problems, though, these individuals may feel difficult to have in the office, and coworkers may complain of "walking on eggshells" around them in fear of tipping them into some form of emotional reaction. It's all about relationships with these individuals, which makes their sensitivity—and coworkers' cautiousness—particularly dependent on how they feel treated by whom. While they may appear needy, angry, or ready for an argument, they frequently feel betrayed or mishandled by those around them.

Many bosses (and spouses) find themselves wondering how they could have hired (or married!) these individuals whose instability seems to come out of the blue. We all experience stress, but we each handle it differently. When the Flytrap can't manage her stress, the entire office can be turned upside down.

So where the Flytrap falls on the borderline spectrum is an important predictor of how disruptive she may be when stressed. Healthier Flytraps generally function well in the workplace but have angry outbursts or dramatic episodes when overwhelmed. Such individuals are commonly sent for consults with me. In fact, it is a well-noted phenomenon with these individuals that they can appear very competent in certain situations but can be grossly unable to handle themselves under other stressors. Their inability to regulate their emotions becomes problematic as raised voices, insults, thrown objects, and even violence toward themselves or coworkers occur. This is when the office Flytrap begins to look like the person in the generic relationship described at the beginning of this chapter. She is valued, perhaps greatly, but her intermittent pattern of acting out causes increasing discomfort to those around her, as everyone struggles to avoid setting her off.

The more distressed Flytrap at work, though, can be a chronic drain on the office's emotional resources and, hence, productivity. Her constant personal drama and attention-seeking gestures are at first interesting and perhaps compelling, but then they are distracting, time-consuming, and often infuriating. Coworkers repeatedly lose time and focus as they are drawn in to "take care" of the outraged Flytrap. It is the chronicity of the distressed Flytrap's symptoms that sets her apart from her healthier botanical peers. Her work life is thus a rocky and unstable one.

Within this spectrum of behaviors and functioning, two species of Flytrap tend to appear in the workplace and in my office. Of the botanical genus *Dionaea* and family *Droseracae*, I have found both the Edgy and Downer species to exist.

The Edgy Flytrap

One type of workplace Flytrap seems to live in an irritable, vigilant state (scanning, thinking, Who's going to screw whom first?), always seeking an enemy to target, always in battle. This is the Edgy Flytrap. She may thrive in a competitive work environment, taking no prisoners as she brings her targets down. This type may appear very competent but then suddenly derail. If she is, say, passed over for a promotion, a targeted person may get blamed for it, or the individual promoted in her stead may get a cold shoulder. She always feels like the victim in these situations—angry, hurt, and wronged—which then makes her think of herself as a "bad" person. The promoted coworker might get lots of damning by faint praise if not outright character assassination. In such stressful times, the possibilities may range from catty gossip to dramatic, uncomfortable scenes in the office. People try not to stare as she paces and curses under her breath, an explosion waiting to happen. "Go ahead and look! But you won't all think it's so great when it happens to you! I've been here for five years, and I'll be damned if this is going to happen because of some arrogant jerk! And if no one sees that, you are all completely insensitive!"

She needs to see who is there for her, who will come to her rescue, and who truly needs her. She can seem excessive in her communications with other people: calling, e-mailing, texting nonstop. "You said you would get back to me about the deadline.

Where are you?" Five minutes later: "Are you serious? There is work to be done!" Five minutes later: "Fine. I guess I won't even finish my part if you can't even contribute to the product. Goodbye!" Outraged when there is a delay or lack of response, she's thinking, *Where are they? What is she doing? He doesn't even care!* She might even enlist others to reach out to the person who wronged her and tell them what they've done. "You should hear the way she's treated me. It's completely unfair. I really need you to stand up for me and let her know how messed up this is. Otherwise, I'll think you are really on her side." And this network approach can happen because of the tendency for the Flytrap to be initially very alluring, engaging, and convincing to others. The Edgy Flytrap may be beloved by her favorites but feared by almost everyone else, and even if she has been helpful to an organization, there tends to be relief when she moves on to her next big thing. If this type's behavior is not contained, it can escalate to destroying office property or even physical assault. When this happens, the Flytrap will still often coordinate the behavior in such a way that she still seems to be the victim, through routes such as spray-painting "you hurt me" on the office door or pushing someone but then falling on the floor. Such behavior moves the Flytrap from the realm of drama to being downright frightening and even dangerous.

The Downer Flytrap

Another Flytrap is the Downer variety. She is always ready with a "glass half empty" perspective on whatever comes her way, is deeply sensitive to perceived rejections, and makes others feel responsible for keeping her misery at bay. Inside, she feels worthless, angry, and misunderstood and will constantly tell others how alone she feels. Coworkers may at first go out of their way to include her, to lift her spirits, to listen to stories of her difficulties at home or her chronic ailments. Attempts at helping are often seen as unsuccessful or even making things worse. She might turn down offers of potential solutions without trying but then sulk and blame others for not helping her. "You just invited me because you feel bad for me! You don't even care. . . . If you really cared, you would know that I don't even like movies," she might say. She might start avoiding people that try to help her and might even start being late or not showing up to work. This type can seem to be a glutton for punishment, and she might act as if she deserves to feel pain. "It's fine—don't worry about me. There's no hope anyways; you should just have fun because people seem to actually like you." She might always sit alone during lunch when others are sitting in the break room but then comment on how it's unfair that she has no one to talk to. Failure ensues as her chronically negative perspective deepens with the ebb and flow of life's stressors. The worst-case scenario can involve threatened or even actual self-harm, and the office can come to a screeching halt as coworkers scramble to ensure her safety. *Why do I even try? If no one seems to care about me, I may as well kill myself. It's not like you would miss me anyway.* But most often, coworkers are simply held hostage by the passive influence of her negativity.

WHEN THE SCHMUCK IN THE OFFICE IS A FLYTRAP

Research indicates that, at least compared with individuals with depression (who already tend to have some difficulty in the office), persons with official borderline personality disorder have much more impairment at work (Skodol, Gunderson, et al. 2002). In fact, poor work history was one of the six criteria proposed by psychiatrist John Gunderson to describe borderline personality disorder (the others being impulsivity, inadequate social contacts, depressed mood when facing loss, brief psychotic episodes, and suicidal gestures) (Stone 1993).

Maintaining steady employment can be challenging for the Flytrap but can also be stabilizing, depending on the role and the environment. Within the workplace, I have personally seen Flytraps in positions of great power, but I have also come across many that simply cannot hold a job because of the chaos they create. Remember, the Flytrap's basic difficulty is emotional problems in relationships. When thinking of the disruption caused by this character in the office, it is helpful to realize that the workplace exists in a network of employment relationships. The Flytrap has relationships to coworkers but also a relationship to the organization itself. In much the same way that she can be distressed about whether Ned at the desk next to her wants, needs, and cares about her, she can also be anxious about whether Green Eggs Food Company wants, needs, and cares about her. The difficult thing about Flytraps in the workplace is that they have the potential to affect far more than their own productivity and to create a truly toxic environment for those around them.

It really is all about relationships. Let's take the seemingly simple example of a compliment. "Hey, Nina, nice job on drafting up that response." When a boss admires the Flytrap's work, she may think, *Okay, he said he likes it, but does he* really *like it?* Now, doing her work is less about the job and more about whether she can keep pleasing this person. The praise sets an expectation of success, which makes the Flytrap nervous that she may not be able to meet such standards. She tries to figure out where she stands and how enduring this relationship really is. Maybe she'll start ugly rumors in the office, make excessive demands for his time, or start misbehaving more, just to see if he still wants her there. And if she sees that her coworker's patience with her is wearing thin, perhaps she'll scare herself and then jump back into shape to try and make herself essential to him again. "Will you engage with me in this endless cat-and-mouse game? Or will you just get rid of me, which is what I knew I deserved in the first place?"

Recall that the Flytrap's life is marked by unstable relationships, an insecure view of herself, and impulsive behavior. She might be the worker who cries when the boss is out of town, who spends inordinate amounts of money, who uses drugs without regard, who is promiscuous without protection, who fights or yells, who flips from angry to happy within a single shift. She might sit at your desk for hours each day complaining about the way her boss, lover, parent, and others victimize her and about the depths of her depression from being mistreated. She may then take it out on you when you try to get back to your own work. Then, too, she may confide that she feels suicidal or otherwise as if she wants to hurt herself and you may find yourself feeling somehow responsible for whether or not she makes it through the night safely.

Does any of this ring a bell? If you are thinking of anyone who might be a Flytrap, stop to consider your own reactions to the person since they might be a hint that you are in the right character ballpark. Do you have particularly strong internal reactions to this person? Do you anticipate interactions with her with particular excitement or intense dread—or more likely both? Does she pull you in certain directions that you might otherwise not go? And do you find that you feel both pulled and pushed? Is there more activity in this relationship than is common for you? Are you going out of your way in a manner you wouldn't expect?

Clues that you may be dealing with a Flytrap in the office are that you feel the person is often acting angry, hostile, or aggressive (Linehan 1993). However, developing empathy for the Flytrap and understanding the underpinnings of her behavior are the keys to succeeding in relationships with her. Underneath those behaviors, it is important to remember that the Flytrap is likely feeling afraid, desperate, hopeless, and out of control (Gunderson 2009). I do not mean that empathy and understanding should lead to tolerance of unsafe behaviors, but it is said that the key to working with these individuals is to understand just how sensitive and vulnerable they really are (Linehan 1993). Everything they do is an effort to lessen the pain they are feeling and to try to get people to care for them, from the frantic phone calls to cutting their skin. Understanding this seeming contradiction and then learning the right way to provide support is crucial to allowing you to do the difficult, and sometimes counterintuitive, things that will contain the Flytrap and allow her anxiety to settle.

DEALING EFFECTIVELY WITH A FLYTRAP

I recall my first psychiatry rotation in medical school, watching my supervising resident introduce herself to a patient, a perfect stranger, and within moments ask incredibly personal and intrusive questions. "Are you suicidal?" "Do you hear voices?" I thought. *How dare she!?* This brusqueness is exactly what we are taught *not* to do in social exchanges. In the world, we are typically taught to value nuance, politeness, kindness. This approach appeared to be none of those things and was completely startling. And yet, seemingly relieved, the patient answered "yes" to both questions as he settled into telling us about why he was so upset. He was there for help, and he wanted to share this information. I learned from this early career conversation and carry the experience with me whenever I'm consulting with people in the workplace.

Time and time again when using effective techniques for dealing with the Flytrap in the office, you may think, Really? But that sounds like it would never work! But have faith knowing that some of these counterintuitive tactics really do work.

Though compelled to act badly at times, the Flytrap wants to be directed to contain herself. She wants to learn acceptable boundaries for her behavior and, though she will test them to see if they're real, their structure will comfort her. As this happens, you will need to clearly define limits and continuously reinforce them. Remember that the Flytrap has difficulty regulating her emotions and relationships so you may need to impose the organization that helps her to do this.

Avoid re-creating the environment of her childhood. That is, don't simply tell the Flytrap *not* to feel a certain way or that there is no possible way she *could* feel that way. "You can't be upset in the office—that's ridiculous!" may be an upsetting reminder of *You can't cry for what you want; you're a ridiculous brat!* If you instead point out that the Flytrap must be feeling angry or afraid, it helps her feel less guilt or shame about what is going on and avoid escalating her attempts to get you to understand what she is truly feeling. "I understand that this seems upsetting to you, but I think we both want to finish this assignment, so let's focus on doing that well. How does that sound?"

In her tendency to drastically switch self-image, the Flytrap often also thinks that she has to do things perfectly or that otherwise they're useless. It can help to have the Flytrap see mistakes as things that need to be gradually improved. For example, when pointing out an error on a report, it might be helpful to say, "Overall, the document had parts that needed improvement, but other sections were right on target. If you want to start by fixing the numbers in paragraph 3 and show me your progress, we can take it from there." This approach of showing gradual steps toward improvement can help the Flytrap from switching to seeing her work or herself as all "bad" and going into crisis mode.

When there are circumscribed problems at work, it can be helpful to take the person aside and break the causes and effects down very explicitly. This technique is called "chain analysis" (Linehan 1993). There should be a very clear conversation about what the problem behavior was. Then you can work together to figure out the chain of events that led to the behavior, step by step, along with consequences, solutions, and ideas to prevent it from happening next time. This conversation should be straightforward but nonjudgmental and explicit to the point that all of the steps are agreed upon and written down for future reference. An additional part of this exercise can be listing pros and cons for acting in a certain manner. Having the person write down all of this can be helpful to have for future reference.

An example of such interaction might occur after an upsetting incident at work. "Aaron, I understand that things were pretty upsetting yesterday. I'd like to help us figure out a plan to go forward. How does that sound?" Hopefully the worker will buy into the idea. If not at first, it might help to bring up a goal such as finishing the project or feeling less stressed at work. "So let's focus on exactly what happened yesterday. What about the way you acted would you want to avoid doing in the future? . . . Throwing everything off of your desk? Okay, let's start there. What was happening at work yesterday that led to that endpoint? Let's write them down." Once the chain of events is established, he can describe what made him vulnerable to acting in a way that he agrees is not constructive. "Do you think anything in particular made you susceptible to being so overwhelmed by that at work yesterday?" The conversation should focus on changeable factors at work (such as the temperature in the office or the uncomfortable seat) or at home (such as not getting enough sleep or not having brought in lunch). Without being clinical, the conversation can focus on workplace consequences, aiming to identify potential solutions that the employee can implement or that the employer can easily make to the workplace environment. A team approach is particularly effective, offering some help but also giving the employee responsibility for implementing change.

Remember that the Flytrap reacts dramatically to feeling blamed, shameful, or guilty. When working to modify behavior at work, it is important to do so from a position of gentle understanding. Instead of pointing fingers, it can help to say that you "understand why someone would get upset when all of one's co-workers go out of town." While acknowledging understanding, there has to be a call for change: "However, I think that there would be a better way to act in that situation to get the help you needed." It is important to help the individual feel competent and in control. Concrete examinations of behavior focusing on simultaneously understanding it and recognizing a need for change are an important method. "When you sent that e-mail criticizing everyone for being out of the office, it made it less likely for you to get help than if you had pointed out that you were the only one at the office and requested help with meeting the deadline."

In moments of escalating drama—crying, yelling, throwing something—it can be helpful to direct the Flytrap to some alternative activities (Linehan 1993). Incorporating some options into the workplace environment itself can be useful for anyone such as having a comfortable and decorated break room, giving out stress balls, or allowing employees to listen to music through headphones when they need to do so. Encouraging employees to regularly exercise or participate in yoga or meditation can have important benefits for employees, including Flytraps. Many employers now incentivize such interventions, which are known to be effective for positively influencing overall physical and mental health, often through provider insurance plans. Programs might reward documenting regular exercise, taking questionnaires about one's own coping strategies, or implementing stress management techniques for reductions in monthly employer-sponsored insurance premiums, for example.

But all of these strategies only work if the individual wants to work. Particularly as a supervisor, an honest discussion can be held about whether the employee actually wants to be at that job. It should not be assumed. Once you're both on the same page and working as a team toward an employment goal, certain stipulations can be put into an agreed-on plan, such as repercussions for specific behaviors that limit the individual's (or coworkers') ability to function at work. For the Flytrap, it is important to position some stable reference point on the other side of breaking the agreement. For example, it may be made clear that on breaking the agreement, the individual could not work anywhere at the company, not just within the department. This technique may be effective if the Flytrap employee truly does value (in her own chaotic way) a relationship with the organization. Clear limits with logical repercussions are important, as is the ability to communicate their value in a nonjudgmental, supportive way.

In working with these individuals, it is important to find out exactly what they are emotionally attached to—be it a boss, clients, or the organization itself—and use this entity as leverage. The recipe for success with this individual is difficult; it takes courage and gravitas to set the limits they need. Someone has to say, "We cannot work under these circumstances. You cannot act in this manner or else . . ." and then use their leverage point. It's a zero-tolerance strategy at work, but one implemented with empathy. It is also very important to reward the Flytrap's positive behavior as soon as possible. Immediate positive feedback, particularly about the Flytrap's personally established goals and values, can be extremely useful in helping sustain the behavior (Linehan 1993). For example, the most effective feedback with the Venus Flytrap might very well be, "It looks like the plan we developed is really working for keeping you connected to and respected by others at work" instead of directly commenting on the work product itself, as one might for another employee. The worst behavior is bound to occur when limits are transgressed without consequence and there is no positive feedback delivered for effective behavior.

This technique of limit setting and structure seems aligned with a managerial dynamic but can be similarly adapted to coworker and employee relationships. One idea is to secure regular, dependable check-ins but to indicate that outreach beyond that time frame cannot be tolerated. The Tuesday-afternoon coffee break can do wonders for holding back dramatic outreach during the rest of the week. "Paul, I understand why you are upset, but I need to continue my work at this time. Why don't you go for a walk and we can catch up about this over coffee tomorrow afternoon?" Though it might seem uncouth, this structured approach can actually be (and be perceived as) quite helpful to the Flytrap. However, the effectiveness of this technique is extremely dependent on actually being there when you promise to be and establishing a pattern of dependability.

The clearer and more consistent one can be with a Flytrap, the better. Initially, one approach that can help with this is to schedule a regular supervision time every single week, for the same amount of time, to help the Flytrap manage her expectations. As this schedule is regularly maintained, she becomes less and less fearful that a boss, for example, will just disappear from her life. She will fear that she "disappears" from the colleague's mind between opportunities to meet, which may cause her to try to contact the colleague, sometimes frequently. In such a case, there needs to be agreed-on limits set for the amount of contact allowed, lest boundaries become unclear. The key to working with a Flytrap in the office is structure and consistency, structure and consistency, structure and consistency.

Obviously, life happens, and one cannot always be at the office or on the phone exactly as planned for all eternity. Down the road, such a disruption can be healthy for a Flytrap if there has been an established trust and pattern of expectation. The Flytrap is prompted to navigate the fear and disappointment created by, say, an illness that prevented a colleague from being on time. Over time, the Flytrap may begin to see such events as reasonable occurrences in the life of a person, any person, who is inherently fallible like all people naturally are.

Jane: Part Two

What could the professor have done differently? Well—of course—he didn't have to sleep with Jane. He could have resisted the ego stroking that she was offering, that filled his emotional holes, and instead he could have simply redirected her behavior.

Why we succumb to temptation is often complex. To avoid discomfort, sometimes it feels easier to cover a tumor with a bandage than to go through the anxiety, pain, and suffering of surgical removal. The professor's frustration with the dean not funding his department, for example, might not have felt as overwhelming as he sought some stimulation, excitement, and distraction. Then he didn't need to confront anything, think about the dwindling resources and declining quality of work, or uproot his home or family in the search for a new job. Right? Or so he thought . . .

When Jane began to demand so much of the professor's time, he might have suggested a regular meeting for supervision, perhaps weekly for an hour. And if Jane was flirtatious or seductive, he might have directly acknowledged it and clarified that he found it inappropriate and counterproductive to their working relationship and to productivity for the department. These decisions are definitely easier to make when sexual or other forms of attraction are not coming up. But the Flytrap has a talent for finding people who are willing to "play ball" and capitalize upon that dynamic.

If Jane was unable to respect the boundaries of the weekly supervision by, say, showing up at a time when no meeting was scheduled or calling or e-mailing too much, the professor might have pointed this out during one of their supervisions. He could let her know that the contact was excessive and help her find ways to become more independent. He could also have suggested assignment of a midlevel faculty supervisor to work more closely with her instead. Whatever the limit set, he would have needed to be clear about the process, and she may have accepted the structure in order to keep the relationship.

Maintenance of the working relationship can sometimes be the only bargaining chip you need to keep things as stable as possible with the Flytrap. Since she will not modulate her own intensity, your ability to frame, define, and limit the relationship will predict its success. Her tendency to overvalue you, her job, a colleague, or whatever other thing is important to her can initially hold great power and might confuse priorities. The almost-prescribed "flip" that occurs when the Flytrap starts to devalue the things she once held in high esteem can be slowed or averted if the intensity of the reaction is contained. So a relationship with very clear limits or a highly structured job with defined roles and expectations will more likely be sustained. However, the real progress is likely to take place by also seeing a therapist and will take years of learning about healthy boundaries, acceptance, and constancy. In this manner, the Flytrap can finally have some stability in who she is in relation to those around her.

I was once referred an employee, a very talented designer working at a big clothing company, who had been upsetting her colleagues by coming to the studio with a variety of cuts on her arms that would sometimes begin to open and bleed at work. After the first time or two, it became very clear that these were self-inflicted injuries—though she refused to discuss them directly, she would often make vague reference to the actions: "Well, at least I know I'll feel better at home tonight, take some of the pain away . . ." Then she would show up the next day with a new wound. Colleagues were concerned about the potential for suicide and unsure how to address the visibility of the cuts. They were also concerned about the potential for transmission of illness if blood were to get on shared spaces. (As a side note, sometimes Flytraps cut themselves in order to make themselves feel better instead of as an attempt to die.)

When I started seeing her in therapy, she began to bring razors into our sessions and actually attempt to cut herself in front of me. This behavior was absolutely untenable, and I had to re-quire a hard rule that this would not occur again. The imperative was that she would not cut in front of me. If she did, it would lead to immediate termination with me. I also advised her office place to enact a similar rule: she was not able to show up to work with new cuts and would have to take her limited sick days instead.

It was obvious that her relationship with her job was an impor-tant one. This fact was made clear when her boss and HR first approached her about coming to therapy if she wanted to keep working for the label. She complied with the firm boundaries we set from the beginning, but she still didn't understand why her actions were so upsetting to me or others around her. Cutting was a normal part of her life, and our sessions sometimes made her feel anxious, so why not just cut there? Why not cut after a hard day at work when others made her feel so bad about herself? With education and time, she began to see the negative effects of her actions on others as well as her own relationships and goals. Eventually, she began to find healthier, more productive ways to self-soothe.

So that was the designer, but whatever happened to Jane and the professor?

Well, the dramatic explosion at work spread far and wide at the university. Academic circles are small, so rumors were spread-ing nationally about the professor's relationship, his boundary transgression, and his inappropriate academic practices with Jane. His reputation was really tarnished.

He was encouraged to find a position elsewhere, but he re-minded all who asked that he had tenure and would not be mov-ing. He was, however, thereafter marginalized and excluded from just about all of the department goings-on.

His wife left him swiftly. It seems that it wasn't a very difficult decision for her since she'd been very unhappy for a very long time, as we so often see in relationships where partners have strayed. His children felt far more betrayed and infuriated, and it was many, many years before there was any comfort among them again. The professor moved to an apartment near campus and just tried to focus on his work and keep moving.

Jane was, at first, full of threats. She asserted that the university had allowed her to be abused and manipulated by the professor and had ruined her chance at a real career in her field. It was difficult for her department chair to reason with her since she was given to loud, angry, and vitriolic outbursts whenever approached. With input from the legal department, I advised that the chair reassign Jane to another division within the department, and I also advised the chair to apologize to Jane for the professor's inappropriate actions but also to remind Jane that she was an adult who had made choices as well. With the professor essentially out of the picture—in that he had little left to offer professionally or in terms of allure at this point—she dropped the threatened lawsuit.

In restructuring the workplace, Jane was able to have a mentor. He was also a very esteemed professor (an intentional move so she could not complain that her career was disadvantaged), but he had impeccable boundaries and no interest whatsoever in Jane's drama. I worked with the department chair to make sure they made everything extremely clear and structured for her. The new mentor assigned Jane the academic deliverables and that was that. He interacted with her as with all of his other mentees and, if Jane needed more attention for work-related issues, she was referred to someone more junior. Try as she did, there was no way in. First, she tried to gain sympathy by detailing how she was "trying to recover from what happened to me here," and then eventually tried the seductive card. "Wow, I thought I'd seen the best there was in our field, but you're really opening my eyes. You're quite something!" No go. The new professor was always polite and responsive to her academic needs, but that was that. There would be no "special relationship" here.

And you know what? She did great. Jane was a smart woman, and she didn't need all of that outside noise to succeed. She learned to derive positive feedback at work from—positive feedback at work! When the workplace was structured so that she was unable to negotiate any special treatment, she stopped spinning her drama wheels and just followed the pursuits that brought her to the university in the first place. With this, she blossomed. Her reputation in the new division preceded her, and everyone around Jane quickly learned the code of treating her with respect but also with boundaries. So, this time around, no one got sucked in when she attempted a play, and eventually she stopped trying.

Now, I'm not saying that this behavior stopped altogether, and I'm certainly not suggesting that it stopped outside the office. Her personal life was still a wreck, and her few friends were running short on patience with her needy, predictable, emotional relationship cycles. But the department managed to create the perfect sandbox for her, and she learned to play like a model citizen.

A Checklist of Ways to Effectively Deal with a Venus Flytrap

- Continuously define boundaries and clearly reinforce them.
- Recognize and redirect emotions, rather than restrict without rationale.
- Practice "chain analysis" to help the Flytrap learn adaptive emotions and behaviors for future situations.

- In the heat of emotional outbursts, redirect them toward alternative activities to distract them and break the negative emotional spiral.
- Implement empathic but firm zero-tolerance interventions directed toward negative behaviors, as well as immediate positive feedback toward healthy behaviors.
- Acknowledge the acceptability of gradual improvement.
- Remember the key to working with the Flytrap is structure and consistency.
- Avoid getting pulled into the drama at all costs.

The Swindler

When we talk about Swindlers, we are talking about people who truly have no regard for rules or for other people. The best example I ever saw of this down-to-the-core criminality was a guy I came across while rotating through a psychiatric unit at a prison. There was an older guy there who had Alzheimer's disease and could hardly take care of himself any longer. He couldn't remember anything, barely knew where he was at times, often needed help with meals—food dribbling down his chin—and wore adult diapers.

However, even in near-complete detachment from the world, he was still orchestrating an entire cigarette-bartering circuit alongside a card-game gambling ring, as if being able to break rules for profit was the essential core of who he was. He had an elaborate system for moving goods and clear targets for whom he could get to trade what. He remained persuasive and manipulative enough to locate a more capable man on the unit and get him to run aspects of the business he was no longer intellectually able to manage, but to do so as his "employee," capitalizing on the man's dependency needs. While he could barely take care of himself, he was still chillingly able to hone in on what he wanted and from whom to get it.

THE SWINDLER'S BASIC TRAITS

The history of scholars thinking about such lawless persons has been largely tied to questions about free will and blame (Arrigo and Shipley 2001). Other questions that have arisen concern goodness versus evil, madness versus badness, sickness versus sin. Are these people sick? Can they control themselves? Are they ill? Are they to blame? Are they just bad and corrupt and responsible for everything they do? Do they deserve help or punishment? Nineteenth-century thinkers were interested in how certain persons could be destructive while nonetheless understanding these behaviors and their consequences (Millon, Simonsen, et al. 1998). They thought about how these people seemed very much in control of how ruthless they were. French physician Philippe Pinel referred to them as having *manie sans délire* (insanity without confusion of mind), while American psychiatrist Benjamin Rush described patterns of "vicious actions" without resultant shame (Millon, Simonsen, et al. 1998). In the 1830s, an anthropologist named James Cowles Prichard described "an irresistible impulse to commit injury or do mischief of all kinds" (Stone 1993). It wasn't that lawless persons didn't know what they were doing; they knew what they were doing and that it was wrong, but they still did it. And often did it again. And again.

Of course, the idea has greatly evolved over time and has proceeded through a series of names, moral judgments, degrees of responsibility, and thoughts about causes and treatment. Throughout its psychiatric heritage, however, the trait of sociopathy has usually been conceptualized as committing patterns of social transgressions without any concern for others. Some of the most common, recent, and related terms employed to describe these characteristics include *psychopathy, sociopathy,* and *antisocial personality disorder.* Typically, use of the words *antisocial* or *sociopathy* is indicative of the patterns of rule-breaking behavior (i.e., these words describe patterns of behavior where *social* rules and contracts are repeatedly broken), whereas usage of the term *psychopathy* tends to refer to underlying personality characteristics, particularly a lack of remorse, rather than the behavior itself. However, there is significant overlap between how and when the terms are used, and many people don't distinguish significantly between them.

These terms became popularized among the American public in the 1940s after Hervey M. Cleckley published *The Mask of Sanity: An Attempt to Clarify Some Issues about the So-Called Psychopathic Personality* (Murley 2008). The conventional picture of this person became one of a man who appeared as a regular citizen but would sexually and violently terrorize unsuspecting women without getting caught. This love-to-hate character type became a popular figure of books, television shows, and movies. We think of Alfred Hitchcock's famous movie *Psycho* or of widespread interest in real-life serial killer Ted Bundy, who confessed to the murder of thirty girls and young women in the 1970s. In contemporary new media, the overwhelming popularity of the most-heard podcast ever, *Serial,* demonstrates the continued fascination with this character type, as this audio series explores whether or not a high school student is in fact a cold, sociopathic killer. Homicidal figures are the very extreme end of the Swindler spectrum, and indeed murdering sociopaths tend to be the most common image brought to mind when discussing these terms, but it is important to remember that in actuality the vast preponderance of Swindlers are nothing of the sort.

The term that contemporary American psychiatrists use to describe severe Swindlers is *antisocial personality disorder*. This condition is estimated to appear in about 3 percent of males and 1 percent of females (Sadock 2000) and is understandably more common in prisons and jails because of the way the disorder is defined (American Psychiatric Association 2013). That is, part of what gains someone the label of having an antisocial personality disorder is breaking rules and laws without regard, which is somewhat defined by the justice system and social norms relative to those who do not conform. To meet the criteria for being diagnosed, such individuals are in touch with reality and understand that what they're doing is wrong; it's not merely criminal behavior. That is to say that just by committing a crime, or even series of crimes, someone is not necessarily a sociopath. A sociopath exists in contrast to other kinds of offenders, who may either not understand what they're doing (e.g., a psychotic individual takes off her clothes in public because she believes God told her to do so and is thus out of touch with reality) or may understand it with a sense of remorse (e.g., a man guiltily robs a bank to get money for his son's cancer treatment).

The Swindler is going to be arrogant and entitled on the one hand, but he will often fall short on following through with tasks and obligations. Swindlers don't follow the rules, and they experience few misgivings about whom they might or do hurt along the way. What often surprises people is how charming these individuals can be. They have a superficial appeal but are insincere in their words and actions. A general pattern of deceit and manipulation runs throughout multiple areas of their life, but it often goes undetected, making them a hard type to spot.

Galen: Part One

Galen was a senior executive at an investment firm whose partners turned to me when an internal audit revealed he'd been embezzling significant amounts of money from the practice for quite some time. He had managed to create a series of "subcompanies" within the firm, unbeknownst to anybody, and was siphoning off funds that ended up in his pocket. These efforts, of course, moved money away from the hands of others who were no less deserving. While the scheme worked and ran along undetected, it was a rather brilliant hoax. His career of bold moves and big financial successes for the firm had earned him less scrutiny, and, when the time proved right, he took full advantage of his access to money and power. Once his hoax was discovered, his fellow partners literally sat frozen—mouths agape at their own gullibility. It was almost incomprehensible that he'd pulled this off. The scandal was a devastating and humiliating blow to the firm. Many people felt hurt that they had been taken advantage of and manipulated. There was a sense of violation, that they had let someone in, trusted him, and—worse—even liked him. They turned out to be completely wrong in their estimations; he had been hurting them all along, using them without a care. There was little solace when Galen was arrested.

Interestingly, his colleagues, the office staff, and his clients truly seemed to love him. There had been no overt pattern of disruptive behavior, and he had been good at his job. He had a magnetism that drew people in, and everyone loved to be around him; in fact, many people had a sense of wanting to *be* him. He outwardly displayed a sort of casual charm that made people trust him. People had known that he drank and gambled, but they hadn't seen any major problems. He was Galen, the seemingly perfect partner with the dazzling life. It was only as investigations were under way that a complicated web of deceit, cheating, and stealing became revealed, to the surprise of everyone in the office. To make matters worse, it wasn't that Galen needed the money or pulled off a heist in the face of desperation; the whole thing was to make Galen richer—while others unknowingly suffered on the sidelines.

It became very obvious that under his attractive, charismatic surface, Galen was hiding a Swindler who repeatedly neglected to care for others over the course of his life. The calculated purpose of that charisma was to be able to get close enough to understand and then manipulate people for his benefit. Everything he did was to get *something* (money, power, sex) for himself, and he always felt righteous in his conquests. He saw himself as a living legend, but he saw others as lesser beings who existed solely to provide for him, justifying his actions by thinking, "It's a dog eat dog world" (Gabbard 2007). One could understand him as having little fear, particularly of punishment, and hardly any moral conscience (Gabbard 2007). In general, he was not able to feel emotions connected to other people as human beings (such as empathy, joy, guilt, or remorse) but instead lived on shallow envy, boredom, hatred, and excitement.

HOW DID THE SWINDLER GET THAT WAY?

Swindlers will show specific patterns of behavior before age fifteen, including aggression to people or animals, destruction of property, deceitfulness, theft, and violation of rules (American Psychiatric Association 2013). Often, Swindlers have learned to be this way by having to figure out how to get their needs met while growing up. For example, though Galen grew up in average socioeconomic circumstances, his alcoholic father often hit him when he made mistakes, and his mother—whom he frequently saw abused as well—passed away when he was young, leading to parenting by a string of various stand-in girlfriends of his father, whom he also often witnessed his father physically abuse.

So, from an early age, Galen had to look out for himself, and he learned to do what he needed to without feeling guilt, no matter how others were affected. He cared only for himself and thought of others as pawns in his game. As a survival skill, he learned how to "read" people, like a card player, to determine who might be able to give him what. As he honed in on a person's weaknesses, he would laud his or her strengths, pulling the person closer into his thickening plot. He made false promises he knew would never be actualized and had a "no pain, no gain" mentality toward people in his path. Success became a need beyond mere existence. He felt and acted as if he were unstoppable, even when he was, in fact, caught. Even then, he had excuses and blamed others for what went wrong.

In fact, Swindlers are often known to use their stories of difficult upbringing or experiences as manipulation tools to gain sympathy from others (beyond what even they feel is actually descriptive of the true events) and to perhaps escape punishment or further scrutiny. Although, of course, it is important to have empathy for a person's background—and particularly for their experience of trauma—it is also important to acknowledge how the Swindler can calculatingly use stories about personal experiences for effect and justification, without a sense of sadness or remorse.

WHO IS IN THIS MOB?

Fast Eddie, the Sleaze, the Big Boss, and the Serial Killer

As with the other schmuck character types, we also find that there is a spectrum among Swindlers. Let's divide them loosely as follows, understanding that there are many gray areas in between. The Swindlers include Fast Eddie, the Sleaze, the Big Boss, and the Serial Killer. It is helpful to think of these divisions as increasingly dangerous and covert.

Many people don't meet criteria for any of this, but they just love to bend the rules. My father was such a man. At the supermarket, he loved to peel labels off food cans in the hopes of getting a cheaper price at checkout. These actions were neither ubiquitous nor defining, he seemed to just have fun with it every once in a while. He liked to jaywalk and race his car through yellow lights, but in all other ways he was a really caring guy. He did not have any pattern of hurting others and still had concern for those around him. In time, I came to understand his toying with rules as a certain immaturity, a need to test social boundaries just as a child tests the limits set by her parents to get some stimulation when life gets boring. Individuals like my father can inadvertently get into trouble, get caught at their silly games, but they aren't inherently bad people.

The rest of the mob is corrupt. Their characteristics pick up where my father left off. Fast Eddie is bad, the Sleaze is worse, the Big Boss is horrible, and the Serial Killer is pure evil. As we move along the spectrum, we get more and more terrified of this gang of Swindlers. Each has less remorse and more callousness than the prior one. They're a bad bunch of rule breakers, and what distinguishes one from the next is the severity of their rule breaking, the depth of their immorality, the absence of their concern for others, and how good they are at conning and manipulating. The spectrum of rule breaking starts with jaywalking and ends with the serial killer next door—or in your bed. That isn't to say that a single individual will progress from jaywalking to clandestine killing, by any means, but this is the gamut of things the mob of Swindlers will do, and understanding this range will help you figure out just who is who.

Fast Eddie

First up is Fast Eddie. Like my dad, he just wants to get away with relatively little things, for sport, superficial convenience, or easy shortcuts. He is a low-level Swindler, but it is a defining feature of his pursuits. Eddie's always cutting corners and looking to worm out of doing work. He may find illegal ways to park in the executive lot or perhaps overstate expenses from his last business trip, creating false receipts to support his claims. This approach defines a way of being for him: trying to get the most for the least, no matter who else has to foot the bill. His schemes often aren't very complicated, but they're repeated over and over again with the mentality that he's deserving of whatever benefits he can accumulate. Fast Eddie commits a lot of acts that transgress social norms, but he doesn't have the same degree of underlying manipulation, callousness, or showiness that some of the other gang members manifest.

I found one example of a Fast Eddie particularly sad. This man worked for a nonprofit company, where he was absolutely beloved.

One of his several roles was to manage the volunteer program, but he was otherwise the "go-to guy" for just about anything. He'd been with the company for over twenty years and knew it inside and out. In many ways, he was seen as representative of the place because of his inclusive, friendly nature. In casual conversation, he might mention some of his financial concerns, putting a daughter through college, managing the mortgage, and so on, but it didn't feel different from what anyone else was saying. The problem was this: all volunteers received a pass card for free food anywhere in the company. The intention was to cover lunch, but it also worked at the coffee cart, gift shop, and at breakfast and dinner, too. Because he ran the program, he decided that he was entitled to these cards as well. He kind of, sort of knew that this wasn't true, but he ran the program so he felt he *should* be allowed to do this. And so, for almost all of his twenty years, he never once paid for a meal or snack. He often had three meals per day at work, and, in the gift shop, he even used the card for other merchandise. As the years passed, this job perk simply became a fact in his mind.

At some point, a cashier questioned him about his card and decided not to take his assertion that it was legitimate as fact. She reported him to her boss, who reported it to her boss, who reported it to Human Resources. A quick analysis revealed that he'd used the cards to obtain items worth many thousands of dollars over the years. He was immediately fired. He insisted that he was simply naive, that this was a misunderstanding, and that he would happily repay any money he'd taken. Nonetheless, he was escorted off the property like a criminal. It turns out that after he left, people began to talk and put things together about all the little ways he had tried to game the system. In his position, not much was available, but he still seemed to take what he felt was due, when he felt he should have it.

The Sleaze

The Sleaze, on the other hand, is a wholly committed manipulator. He tries to be charming and smooth and thinks he's the bomb. In truth, he comes off as rather gross and dodgy. Regular work is beneath him—he gets by on his street smarts and by exploiting others, with absolutely no empathy or consideration of how his actions might affect them. He's a self-proclaimed jack-of-all-trades, will readily tell you of his many abilities, is constantly manipulative, and can never be trusted. He's the mugger, the exploiter, the day-to-day criminal. He does not try, or is unable, to hide his slimy ways.

It's hard for him to maintain steady employment. When things don't go his way, he may unfortunately end up imprisoned, homeless, and/or addicted. He is in all ways irresponsible and lives by and for himself. Any involvement with him is eventually going to sting you in some way, so best to stay away when possible. Distance might be hard, however, because the Sleaze's modus operandi is the con. He puts it all out in the open; there are all these red flags that he was going to screw you over, but for some reason you engage with him and find yourself surprised in the end. You're left with your tail between your legs and a huge bill to foot.

A prime example of the Sleaze is a residential home contractor who was hired by an acquaintance of mine. He had suffered from a roof problem for several years. He'd had an addition built to his home, and it seems they placed the rafters in the wrong direction. The result was a chronic leak that revealed itself two years later when his walls just buckled. Behind them was a tremendous patch of mold.

He went on one of those Web sites that rates servicemen in the hopes of getting someone good to fix his roof. When the roofer appeared, he told my friend that this was the "worst" roof and mold problem that he'd ever seen but that he was prepared to handle it. The roofer described his past work experience with similar problems in a veneer of pseudotechnical language. He dodged questions about other projects in the area he had completed and seemed to forget his list of references when asked for them. He commented on how my friend was lucky to have reached out at this point. Seeing some children's toys strewn about the house, he talked about the negative effects of mold on a child's health and stated that he wanted to get things done as soon as possible. He appeared sure of himself and said he understood how upset my friend must be. His price was steep, and the guy seemed a little slick, but the situation was undoubtedly bad.

The roofer worked on the roof for about two days—still laying on the charm—before he requested that my friend go on that Internet site and give him a great rating. He talked about how he was using the very best materials that he had driven far out of his way to purchase. The work wasn't done, so my friend was reluctant. At this point, he had a bad feeling about the whole situation, but the guy asked over and over until my friend felt bullied into doing it. Once his great comments were posted, though, the roofer's attendance became very spotty. He'd call every few days with an ever increasingly absurd story about why he couldn't get there. And when he promised to come, he wouldn't show. After a long period and lots of complaining from my friend, with many fits and starts, the job was proclaimed to be finished.

Perhaps not surprisingly at this point, the roof kept leaking. But my friend kept sticking with this roofer because "he knew the situation." Suffice it to say that he was strung along for many months and many tens of thousands of dollars. When there was no end in sight—he never got the roof to stop leaking—my friend finally requested a recommendation from a contractor he knew and trusted. The roof was fixed within a week for a few hundred dollars and never caused him trouble again. And, no, my friend did not go online and update his comments to reflect this chicanery for fear of some form of retaliation from the roofer. So the roofer went on, scot-free, to the next unfortunate sucker.

The Big Boss

Next up is the Big Boss. There's the lower-level Big Boss (Big Boss, Jr.), who is in many ways an extended version of Fast Eddie and the Sleaze, and there is the higher-level Big Boss, (Big Boss, Sr.), whose acts can truly be characterized as crimes, sometimes as parts of organized criminal activities but sometimes through individual scamming. Big Boss, Jr. cuts corners and doesn't follow any established protocols. He is often in positions of relative power, which he can exploit to his own financial or other advantage. He is more sophisticated than Fast Eddie or the Sleaze but still somewhat less nefarious than Big Boss, Sr.

I once knew an "upper-level middle manager" whose actions at work really fit the bill for being a Big Boss, Jr. He wasn't the top dog in the organization—a large computing company—but he reported to some of the senior executives and had near absolute authority over the software development area, overseeing hundreds of employees in the broader innovation analytics department. He was likable and warm, and those in his inner circle felt loyal to and protected by him. The question, however, came down to just why did they need to feel protected at work?

It was clear that those on his wrong side did not flourish at the company and usually either left or transferred. And if a job needed to be filled, he had no regard for employee preference, choice, or often even appropriate skill set—he'd fill the hole with somebody (anybody?) and be done with it. So there was a fair amount of disgruntlement alongside feelings of invalidation, devaluation, and fear. Fear was present because anyone who complained or talked back was immediately punished in some way, often in a manner so vague that one couldn't really know, or certainly couldn't prove, that it was really happening. Suddenly, such an employee would feel as though she was on a blacklist of some sort and just knew to keep her head down and hope the cloud passed over her. The only alternative was to start looking for a new job. There was such loyalty from his core team that his authority seemed impenetrable. So everyone just worked, kept her mouth shut, and hoped not to come to any negative attention.

There were some overtly distasteful features that made even his core team uncomfortable. Like the line staff, they were also afraid to question him. Members of the core team were often asked to do things, little things, that weren't quite right but not quite illegal. He would lay out plans to get projects completed that sounded more like game strategy than business, involving steps to manipulate one person into doing something so that the next person in the game would do something else, all neatly scripted to guarantee his desired outcome. Friends and relatives were frequently hired into jobs that were never officially posted; business deals and contractor choices were often made because someone involved was "a friend of a friend." Projects seemed to move unusually quickly in the wealth-management department, whereas other managers in the company felt held back by the associated bureaucracy. It was hard to understand how the budget always balanced despite his obvious extravagances, like expensive dinners out, personal equipment purchases, and even whole vacations, all on the company's dime.

As you might imagine, he was eventually caught in several of these activities when the budget numbers didn't make sense and an investigation ensued. As he endured the process that eventually led to his dismissal, his core team wrung their hands, wondering whether any of them would be implicated as well, even though they were just following orders. He outwardly acknowledged his mistakes, apologized, and promised to be more thoughtful moving forward. Shockingly, though, even up to his very last day, he was still cutting corners and asking his team to lie for him, certain that he'd find a way around it all.

The higher-level Big Boss, on the other hand, is truly antisocial, and much of his time is spent in pretty awful Swindler activities. Often appealing and charismatic, he may have a manifest "career" and even be quite successful in it, but his life is otherwise spent pursuing nefarious illegal activities. A leader, he comes off as smart and appealing. You want to be around the Big Boss, even if it feels a little dangerous. You might sense something risky about him, but you can't quite put your finger on it. You follow him, engage with him, feel connected to him. He may be a family man or otherwise engaged in things that are considered conventionally good, but he compartmentalizes his home life separate from his work life.

There is, of course, something superficially enviable about living in two simultaneous worlds, and many movies and television series chronicle the lives of such people. Psychologically, though, separating the self like this is deeply pathological. This division of worlds reveals an inability for one part of the self to confront the other. The Big Boss is able to hurt others with his criminality, while the part of his mind and life that would criticize the criminal part is kept completely separate, allowing the corruption to endure.

But for most Big Bosses, those two worlds eventually clash. Our above example of Galen is one of a Big Boss. In the end, we find out we've been totally duped by him, and the shocking truth is that he's truly a bad person. We all hear about financial advisors engaged in Ponzi schemes that ruin people's lives. These people were often considered a trusted advisor or a close family friend. There are also the individuals with seemingly legitimate businesses that turn out to be "fronts" for drug trafficking or other illegal activities.

I once treated a police officer who lived a double life, and it ended up becoming sheer hell for him. He was a nice guy and had a lovely wife and two kids. He was known for having a "tough on crime" approach and was thought to be a well-respected public servant.

However, seduced by the opportunity to make lots of extra money, he became involved in a scheme where he used the power from his position to facilitate a network of black market trafficking. He acted as a look-out during exchanges, keeping onlookers away by making everything seem like official police business. Sometimes he would use persons he could have arrested to negotiate deals and connect them with other individuals buying and selling everything from cocaine to stolen cars and even art. He would threaten people into submitting to his requests by holding ever escalating possibilities of punishment over their heads.

He ended up in my office for an evaluation near the beginning of his underhanded career because he was about to be disciplined for a much more minor infraction—he kept a small amount of money from a bust. He claimed "anxiety and insomnia" as culprits and was mandated into treatment by the chief of police. I smelled his Swindler tendencies and advised the department to use their HR processes to cut ties with him, but they felt strongly that they wanted him back on the force, so I referred him to a therapist near his home. He completed only a short course of therapy and was back on the job as soon as permitted. Only years later did I find out the true extent of his criminal nature when it all exploded on the front pages. In fact, without knowing the details of his therapy, it's quite likely true that while he had been caught keeping some money from a bust, this was likely not the first or deepest of his transgressions at the time—just the first one that got him caught! I imagine his wife, and quite possibly his therapist, were convinced that it was a one-off act, that the theft wasn't something that he would repeat, that he had learned a lesson. But how wrong they were. . . .

This becomes an important part of understanding the Big Boss. One would be hard-pressed to imagine that his wife did not know, at some level, that he was or could be so deeply manipulative and deceitful. One cannot overstate the attractiveness of the Big Boss for some people. It's exciting to live near the edge, be near the power, flirt with the danger, even if it's just a vague set of feelings without conscious awareness of how dangerous those interactions might be. As opposed to the Sleaze, the covert sociopathy of the Boss can seem intriguing and sexy. As a relationship persists and appears to deepen, one imagines that she might be able to "tame this bad boy." But the extent of that "badness" is woefully underestimated at times. Just as this Boss's wife and department came to learn.

Even when the lives seem separate, there are often underlying violent tendencies that intermittently cross over. For example, a supposed "family man" might still go home and beat his wife after a bad day in the office. This Swindler may function in the workplace, but when things don't go his way, he is more likely to resort to violence. It's as if, despite the separate lives, there is an underlying thread of violence just waiting to break the surface. Because of the need for compartmentalization, this type is often seen in positions of power, where authority can be used to manipulate, assault, terrorize, and victimize others under a seeming guise of doing one's job until the pattern is revealed.

The Serial Killer

From the Big Boss, we go to the most chilling of the Swindlers. This is the psychopath, he who embodies true-blue evil beyond comprehension. The Serial Killer is, of course, the worst breed of sociopath, and, thankfully, I don't believe I've ever seen one. And, hopefully, you won't either; despite making big headlines, they are actually quite uncommon in the population overall. We all hear the terrifying stories of the nice guy next door who has been chopping people up for years. For example, Scott Peterson was said to be a good husband and was noted by his sister to "light up a room" before he was convicted of murdering his pregnant wife (Bird 2005).

Dennis Rader, also known as the BTK strangler, is one example of a person who horrifyingly fits so many of the worst Swindler characteristics. *BTK*—the name he gave himself in a written letter to authorities—stands for "bind, torture, kill," describing the sequence of events that he would proceed through in his murders, usually including tying victims down, strangling them, and sexually stimulating himself at the scene of the crime (Beattie 2005). Rader was convicted of killing ten people over the course of three decades. In a documentary, he was noted to have been happily married with children, served as a church leader, and involved in both Boy Scouts and community policing. He epitomized the tendency to live multiple lives. In an interview with reporters, he said, "I've compartmentalized somewhere in my body . . . where I can just do those sorts of things and then go back to normal life." He knew that there was something wrong with him in middle school and has said that he had to cover up the sense of a secret self throughout his life.

While engaged in the killings, he ended up going to college to study criminal justice and worked at ADT Security Services to gain knowledge in order to better be able to invade houses. In fact, he would sometimes change clothes and kill during his lunch break, coming back to work for the remainder of the day. A coworker at ADT said that he wouldn't allow others to swear in her presence. He even took victims to the church where he was elected president of the Lutheran community. There was Dennis, and then there was BTK, and they were able to lead separate lives in the same body. The only arena in which both faces seemed to overlap was in his role as city compliance officer, where he would often harass women while enforcing community standards by being manipulative, controlling, and threatening. When he finally went to trial after decades of killing, the public reacted strongly to the emotionless way in which he described killing his victims (which he called "projects," denoting the completely objectifying way he saw the murdered victims as a way to sexually please himself). After imprisonment, in one letter, he wrote about the tendency for some to have "dark secrets" alongside "normal Family lives" (Wenzl 2014).

This person is the absolutely most horrifying and chilling that any of us could meet. The depths of his violence, the terror of his acts, the distance from humanity create a truly shocking and gruesome person.

WHEN THE SCHMUCK IN THE OFFICE IS A SWINDLER

In the workplace, Swindlers are often initially seen as likable and trustworthy (Ray and Ray 1982), allowing them to attain important positions. They can frequently fly under the radar until they potentially, eventually get caught for their malevolent behaviors. Nonetheless, even before any large misdeeds come to life, you may be able to notice that this is the person who can't function well on a team, can't share with others, mistreats those around him or her, can't accept blame, can be unpredictable or aggressive, and repeatedly lies for self-benefit (Babiak and Hare 2009).

It is important to recognize that isolated Swindler traits can actually be adaptive in certain industries and do not necessarily cross the threshold for indicating the presence of one of our gang members. For instance, a talk show host may be glib, an actor may be grandiose, a tightrope walker may thrive off adrenaline, a spy may need to lie repeatedly; we may see used-car salespersons being manipulative, soldiers protected from remorse, and undertakers with limited emotional expression (Stone 1993). Of course, such statements are working off of broad stereotypes, and an individual in these professions or others may or may not demonstrate any individual personality characteristic. What the pairings demonstrate, however, is the need to consider workplace context and culture in thinking about an individual's characteristics.

So what do office Swindlers tend to look like? We may see every variety at work. They are likely to work hard to build relationships that will benefit them, while at the same time they disregard people they think they don't need through manipulative comments and power plays (Babiak 1995). The Swindlers try to have power over the entire workplace and eliminate any potential competitors. Those who reinforce their schemes—and particularly their position of power—end up rewarded, but most employees feel a lack of recognition or appreciation (Boddy, Ladyshewsky et al. 2010). Such lawless individuals desire the power and wealth that can accompany top positions and are often seen as successful because they can work hard for what they want. As leaders, however, Swindlers are known for mistreating their employees, suddenly terminating contracts, maintaining unsafe work environments, constantly changing business partners, deceiving customers, and even breaking employment laws and human rights standards (Ketola 2006). One red flag is that these people tend to take credit for the work of others (Babiak and Hare 2009). Often, the people around them feel intimidated into silence—the Swindler ends up possessing an air of immunity, which makes coworkers feel ineffective in confronting them. Those who witness the behavior but feel powerless to confront it—often subordinate employees—may lower their productivity as morale drops and people feel less committed to completing their jobs (Pech and Slade 2007).

Studies show that organizations with Swindlers tend to be less likely to engage in projects that are positive for the environment or community (Boddy, Ladyshewsky, et al. 2010). Some scholars have even proposed that recent global financial crises have been caused by the ascendance of true sociopaths in business positions (Boddy 2011). A couple of factors have made the business world particularly ripe for the Swindler's swindling, and in fact some estimate that up to 10 percent of persons in financial industries would qualify as true Swindlers (DeCovny 2012)—a rate that is 300 percent above that of other industries! One factor is that such positions provide natural conduits for accessing (and manipulating) success and power. Money isn't a by-product of the financial world; it constitutes the very rules and goal of the game.

Another reason for this number is that the Swindler is able to hide his deceit, manipulation, and motives in the anonymity of a large company much better than he would be able to as, say, the neighborhood tailor. Over the last decades, organizations have grown dramatically and have simultaneously become increasingly complex, particularly as more and more workers are managers, professional personnel, and specialists. Organizational skills and technical knowledge are often less productive to accomplishment in such environments than are, say, charm and social skills. This scale favors the Swindler's success over a more competent—and ethical!—employee. These complex organizations do not allow for close evaluation of behavior and instead promote selective communication of information. Whereas this trend may be true for all employees, the Swindler is actively seeking to manage and control this filtration of information in a way that benefits solely him.

Swindlers are not likely to be found in positions that are less hospitable to their schemes, such as on teams or in tightly structured bureaucracies. Instead, these character types are likely to be found in large, anonymous, fast-paced, quickly adapting workplaces where their underhandedness can carry on undetected. People are now working from home and all over the world, additionally allowing the clandestine Swindler to swindle unnoticed. And when these individuals are terminated from or leave a position, they just hop into the next unsuspecting organization, pockets still stuffed from their last conquest. Often, the incident that causes a change in position may not be high-level enough to cause an arrest or be newsworthy, so the Swindler maintains somewhat of a clean slate. This trend makes reporting events to associations like the Better Business Bureau or Federal Trade Commission important for tracking patterns.

An additional influence for these business-place trends is that a global marketplace focused on the production of wealth often aligns well with the Swindler mentality of success over empathy; "it's good for business" becomes a workable motto. The Swindler's overemphasis on such success at all costs leads to unethical decisions, low employee morale with rapid turnover, and often expensive errors for the organization at large (Pech and Slade 2007).

An even scarier possibility with Swindlers is the ultimate concern of violence in the workplace. In fact, rates of workplace murder have drastically increased—perhaps even doubled or tripled—over the last several decades (Fox and Levin 1994; Johnson and Indvik 1994), and such acts are usually related to reprimanded workers or financial disputes. With Swindlers, the risk of violence is increased if there is a history of aggression and defiance toward authority or if the person is also using alcohol or other drugs. All potentially serious threats of violence should be reported to the authorities so that proper legal and/or psychiatric proceedings can be undertaken. Think of any such situation as an utter emergency, even if you are unsure of its probability. Companies have been found to be legally liable for incidents of violence, in situations such as not taking threats seriously or having inadequate security (Johnson and Indvik 1994).

HOW TO DEAL WITH A SWINDLER

While I'll explore various potential interventions for some kinds of "lower-impact" sociopathic behaviors or types, it's important to look out for the red flags and warning signs that indicate the presence of these potentially ruthless criminals. Part of this approach comes from the fact that Swindlers can be charming and successful at work, and the organization might not have any way to deal with them on a day-to-day basis until their swindling is uncovered. In this way, the general method of dealing with a Swindler differs from other character types in that it is more about keeping or getting them out of the office than managing them.

For most organizations, it's essential to cut ties with such an employee as soon as possible, particularly given the increasingly prevalent legal reality that employers have a duty to protect others, including employees, customers, and clients, from potential harm in the workplace (Clarke 2005). These are high-stakes decisions, and it is imperative to figure out just who might be a Swindler and how to get them out. Unfortunately, Swindlers in the workplace are often initially seen as pleasant and responsible, allowing them to attain important positions and fly under the radar until they get caught for their malevolent behaviors. The goal is to not allow the behaviors to continue, to do as much as possible to stamp them out as they arise, and to create an organizational environment where these actions are not rewarded, tolerated, or even allowed to develop.

The most beneficial, safe method would be to stop Swindlers before they get in the door: don't hire them, don't work for them, avoid them every step of the way. But, of course, that's easier said than done because of the ease with which they con, manipulate, and even charm. Such tactics are likely even to make their way on to a résumé through fraudulent claims, such as positions never held or papers never published, so one countermove is to verify all the provided history by calling references. Since very often past employers will not give information about a hire's performance (usually out of concern for legal ramifications), it can be essential to at least validate facts with registrars' offices, licensing boards, and so on. Such precaution may require a little time and energy up front, but it is a very important step in keeping a Swindler out of the office—and one that many who end up conned wished they had taken. In fact, in many states companies can be held liable for negligible hiring practices, which includes inadequate investigation of background history and references (Wang and Kleiner

2004). There have been successful lawsuits for negligent hiring when employees who perpetrate crimes turn out to have a criminal record that was not considered at hiring. Of course, this doesn't mean that people with criminal backgrounds can't be hired, but you should do the research and know what you're working with.

In interviews, avoid being seduced by a superficial discussion of past roles and obligations. Ask for specific details about a given job and press further if the interviewee seems to be glossing over anything—for example, describing how well he did rather than *what* he did. The Swindler will be glossy—using lots of jargon without any specific content—and is likely to know how to angle their résumé and interview to make himself seem successful, liked, and valuable. He would likely be particularly talented at making himself stand out as a hirable and desirable candidate.

In fact, it may be worth looking out for candidates that seem to portray excessive charm or boldness during their interview, since Swindlers are much more likely to display these characteristics up front than any underlying lawlessness. Your initial impression might be, "Wow, this sounds too good to be true!" That gut feeling might indeed be the case. You need to press for more information, specific information, and for examples as many times as necessary to convince yourself that the candidate is the real deal.

A close friend told me about someone he tried to hire in a HR capacity for his company. He had interviewed the guy, who had a fitting background with prior HR roles. He told me all about how affable and smooth he was. My Swindler radar got activated. I told him to look into the guy's background more. Turns out, he was better at selling himself than doing any real work; when my friend described the follow-up interviews, we noticed he was using lots of business speak to say nothing at all. I told my friend to press him for well-defined specifics, and the more precise he asked the applicant to be, the more bullshit was slung. It was crystal clear by the end of the process that, sure, he had held HR positions but that all he ever did was delegate the actual HR work. He knew close to nothing about the field for which he was applying and, needless to say, was turned away.

Be on the lookout for any gaps in education, training, or working. If these appear on a résumé or interview, be sure to follow up regarding what happened during these time periods, since they may represent periods of transition associated with swindling events. Pre-employment screening can verify criminal history in addition to such purported facts as social security number, ID data, driving record, educational history, previous employment, credit history, workers' compensation, military discharge records, professional licensing, and civil litigation history—all of which can provide potentially useful information (Wang and Kleiner 2004). It may be important to consult with legal services to establish specific hiring protocols or to figure out what information can be used to rule out a candidate without being discriminatory or violating any disability rights. There is an important political movement called "Ban the Box," which seeks to remove the box for checking off and revealing criminal history from initial job applications so that people with a criminal record are better able to find employment and integrate into society. This movement seeks to give individuals with previous criminal records the opportunity to put their lives back together, since they have otherwise been shut out of obtaining employment, housing, and other resources.

It is important to keep in mind that these tips are merely that—tips—and cannot be used indiscriminately. Gaps in work history may represent an infinite number of pasts other than swindling. In fact, they may point to a kindhearted son who left work several times to care for an ill mother or an adventurous person who wanted to travel between positions; it might be a mother or father who stayed home with their child or—hey!— maybe someone who wanted to write a book. You want to be sure that these hiring recommendations are taken as pieces of an overall picture: multiple job transitions with sketchy reasons and poor references? Pouring out charm with little substance? Take notice and pay closer attention to this candidate as a potential Swindler. However, you do not in any way want to blindly follow this word for word, or you will end up not hiring plenty of good, caring people.

In addition, it has been suggested that—particularly for individuals in the financial industries—it may be beneficial to hire individuals who have interests outside work (DeCovny 2012). This may mean hobbies or family, but it is important that the individual be able to talk about and spend time with something other than money, success, and power. While it's important to recognize and reward those with motivation to do well, an obsession with these markers of attainment may very well indicate the presence of someone who would swindle in the office. Another screening question would be to create a scenario about the individual and company beginning to fail and see how distressed the interviewee becomes and what their natural responses for dealing with this are (e.g., How focused are they merely on success and not on a broad consideration of factors?). There should be a healthy skepticism of anyone who presents an unforgiving willingness to do anything to get ahead.

But let us assume an applicant does get past these initial screening and interviewing stages to being hired. The next step is to appropriately orient them to the company. It's very helpful to employees (and managers, even coworkers) when an organization has a defined mission and culture, and where expectations for appropriate behavior are set. Defining the playing field also makes it far easier for employers to decide when rules have been violated. This discordance has come up frequently in my work with disruptive physicians of all character types. When behavior gets an employee into trouble, a common battle cry is lack of knowledge that the behavior was inappropriate. And, as I mentioned early on in this book, what is acceptable in one company may be absolutely taboo in another, even within the same industry. Mission statements, visions, and clear HR policies are all important for companies to write, distribute, and regularly refer to. This is important not merely to weed out the true Swindler but also to help keep innocent bystanders from starting to mimic their patterns. While rewarding productive behavior is important for creating organizational culture, so too is literally defining that culture. Most important is for the rewarded behaviors and described policies to closely align. Often, colleagues will witness a Swindler being rewarded for her various tactics; even if these workers are naturally more honest and humanistic, they may be rightly confused by a Swindler's success and perhaps even unconsciously start copying his behaviors in an attempt to keep up. For example, an assistant might witness her Swindler boss taking liberties from the company like writing off personal expenses as being used in the office and so on. In seeing the Swindler do this, she might feel that it is okay for her to start bringing office supplies home, even though she knows what she is doing is wrong. A simple enough action in that case. However, such patterns start to accumulate, coworkers feel exonerated, and the moral compass of the office can continue to veer further and further off course.

A common mistake is to make the HR policies too abstract, since this can actually worsen the Swindler's behavior as he focuses on maintaining an overall and superficial impression of "integrity" or "quality" through networks of allies instead of accomplishing any true productivity. It is important to specifically delineate potential transgressions and repercussions alongside any declaration of more lofty values or goals. Of course, you will not be able to literally list every potential transgression that an employee can make, but instead of simply stating that "professionalism" is a value of the institution, be sure to specifically describe that plagiarism, threats, and racism, for example, are prohibited.

A tactic that can help buffer the rise of the Swindler in the organization is to focus on metrics that evaluate individuals' contributions to the overall goals of the company instead of solely personal success (Giblin 1981). Has an individual spent time on a long-term quality-improvement project that perhaps interfered with maximizing personal productivity for the quarter? This kind of trade-off should be rewarded and expressly valued.

Another technique involving clarity of expectations can be helpful if instead the Swindler is your boss. Try to document your conversations in a way that makes it seem like your natural work style. Follow up your phone conversations and meetings with clear indications of what you understood plans to be, what your obligations are, and what your contribution to the work is. *Mr. S, very good to meet with you today, and thank you for explaining the marketing strategy at this point. I will be sure to follow up by reaching out to new client X and distributing our material. As we discussed, if she doesn't respond by next Tuesday, I will approach her supervisor. I appreciate the opportunity to work on this project and look forward to executing the plan in place. I will be sure to update you along the way.* Even if he doesn't respond, there is a paper trail that can be helpful later on if the Swindler tries to take you down.

In the contemporary business setting, there are pretty interesting technological screening tools that allow one to look for the presence of a Swindler among the ranks. These applications are not psychological assessment instruments but rather electronic applications that monitor activity in the company for potential anomalies that might need further intervention. For example, such programs can integrate data from company databases and screen for patterns indicating potential intellectual property theft or abuse of access privileges. They may be worth the investment depending on the type of organization one is embedded in.

If the rules are clear and a violation still occurs by a Swindler employee, consistent enforcement is key. Bending rules or indicating that there's wiggle room leaves the Swindler in the game, and more bad behavior will ensue. If Fast Eddie is caught in the act, it's important to sanction him. Hopefully, getting into trouble will help him define the boundaries of what is and is not okay at work, and he'll make better choices next time an opportunity to Swindle presents itself. It also sets a precedent for any Swindlers waiting in the company's sidelines.

Just remember that when the Swindler gets into trouble, there are things to look out for in the confrontation and resultant aftermath. Know that engaging with these individuals may leave you or the company open to additional deception and manipulation. The person may try to "con" the individual who is confronting them, making him feel that the accusations are wrong, that he himself might get in trouble, or otherwise manipulate and exploit the situation. They may even seek others as allies to defend the accusations against them, pulling alleged comrades into the office or the e-mail chain. Such actions should raise suspicion that you are not just dealing with a Fast Eddie but instead another member of the gang.

Unfortunately, some of the best Swindlers will use their superficial charm to feign apology or regret. Flowers on your desk? Tickets to the opera? They may use intellectual, logical, or expert opinion to seemingly logically present convincing alternative explanations (read: excuses) to the alleged behavior. Remember that this charade is what they are good at, so that even if they are agreeing to limits or interventions with a mask of truthfulness and good intent, they may nonetheless be actively plotting otherwise. It might be a good time to review the person's history—at the company, at their previous job—and consider rechecking facts and references if you want to reveal any patterns of behavior.

There isn't a quick fix for the Swindler's patterns. For lower-level behavioral problems, one can try to tie productive, positive behaviors to whatever outcomes are desired by the individual, such as money or other rewards. Be sure to have a very, very clear delineation of the hierarchical structure of the organization as well as the rules that are in place if the person is to stay. If the individual expresses regret and genuinely seems to want to change their behavior, it might be the appropriate time to refer them to therapy through consultation with legal or HR. In order to avoid feeling crummy about oneself and one's decisions in the future, the person may be willing to take steps toward changing his or her behavior. A number of studies in fact show that depression is a favorable indicator of treatment response in an individual with antisocial personality disorder (Stone 1993). This connection makes sense because, as previously discussed, the most chilling Swindlers have no capacity for remorse or ability to feel any emotion—positive or negative. If someone has depression or regret, they may be a low-level Swindler who is more capable of making change than are the bad-to-the-bone bosses who should be immediately removed from the company. Though there are numerous reasons why someone might not agree to a therapy referral, following through with a therapist is a good sign, especially if it is not forced and they seem to actively want to correct their behavior. A scarier

Swindler, on the other hand, is likely to downplay or sweet-talk the transgression and need for rehabilitation. For many individuals, however, engaging in some of the worst behaviors tends to naturally decrease after age thirty to forty (Stone 1993; Sadock 2000).

If repeated transgressions clarify that the company hired a Sleaze or worse, it is crucial to urgently move him out through the appropriate administrative channels. The true Swindler in the organization will not learn from mistakes or reprimand; instead, he will just try to improve her swindling so that she doesn't get caught in the future. You need the Swindler out of there—and quickly! The behaviors aren't going to get better with coaching or therapy, and the sooner you act, the less damage you are likely to incur. If you're working with the Big Boss and he gets discovered, he is likely to be summarily dismissed from his job, no matter where he sits in the organization. His actions usually directly negatively impact the company. But perhaps you're working for the Big Boss, and you know it. You're aware that there's shady business at play, but, well, it's a job, and you yourself aren't doing anything bad, right? Just be aware that you could be financially, legally, morally, or otherwise implicated when it hits the fan.

It is very common for someone to have high suspicion that someone is a Swindler but be afraid to take the necessary steps for extraction. Whether an employer or employee, you might be afraid that the Swindler could retaliate or you might be ashamed that you've been conned. But, really, this is about safety and ethical treatment of yourself and those around you. Try to remember that the best backing you'll have in any turn of events is to have the most documentation, the most institutional support, and the most overall structure behind you. Start saving e-mails and transcribing conversations and meetings—remembering that audio or video recordings of conversations are illegal in many places. Nonetheless, make sure the data you collect is as objective as possible: events, statements, actions. Consider instituting anonymous feedback surveys from coworkers—collecting both numerical ratings and narrative descriptions of behavior—for everyone at the organization. Include categories such as ethics and professionalism in these evaluations. If helpful, figure out where this individual stacks up in relation to his colleagues. As the process moves forward, do your best not to confront—or even converse with—the individual alone. Have third-party witnesses present whenever possible so the Swindler cannot lie about what happened in your interactions. Report any threats that arise during this process to the proper authorities, even covert threats that use power, money, or body language to intimidate you.

The Swindler is going to swindle; there isn't any doubt about that. Think of his presence as a potential threat to you, your colleagues, and your company! Whether you are a pawn in his game or merely watching from the sidelines, know that you could be protecting both yourself and others, however difficult it may seem. While there is some urgency to the situation, unless there is a glaringly egregious violation, you also need to be careful and calculated in your approach to collecting (and eventually bringing forth) information. You will likely benefit from seeking out advice, perhaps legal or from a fraud-reporting agency.

Unfortunately, if your boss is the Swindler, it may very well be you who ends up leaving the organization in order to avoid being involved in a potentially harmful scandal that would end up hurting you or your family, your reputation, or your career. It may be unfair, but it may also be wise. Particularly if you feel unhappy and abused in the situation, this may actually be a smart and productive move. At some point, it may require asking yourself why you are so intent on staying in a relationship with the organization if it is truly detrimental to your well-being.

When I was a psychiatry resident, one of my senior supervisors told me a story in trying to explain why Swindlers are so difficult to treat. He described an experiment in an inpatient psychiatric facility intended to "cure" sociopathy. I've never actually located the study in print, but the anecdote serves as an excellent educational tool—one I've never forgotten. In this study, a small cadre of individuals with diagnosed antisocial personality disorder agreed to an admission to the hospital that would last exactly two years. These men were already down on their luck, homeless, and unemployed, so two years of good food and clean, safe surroundings seemed like a pretty good deal. These were the "old days" in psychiatry, and the hospital was a sprawling, open campus amid beautiful surroundings.

The plan was as follows: orders would be written on day 1 of the admission and would never, ever be changed. So on day 1, each participant knew his room, his diet, his medication orders, when he could be outside, and so on. There would be no negotiation. The study was based on the premise that Swindlers function by zeroing in on people and situations where they feel they can "make a play." They can have an almost uncanny ability to read people and draw them in, with the goal of meeting personal needs and desires. Those needs tend to be shallow and immediate, which makes the Swindler, in many ways, little more than a mirror of other people's vulnerabilities.

So the participants knew the rules going in—the orders were the orders, and there was absolutely no room for alteration of any sort. Nonetheless, each man spent his time attempting to learn the idiosyncrasies of his peers and the staff, looking for cracks in the china, finding buttons and weak spots to push, trying in little and then ever more desperate ways to get those damn rules bent. They did this for no particular reason other than to know they could do it and maybe enjoy some minor advantage.

But as the months passed and it became increasingly clear that the plan was ironclad, the men began to stop. Slowly but surely, they became engaged in other activities, started interacting with others, worked on community projects, and even spoke and listened to their peers in group therapy. They became citizens. They developed interests. They reported that they felt better.

At discharge from the hospital, each man was given ongoing outpatient psychotherapy, housing, and an employment opportunity. They left grateful, promising to maintain this "new start." At one-year follow-up, however, all had left or lost their jobs, none had maintained stable housing, their relationships had again disintegrated, and several were in prison (even more had likely committed acts still uncaught). The stimulation of too much opportunity to Swindle overrode any apparently superficial change. The world at large simply cannot be the controlled environment required to make them stop.

Even prison, which in many ways should offer the environmental control of this study, often becomes a hotbed of aggression and illegal activity. The above study required twenty-four-hour close supervision and support by trained behavioral health specialists for a small number of men. Though prison is the closest approximation to this, we know it is often not focused on rehabilitation. It would be near impossible to offer the same level of intervention as the study in most treatment, let alone workplace, environments. So this anecdote clearly reveals the need for removing the Swindler—as quickly as possible—from any organization they might be entangled in since it's simply not worth the risk of keeping one around.

A Checklist of Ways to Effectively Deal with a Swindler

- Avoid hiring the Swindler by talking to their references, conducting background checks, and looking for warning signs during interviews or on their résumés.
- Develop a specific code of conduct with HR, distribute a handbook describing it, and reward adherence to it; this prevents the Swindler from pleading ignorance about unacceptable behavior and dissuades potential copycat swindling.
- Prevent the Swindler from rising in the ranks by evaluating performance based on contribution to the company over personal successes.
- Sanctions against rule violations should be consistently and uniformly enforced.
- Ideally, the Swindler should be removed from the company when detected.
- Confronting the Swindler is best done with institutional support and clear documentation of the inappropriate behaviors.
- If unable to remove the Swindler from the office (i.e., your boss), sometimes the best option is to remove yourself.

PART III

Distraction, Disorganization, and Delays at the Desk

Cognition at Work

Let's now turn to another factor that affects how people interact in the workplace: cognition along with the various complex mental functions of the brain. Part II ("In the Spotlight") demonstrated how various types of personalities and interpersonal interactions can cause disruptive behavior. Now, we will look at what cognitive processes are, how they are affected in certain character types, and how that can be disruptive at work.

The last section focused on the relationships and emotions of several character types, while this section focuses more on the brain and thinking—so called *cognition*—and how they can affect the workplace for better or for worse. *Cognition* can be thought of as all the ways in which the mind takes in, manipulates, and uses information from the world around us. It includes, for example, perceiving sound and sight as well as remembering, thinking, and speaking.

Psychiatrists currently divide cognition into specific domains of ability. A person can have problems or difficulties in just one or multiple domains. There are several domains of cognitive functioning. The first realm we will explore is called *executive functioning*.

Executive functioning provides the ability to foresee various outcomes, to process events, and to solve problems. This domain coordinates actions, behaviors, speech, rules, and goals. It helps one start, stop, and switch thoughts and behaviors. It allows for planning, strategizing, and decision making by overseeing other functions of the mind, playing a role similar to that of a football coach or orchestra conductor. Interestingly, conceptualization for this type of brain processing originated in the field of engineering during the 1960s and increasingly through computer technology, with ideas such as *information processing*, *networks*, and others (Arciniegas, Anderson, et al. 2013).

Oftentimes, researchers learn that a skill set is controlled by a certain area of the brain when there is a problem with that area. For example, in one famous case, Phineas Gage, a nineteenth-century railroad engineer, was impaled by an iron rod passing through his head and hitting a specific area of the brain called the frontal lobes (in the front of the skull, above the eyes). This injury left him newly undependable and bad mannered (Parkin 1999). After the event, his mind was described as "radically changed, so decidedly that his friends and acquaintances said he was 'no longer Gage'" (O'Driscoll and Leach 1998). He was now noted to be impatient, use profanity, and be unable to control his behavior—a marked change from the efficient and kind man who lived before the accident. Gage's experience and other studies have led neuro-psychiatrists to understand executive functioning as residing in the brain's frontal lobes. When psychiatrists think about commonplace difficulties in executive functioning, the problems that come to mind are with multitasking, complex projects, planning, and organization. However, because executive functioning coordinates so many different parts of the mind, problems can arise almost anywhere, including with the other subsets of cognition described below: attention, learning, and memory. Completing routine behaviors and processes may be less affected, but adapting to anything new or unexpected is very difficult with impairments in executive functioning.

Another domain of cognitive functioning is that of attention (American Psychiatric Association 2013). Skills in this area allow someone to concentrate on something over time, to focus on one thing instead of others, and to successfully switch between noticing different stimuli. The world has almost limitless things to focus on at any given time. From thoughts to sensations to sounds to emotions to sights, all going on at once, we select which stimuli to pay attention to and which to ignore. As you read this book, you might be focusing on the words, but you might also be thinking about what you have to do, noticing that you're hungry, listening to sounds outside, or otherwise be dividing or alternating the focus of your attention. Sometimes, we can choose what to focus on; at other times, intensity automatically brings something into our awareness—like the pain of breaking a bone. Typically, attention is required to move toward finishing any goals; otherwise, we would be simply and continuously bombarded without ability to move forward. Someone who has attentional difficulties may take longer to complete tasks, make more errors, or have difficulty blocking out the environment.

A third domain of cognitive functioning is learning and memory (American Psychiatric Association 2013). Of course, this set of skills provides for remembering experiences, facts, people, and skills. To be able to remember, however, is a complex, multistep process that starts with learning. First, one must be able to acquire the memory and then one must be able to store it and, later, retrieve it. Memory itself is also divided into different categories. One classification is between short-term memory (that is, holding on to information in the mind for mere seconds) and long-term memory (that is, holding on to information for longer periods of time). There are also separate types of memory for recollection of facts versus events versus skills—the name of the third president of the United States, what you had for dinner last night, and how to ride a bike. Commonplace difficulties with learning and memory are academic problems, repeating oneself, or needing frequent reminders for tasks. One of the most famous cases of impaired event-related memory was a patient called HM, who, after surgery for his seizure disorder, was left with complete amnesia for anything that happened to him.

In addition to executive functioning, memory, and attention, some of the other areas of cognition are language, physical movement, and social understanding. To understand more about how all of these different pieces of cognition fit together, let us take the example of someone, say Gary, completing a task like giving a speech to an audience using his various domains of cognitive functioning. First, executive functioning would come into play as Gary makes the decision to accept the invitation to speak and then as he plans and organizes a schedule to prepare for the speaking engagement. As he sits down to write the speech, language functions operate by allowing for syntax, grammar, and word production. Gary must use social cognition as he considers his audience, what they would like to hear in his speech, and which jokes may or may not be appropriate. Then, Gary decides to memorize the speech; to commit the words to memory, he must use the cognitive domain of learning. During this process, Gary exercises attentional abilities in order to avoid being distracted by the noise around him while trying to learn. On the day of his speech, Gary must arrive at the lecture hall and walk up to the podium using his perceptual and motor abilities.

Each of these cognitive domains can be affected in numerous ways that lead to different types of problems and different disruptive styles at work. In the following sections, we will see how various people who might have too much attention to detail ("The Bean Counter"), have too little attention to tasks ("The Distracted"), have general cognitive decline ("The Lost"), or experience the drastic cognitive effects of drug abuse ("Mr. Hyde") can be disruptive at work. It's important to note, however, that disorders of cognition often do not entail a single problem or even a single domain of problems. Instead, the various cognitive functions of the mind are interrelated and affect one another in their various modes of processing information.

The Bean Counter

Have you ever had a great idea that you organized in a thoughtful, rational, and clear proposal? After spending time preparing it, you presented it to a boss. But then were you made to jump through hoop after hoop after hoop in cycles of revision and clarification, reorganization and reordering for no apparent reason? These endless requests made you feel like you were being actively blocked from moving forward. "The table needs different spacing, the graph should be different colors, and please adjust the margins by half an inch while you're at it!" This has certainly happened to me, and it can be absolutely maddening. You become frustrated by the person that needles you constantly, asking question after question, requesting more and more data, asking for repeated justifications of items you already rationalized. You feel as if you are being held hostage by someone else's need to control, and unfortunately this same person is able to influence the outcome of your project in a significant way. Say hello to the obsessive, demanding Bean Counter.

Growing up, I had a friend named Mollie, and we always went

to one another's houses, got along quite well. The problem was her mom. I simply didn't understand her, and I doubt Mollie did either. She had these weird collections all over their house of what seemed like junk but were apparently extremely important to her. The family room was stacked to the ceiling with newspapers that you had to walk around even to sit on the couch. She always asked odd questions about what we were doing and never seemed to leave us alone. Despite her piles of newspapers and drawers of receipts (she held on to any local newspaper edition that might contain stories she would someday want to refer back to and every receipt that she may one day need to prove a purchase with—all organized by date of publication or purchase), she wouldn't let us make any sort of mess and definitely protested when we tried to take the cushions off the couch to make a pillow fort. Every time we were over there, she would be making lists of things to do. If we helped with chores, she always had very particular ways she wanted us to help: like sorting all of the cans by color after grocery shopping.

Mollie's mom, I now realize, was being obsessive. Although some people think of obsessives as being extremely neat, an obsessive Bean Counter can be either painfully spotless or abhorrently messy; they might spend all of their time cleaning or all of their time collecting. Often, like Mollie's mom, there may be a mix between obsessive neatness and obsessive messiness. No matter how his house or office looks, however, there is something about this person that has extreme difficulty going with the flow, clings to his way of doing things, and wants to control every step of the way.

The first recognized form of obsession seems to have been religious. The term that applied to such obsessions was *scruples*, and even now religious obsessions are called *scrupulosity*. In 1730, Saint Alphonsus Liguori defined *scrupulosity* as "groundless fear of sinning that arises from erroneous ideas" (Taylor 2002). The

Catholic saint Ignatius Loyola described his religious obsession: "[T]he idea occurs to me from outside myself that I have sinned whilst on the other hand I do not think I have; however I go on feeling this disturbance of mind, partly doubting and partly not doubting; this properly is a scruple" (Taylor 2002). These early obsessions were recognized for the way in which the religious thoughts and doubts would continuously enter the mind without clear reason. These doubts about sinning are often accompanied by drives to perform religious behavior or rituals.

Eventually, psychiatrists too began to think about obsessions outside religion. In fact, obsessive types like Bean Counters became a fascination of the early psychoanalysts. Sigmund Freud described obsessions as thoughts that could not be dispelled; he characterized such people as being clean and tidy, stubborn, and frugal, as well as often being hoarders (Blaney and Millon 2008; Gordon 2010). He felt these problems stemmed from parenting battles, primarily around toilet training (Gordon 2010). In 1903, a French psychiatrist named Pierre Janet wrote about severe pathological obsessions in a book describing not only obsessive worries but also "a need for precision or perfection in perception and actions" (Pitman 1984). He described obsessive individuals as being perfectionistic, indecisive, and devoid of emotional expression (Mancebo, Eisen, et al. 2005). William Reich famously called these individuals "living machines" who are focused on always staying in control (Curtis 1991).

THE BEAN COUNTER'S BASIC TRAITS

The difficulty with obsessive people is that they just can't let things go. Sometimes these *things* are thoughts (as in the religious scruples), and sometimes they are possessions (as in the newspapers of Mollie's mom). An *obsession* is a thought or impulse that keeps intruding into someone's mind. Obsessive people hang on to details and want them to be organized very particularly—even if not neatly. In fact, their over-the-top efforts to hang on, collect, and organize usually interfere with productivity, efficiency, and tidiness. They can't see the forest for the trees.

Everyone can have obsessive thoughts from time to time: when we're in love, when we're new parents, when we're preparing to skydive. In all of these scenarios, we likely overfocus on one idea or worry or person, and hanging on to those thoughts makes sense. However, true obsessive compulsive personality disorder is also quite common. It is estimated that 1 to 8 percent of the general public has been given the diagnosis (Mancebo, Eisen, et al. 2005; Blaney and Millon 2008; American Psychiatric Association 2013). It appears to be up to twice as common among males. In many studies, it is considered the most common personality disorder and the one that may be the least impairing for the person (Mudrack 2004). Such facts should be considered in context of the fact that Western culture—at least since the Enlightenment—tends to value logic and pragmatics (McWilliams 2011). Interestingly, it has also been suggested that this personality pattern is becoming more subtle or rarer in recent years (Gordon 2010).

As with narcissism, a healthy amount of obsessiveness can be highly adaptive. Attention to detail can help a person do things neatly and correctly and in an organized manner. Handling tasks in an orderly, stepwise way can make an individual decidedly more efficient, and by carefully mastering the steps in a process, fewer mistakes are likely to be made. But when an obsessive personality becomes a problem, we note that individuals will veer away from mindfulness toward intense preoccupation with order-liness, perfectionism, and control, often making them appear very anxious. On the other side of the coin, the individual has difficulty with flexibility, openness, decision making, and efficiency. He intentionally attempts to avoid any association with aggression, sexuality, or neediness. As with other personality problems, his obsession interferes with the ability to function, and at times this impaired performance can be severe and drastically affect others as well. They are so tied to their vision of structure that it gets in the way of accomplishing what they want. Since there were too many receipts to sort through—even if they are ordered by date—Mollie's mom would likely have never been able to find the one she needed to make an actual return. And even if she had, the refund would likely not have been worth sacrificing her living room and so much time for.

Underlying everything the Bean Counter says and does is a need to control the inherent uncertainty of life swirling around them. They plan and plan and plan to avoid any potential surprises. These obsessive Bean Counters try to artificially impose organization through rules, laws, and protocols. They defer to authority and hierarchy, follow conventions and standards. They desire stability and security but often end up overwhelmed and lonely, angry and afraid, guilty and ashamed. The Bean Counter ends up clinging to an ideal of perfection that gets in the way of accomplishment—despite accomplishment being the thing that gives meaning to her life and self-respect. Her worries often accomplish no objec-tive: they're way past that point.

The interesting thing is that the Bean Counter *likes* to live this way. For the Bean Counter, being "in control" is a philosophy of life that he fully endorses and means to continue. This feeling of really enjoying having everything a certain way, which is associated with obsessive compulsive personality disorder (OCPD), helps differentiate from the upsetting feeling of being trapped that an individual with obsessive compulsive disorder (OCD) has. Yes, these appear to be quite similar terms and diagnoses, but in fact they are significantly different in terms of underlying thoughts, feelings, and even recommended treatment. In obsessive compulsive disorder, the individual spends significant time doing things like washing, checking, counting, or confessing but feels compelled to do so despite experiencing significant distress. The person doesn't necessarily want to be doing these things but feels as if they have to. This discordance will often drive someone with OCD to seek treatment, whereas a Bean Counter will most likely only consider changing because of the effects his patterns have on other people in his life, difficulty at work or in relationships, or associated anxiety or depression. Otherwise, they really would prefer to just keep obsessing.

Pierre: Part One

I was once asked to see a mechanical engineer named Pierre. Pierre was known for his thorough and accurate work and, though he was proud of his fine products, he knew that this pressure to be perfect kept him in a somewhat constant state of anxiety and limited his social life. He felt he only wanted to do things flawlessly, and he liked paying very close attention to detail. He progressed through his career pretty well, though, of course, people thought of him as plodding and nitpicky. For the most part, however, he was unobtrusive with his habits, and his teams appreciated his work. However, he had significant difficulty working with others and never really achieved significant promotions or awards.

Despite his careful and cautious ways, the concern with perfection ultimately caused him more serious trouble. At one point, for reasons that he will never truly understand, one of his projects went terribly wrong, and several people were injured as a result. It wasn't his fault. His calculations were accurate; it was just a bad outcome. There were multiple root-cause analyses and minor adjustments made to the process, but ultimately nothing significant went wrong . . . except that everything went wrong because the project fell through. Time passed, and the episode was pretty much forgotten by everyone except Pierre. He'd become paralyzed with anxiety, second-guessing every move he made, unable to complete projects for fear of hidden mistakes. He stopped sleeping, lost weight, and ruminated constantly. After that incident, Pierre pretty much couldn't work because he was so focused on the details and possible risks of each step in his processes.

I saw him as a Bean Counter. As this type tends to be, he was perfectionistic to a degree that interfered with his productivity. Even before the project with the bad outcome, Pierre had always had a difficult time working with others. He was always first in the office and last out. His work on projects was generally individual in nature—he had only himself to rely upon to complete them. This was a good thing, he thought, because Pierre could not assign his work to others—believing beyond doubt that only he could finish anything correctly and with adequate quality. Though there was a certain arrogance to that posture, Pierre certainly didn't process it that way. He liked to live and feel like this. To him, the potential future anxiety associated with any form of failure was truly too much to bear, and if he let go of even a single task, he would wonder endlessly about whether it was done right. He'd worry so much about it that he'd often just trash whatever someone else did and redo it himself. Putting in absurd hours, often twice those of his peers, meant nothing to him, because if he went home before his work was done—as if his work were *ever* truly done—he'd be up much of the night obsessing anyway. His mind would turn the problem over and over, he'd become overwhelmed with all he had yet to do, would wonder whether he should recheck the work he'd already done (had he inadvertently forgotten something?), and would catalog all the things that could go wrong if he screwed up. The next morning, he would arrive to work even more anxious and fired up—and exhausted to boot.

Pierre had been assigned to group projects before, but these arrangements never really worked. He wasn't a team player in that he'd alienate or enrage members by repeatedly correcting their work. Otherwise, he'd just take on the entire group project himself. Some people, of course, loved to pair up with him and just sit back and wait for the project to magically appear. Although Pierre didn't like when others took credit for work they didn't perform, he also didn't really care. The work was good, and no one got in his way.

So, eventually, after too many people complained, his superiors just stopped putting him in any group settings and allowed him to work solo. He couldn't play well with others even though he was generally a pretty nice—albeit anxious—person, and he became the company's valued "detail guy." His bosses were thrilled that they found a way to keep Pierre happy but away from his peers while still ensuring output of product. This setup worked out for quite some time, until Pierre's fateful project failed and he had only himself to blame.

HOW DID THE BEAN COUNTER GET THIS WAY?

Like the childhood of many such Bean Counters, Pierre's parents were harsh disciplinarians when he was growing up (Eskedal and Demetri 2006). Both of his parents had high expectations for his success, and they made it appear as if their love was tied to his accomplishments. However, they did not respond with support when he met their goals and always expected him to act very "grown up" for his age. When he did achieve something, it made him feel merely adequate to them. He tried to behave perfectly in order to avoid criticism in a family that emphasized obedience, authority, and tidiness. His parents made him feel guilty and in-adequate when their standards were not met. He found them very hard to please no matter how well he did. The overall feeling in the house was one of anger and hostility, and there were many power struggles centered on the theme of respect. Pierre began to have the same exhausting expectations for himself as his parents did and to feel extreme stress when things were not perfect. This Bean Counter to be had difficulty developing a sense of security in the world. The high-pressure, hypercritical environment fos-tered a fear of imperfection, and he had trouble with any uncer-tainty. One can understand that the Bean Counter's traits developed to help protect him from the criticism and punishment of his par-ents by trying to be perfect and in control. He learned that fol-lowing rules was the best way to win approval from his parents, and this assumption carried over into all other relationships and aspects of life. He learned to seek security through stability, fa-miliarity, and constancy.

Pierre actually experienced his most successful time period during college. He found that he could win over professors with attention to detail, thorough analysis, lengthy submissions, and extensive lists of citations. He was occasionally late turning assignments in because he just couldn't seem to get them just the way he wanted, but he always seemed to impress graders with his exhaustive reviews. Most of the classwork was solitary, and he did well on all the exams. After college, however, he started having more difficulty as projects required more flexibility, spontaneity, and teamwork. Also, the workplace environment changed over time, and Pierre had trouble adapting.

COUNTLESS BEAN COUNTERS

The Bean Counter is so ubiquitous in the office that, quite frankly, I had a difficult time choosing whom to write about. Eventually, I realized that this was because I have spent decades at work either treating or trapped by Bean Counters. I have had many patients of this type given that such behavior is so common. And in a field of rule followers like medicine, I am particularly destined to encounter them as colleagues. Just as in so many of our character discussions, obsessive personalities run along a spectrum, and two major subtypes emerge: the Hostile Bean Counter and the Hermit Bean Counter.

The Hostile Bean Counter: Hard on Others

The hostile variety of Bean Counter is the most obviously vexing. He is either simply unable to delegate tasks (and says so!), is utterly self-righteous in his assertion that only he can get the job done right, or offers the pretense of delegation but corrects and controls every last detail. He seems controlling from the get-go. Water-cooler gossipers will call this variety a "control freak," and few will relish work interactions with his micromanagerial style. The Hostile Bean Counter is patronizing, rigid, and often given to displays of angry, punishing outbursts when he perceives that something has gone wrong or is interfering with his personal obsessive goals . . . particularly if someone else tries to exert any control over his work! He may always talk about how his way is the best, most efficient, and most productive manner of doing things; he is sure to insist on being right at all costs. He may criticize others for "not caring as much" as he does.

The Hostile Bean Counter is particularly long-winded in his demonstration of knowing all the facts about a task at hand. He comes off as trying to appear very logical and intellectual but is, in fact, very long-winded, hypercritical, and dogmatic. Soliloquies might be delivered concerning a topic as minor as the position of paper clips on reports—often with the same seriousness and rigidity as detailing the structure for the content of the report itself. In meetings, he is an obsessive note taker, jotting down every single word that is uttered. He is sensitive to the criticism (or humor!) of others about his work; however, in other arenas of life, he may not appear as arrogant or delicate. He can be ruthless in his efforts to gain control of functions in the office, and, even if he is successful in many arenas, his need to run the show will eventually get her into trouble. He will appear constantly demanding, asking for multiple revisions of anyone else's work. "Why can't you see how important this is?! I need it done, and I need it done right! It's not that hard to figure out the algorithm: if you just refer to the appendix on 3B of my protocol, it is clearly laid out. I'm not sure why everyone has to be so incompetent! Just do it again!" The Hostile Bean Counter's work may be valued if the products are successful or of high quality, but his inability to work well with others will lead to disgruntlement, fear, and an eroding, paralyzed team. He will either not notice or not care about the insidious side-effects that result from his ways, immersed instead in satisfaction of the immediate goals achieved. Any attempts to point out this impact on others will likely result in verbose explanations of why this isn't the case with the inclusion of all sorts of alleged yet invalid supporting facts and details.

Through the grapevine, I heard the story of one such Hostile Bean Counter who was an impossible operations administrator and treated every penny at his firm as though it were his own. He would bring accountants to tears over eight-dollar discrepancies in the multibillion-dollar budget. New managers learned quickly to take their entrepreneurial ideas and throw them in the trash unless they were coming to him having developed viable, thorough business plans; having completed due diligence; and having modeled the plans on comparable projects that were well established. And, of course, how could the firm be expected to support the start-up fees without a guaranteed return on investment? No chances were to be taken unless you came to him with cash in hand, and, because of structural limitations at the firm, no one could do that.

So the firm was frozen in time, doing what it had always done, and did not pursue anything new since it would make the Hostile Bean Counter extremely uncomfortable. Managers tried to get along with him superficially but avoid business interactions when possible. Reports would be returned sprayed with red pen and then delivered and returned, delivered and returned, again and again. Once the content was "corrected," the language would go under attack with question after question about the most minor details. Everything was deemed inadequate or just plain wrong. And they were merely internal reports! Everyone wondered how so much time could be spent on this minutiae, all for the apparent purpose of ending up in a series of binders neatly stacked in his office bookcase.

Business ran as usual, but eventually his rigid and parsimonious strategies began to shrink profit margins. Equipment was getting old, and competitors were investing in state-of-the-art products. He kept saying, "If it ain't broke, don't fix it." His only response to financial losses was to yell at others and then cut back, tighten the belt, and lay people off. Everyone felt trapped, disgruntled, and vulnerable. It got even worse when a new CEO was hired from the internal pool and promoted him to control even more of the operations, convinced that the administrator was the only person who knew the organization well enough to manage the details and keep the place afloat.

As the company moved squarely into the red, the new CEO jumped ship and an external "turnaround" person was hired. In less than a year, she saw where the company was stalling, fired the administrator, and reassigned his tasks. The company was well back into big profits within five years. Most remarkable to those in the company who survived the debacle was the fact that those reassigned tasks took almost no time for the new administrators. The previous amount of effort and detail spent on them had been of almost zero yield, despite so many cycles of revision. And, at the same time, huge chunks of important work that the prior administrator should have been doing were simply left undone, deemed "not as urgent," according to those workers who were left paralyzed by years of neglect. Despite the offer of a year of severance, the administrator sacrificed the cash to get back in a similar job at a new firm within six weeks. His decades of pristine performance evaluations proved an easy entry just about anywhere. And so began his next round of obsessive persecution.

The Hermit Bean Counter: The Hard-on-Herself Thinker

The Hermit Bean Counter, much like Pierre, obsesses quietly in his office about things going perfectly. He might not come off as so overtly controlling but acts through more subtle ways. In fact, he likely appears polite and accommodating at a superficial level. When things are operating smoothly, he can keep his overt anxiety to a minimum. But any curveballs can throw him into a frenzied state of agitation and incite increasingly frantic efforts to correct whatever he feels has gone wrong, to meet what feels like an impossible deadline, or to avoid the perceived threat of losing his job or someone's respect. Even when somewhat calm, this worrywart is always on the lookout for potential danger: signs that things are not going exactly as planned and that he will disappoint others. He is always doubting himself and wants to be seen as obedient. "Are you sure? . . . Is that okay? . . . Do you mind?" He depends on others for approval and guidance and has great difficulty asserting himself out of fear of humiliation. Instead, he makes lists of pros and cons in his head.

He worries, worries, worries. As he runs through his personal catastrophic algorithm, his anxiety escalates, and he can become so overwhelmed that he undermines efforts to move forward. Even having to make a simple decision can completely unhinge him. He may let other things go, like returning e-mails or phone calls, because he's just too busy overinvesting in his current focus. His outcry is, "There's just so much to do!" Tremendous time can be wasted obsessing over the most minor details as self-doubt and fear make project completion even more difficult. He is incredibly indecisive and spends an inordinate amount of time preparing for the next step. This type would rather not make a decision than make the wrong one; he wants everything to be "perfect" before choosing, which of course never happens. You might find yourself wondering, "Just exactly what does he spend all that time doing?!" as he hides behind closed doors in his "mad laboratory." In reality, he literally might be straightening out the rug on the floor, alphabetizing last year's expenditure receipts, or switching between different fonts on an e-mail to send out to colleagues.

The Hermit Bean Counter may also become enraged if he is interrupted at work or has external factors interfering with his efforts. However, he very likely fears letting others know he is angry and actually tends to avoid conflict or any expression of emotion because it feels "out of control." Hermit Bean Counters are easily embarrassed—they have an intense fear of social disapproval and rejection by others. The anger just simmers inside, making him feel increasingly guilty. He may compensate by excessively apologizing—of course, without actually taking responsibility or making change. "The e-mail? I'm so sorry I haven't followed up yet; I've just had so much to do. I really am sorry, though." Like Pierre, he functions best working solo but, despite this clear personal preference, can also become resentful for all the "extra" work he feels she must do. He stays late in the office, just waiting to clean up after everyone else, redo his work, and make sure everything is set for the next day.

The Hermit Bean Counter's fear of being fired is often the endpoint of the swirling, anxious, catastrophic ideas that arise with change or uncertainty. They are always imagining the worst-case scenarios. At times, this fear can take over, obliterating whatever the inciting crisis may have been. For certain Hermit

Bean Counters, the fear of doing or having done something wrong can lead him down a path of increasingly anxious data collection as he seeks "evidence" to prove that the boss is trying to get rid of him. This is when it becomes hard to distinguish the Bean Counter from the Suspicious, whom you will meet later in this book. As he builds the case against himself, he may become increasingly certain that his fears are well founded within the reality of her data points—"on this day you said this" or "you looked at me this way"—and is emboldened to confront his managers or to place a call to Human Resources about his untenable work environment. Repeated efforts at reassurance by bosses seem to have no impact as the fear has taken on its own life, and the managers' frustration becomes more evidence to the Bean Counter that they are against her. Talk about a vicious cycle! At this point, the Hermit Bean Counter moves from simply annoying to terribly disrupting the office, as more and more people are implicated in the story and more and more time gets wasted dealing with the situation at hand. Unless something can "reboot" this process, it can paralyze the workplace and be very destructive.

I recall one particularly poignant patient, an older financial advisor in the midst of a severe and psychotic episode of depression. A Hermit Bean Counter at baseline, his story was complicated by also having periods of depression during his life. Not unlike Pierre, he had a pristine reputation for rational, careful investing that made his clients feel very happy and secure. At one point, though, he made some investment recommendations that went awry. He was following his tried-and-true investment principles, but in this particular market they didn't seem to be working. Increasingly agitated, he froze the investments—worried about moving the money around and afraid of making a wrong decision. He became increasingly fearful of touching anyone's money at all and began to stay in bed all day instead of going to work. He stopped sleeping and eating, couldn't concentrate, had zero energy, and couldn't enjoy his usual leisure activities. It was utterly humiliating for him, and he just couldn't face the fact that he had really and truly made any mistakes. He started to think he was dying because he believed his bowels were constipated (they weren't) and imagined that eventually his insides would explode and kill him. His depression became so debilitating that I recommended a course of electroconvulsive therapy while starting antidepressants in an effort to get him to feel better sooner. Alongside talk therapy focused on gradually feeling less grief about his loss and being more flexible in choices, these interventions helped him have a more comfortable, if not entirely relaxed, future.

WHEN THE SCHMUCK IN THE OFFICE IS A BEAN COUNTER

Because many of their characteristics—in moderation—are seen as desirable to the workplace, so too are Bean Counters often initially valued. These individuals frequently pursue jobs in law, accounting, computer programming, or other rule-based fields where they can feel in control of the algorithms (Curtis 1991). They appear organized and dedicated, responsible and detail-oriented. Who wouldn't want an employee that seemed to adhere to standards and want to work hard? In the workplace, Bean Counters are usually seen as workaholics (Mudrack 2004) or the so-called "type A" personalities.

However, as they begin to take on more tasks and responsibilities, coworkers become aware that these same tendencies interfere with getting the job done. As the individual has more group projects and interactions, they have significant difficulty sharing tasks with others. The data shows that despite their often intense dedication to work, they underperform compared to their abilities (Furnham 2007). Further, regardless of their seeming desire to work long and hard, they often do not seem to enjoy their work. The Bean Counter may spend significant amounts of time making lists, categorizing, and organizing without actually accomplishing much at all. The Bean Counter may have a neatly arranged workspace, but he also may have difficulty throwing things out such that the desk is covered with piles. He is likely seen as extremely indecisive when it comes to making and enacting plans. Others at work also perceive the Bean Counter to be formal, moral, and respectful when not angry.

Bean Counters often have difficulty taking time off from work and may even not use their allotted vacation days. If and when they do, they feel extremely guilty. This blurring of the office into other aspects of life is particularly prominent in contemporary society with constant access to work e-mails and conference calls on phones and laptops. For Bean Counters, workaholic tendencies lead to stress, burnout, and job turnover. Because they place so much value on mastering their work, any small change in their role or the office can overwhelm them. For this reason, they have particular difficulty with quick-paced environments or may demonstrate more difficulty during periods of growth or transition for the company. The Bean Counter often has difficulty with tasks requiring creativity, spontaneity, or flexibility, such as speaking in meetings or on-the-spot problem solving. They frequently have difficulty turning tasks in on time and can seem to procrastinate despite working long hours. The common pattern is that a need for control actually interferes with the desired outcome for the office.

Bean Counter leaders also have the effect of increasing a general sense of mistrust and conflict in the workplace. Even with a position of authority, they have difficulty delegating tasks to others. At the same time, he might set impossible standards, which in effect dooms other employees to failure. Despite the focus on organization, the Bean Counter boss often has difficulty scheduling, structuring, and planning. As subordinates, Bean Counters can be competitive with their bosses (Stern, Rosenbaum, et al. 2008). Bean Counters also often feel as if they have been unfairly passed over for promotions in favor of others whose work is not as good. The subordinate might also excessively ask whether they are "allowed" to do things, whether everything is going smoothly, or for help with making decisions. At all levels, Bean Counters focus on regulations and procedures. They often tend to avoid seeking, or even directly reject, help from others and have significant difficulty working in teams.

As might be imagined, Bean Counters don't just reserve these behaviors for the office. Unless the Bean Counter has paired with a significant other for whom these traits work well, the long hours, rigid postures, and poor frustration tolerance can cause quite a bit of interpersonal conflict. Because they tend to hyperfocus on one specific area at a time, other parts of life are often neglected, such as interpersonal relationships or other obligations. Sex and leisure may be particularly disregarded.

HOW TO DEAL WITH A BEAN COUNTER

If the way of life of being a Bean Counter is the need to feel in control, the philosophy of dealing with them is to let them feel in control. The various techniques center on reassurance, reality testing, and external structure to help lessen their anxiety. At the same time, the methods avoid direct challenges to their detail-oriented nature.

When dealing with a Bean Counter, it is important to recognize that they usually don't think that they're doing anything wrong. Because, after all, they are working toward perfection! Oftentimes, suggestions to change will be met with lengthy arguments and criticism about the standards or person suggesting them (Gabbard 2007). All in all, the best strategy—when possible—is to give the appearance that you are understanding and valuing their dedication. Overstating your personal investment in a project, appearing as committed as possible, may help them step away from micromanaging just a little bit. It is best not to argue about details (which is likely to make them ramp up their involvement) and to instead agree on the process moving forward.

Once again, remember this all may be very difficult because you likely think they are wrong. The reason you are accommodating them is to avoid what may be worse—their controlling takedown of the office. It may be helpful to try to remember just how worried they probably are. In most cases, you are simply assisting them with their overwhelming fear of uncertainty. When possible, help them avoid being hard on themselves if they seem down on their confidence. To avoid a blowout, try to take notes about what they say, follow their instructions, and (at least appear to) fully agree with the plan. They are likely to be impressed by your own timeliness and attention to detail—neatly organized work and space—even if they can't achieve it themselves.

What if there is a disagreement about something that already happened? Since the basic motivation of the Bean Counter is the need to control risk, an excellent strategy is to help him feel as if he is indeed controlling any given situation. Let's say a manager is giving you a hard time about a reimbursement, after the fact. You expected your money and now he's saying you spent too much and he doesn't know what he can give you, if anything, citing how you didn't accurately estimate the costs, even though he approved the purchase. Assuming you didn't overspend wildly, this is a very annoying development. What do you do? The natural instinct is to go head-to-head through the numbers and explain why they're reasonable. And you may gently do this. However, if you add in some deference to their logic, such as acknowledging the importance of accurate estimates, you will likely diffuse the intensity of the manager's anxiety. In so doing, you will tap into the manager's empathy—you did spend your money expecting it back, after all—and your show of reason is more likely to get you what you deserve. This move will encourage him to think more highly of your competence, which may get you more reimbursement than if you had argued about the details of numbers and expectations.

When you can't magnanimously "offer" control to your manager, you may well be held captive to an endless justification process. You'll have to grit your teeth and hope it doesn't last too long. Again, take a look inward and ask yourself why it's bothering you so much. You'll do best when you can accept that, while it's incredibly irritating, it may simply be the way it goes. Think about waiting in line at a state or federal agency of some sort. Some people stand there, patiently accepting that they're going to be in line way too long but keeping their eyes on the prize of achieving the task. Others will fidget and mutter under their breath and be in a constant state of exasperation. Both will reach the window at the same time. It's simply how it is, and there's not much you can do about it, unless you're ready to walk away from it all.

Comparable to any negotiation, the most powerful bargaining posture is the ability to leave the position, particularly as a subordinate. If I indicate that, ultimately, I don't need what you're giving badly enough to really compromise myself, you will fear that I'll walk away from the deal (leaving things spiraling out of control!) and therefore be more amenable to settling with me. This is, of course, not always possible.

If the Bean Counter is your boss, some techniques can be particularly useful. These will also apply to other relationships with obsessives but are particularly helpful given the limited flexibility of dealing with a supervisor. She may find some relief from her anxiety when you demonstrate over and over that you understand the level of detail and perfection she requires and you meet her needs at every turn. Never break a promise; only commit to what you are able to actually do, lest you risk upsetting the Bean Counter's carefully mapped plan for the future. This strategy includes being on time for appointments and meeting all deadlines as expected. Make sure to take responsibility when you do make mistakes and avoid excessive defense of yourself (or criticism of the Bean Counter's plan) when you don't. The last thing you want to do is get into any power struggle over details. This approach also entails avoiding disrupting the hierarchy when at all possible. Defer to the Bean Counter's authority and don't go around them—unless you really need to. If you do, in fact, have to go to a supervisor for advice, be sure not to let the Bean Counter think that you were directly testing their authority.

In contrast to some of the other character types, supervisors do have some efficacy with Bean Counters given their reliance on hierarchy and authority. Their rule-based nature makes them more likely to listen to directions for change. The important piece of this technique is understanding what the problem is and directing them to make the appropriate change. It is most important to focus the employee's attention on his process (making too many revisions, spending too long at the office, turning in assignments late) rather than on the quality of the work (which would have the reverse effect of aggravating his self-defeating tendencies). It is usually better to point out the need for perfection as the culprit requiring change rather than the resulting inefficiency, which could cause the individual to try to be even more perfectionistic. At the same time, too much contact with authority may be distressing, so a mentoring system for employees may be helpful to provide supplementary advice and encourage a socialization, such as weekly coffee meetings (Langan-Fox, Cooper, et al. 2007). When working with a Hermit Bean Counter, gently encouraging them to say no to things they don't want to do, voice criticism, or choose an unpopular option can be very freeing for them if they are able to handle the anxiety.

If a manager catches a Bean Counter during a period of increased anxiety, direct reassurance and reality testing may be helpful. You might simply point out that making mistakes is a way to improve one's skill set. At the same time, you want to reinforce his self-conception as someone who does well at her job and is careful with detail. "Don't worry about the edit—I still know you're a hard worker who cares a lot about this project." Remember, his self-esteem depends on meeting the expectations of others. Clarifying that the particular issue at hand will not lead to unemployment might help mitigate anxiety. Because they are somewhat soothed by rules and structure, it may be helpful for this person to realistically try to estimate the plausibility of their worst fears. When he comes to you terrified that he made an error by not knowing about a recent review process, convinced he will lose his job, you might say, "Margaret, it's understandable you didn't know. It's definitely stressful to not know about the review, but there's no reason to think you'll get fired." He likely will not respond well initially, so you will have to add, "Who else can you think of who has missed review processes? Did any of them lose their job? So I don't think that's even at stake here." Reality testing their fears with facts and structure can be important and useful, particularly in an uncharacteristic time of stress. Distracting the Bean Counter, perhaps with another, more realistically pressing project might help move him forward. Any of these strategies, though, will only briefly mitigate the symptoms. In particular, the Hermit will surely find another apocalyptic crisis to chew on in good time.

If a Bean Counter works for you, give him structured tasks with boundaries that require great attention to minutiae and "reward" him with unstructured leisure activities like informal get-togethers with colleagues after work, time at the gym, and so on. It may be important to even strongly encourage or enforce taking vacations so that the employee can step away from the job for just a little bit. Though relaxation and leisure can often seem uncomfortable to Bean Counters because of their inherent lack of structure and productivity, encouragement of such times by a superior can be meaningful given their typical deference to authority. Company retreats, happy hours, and dinners can help structure and model enjoyment activities.

If initial attempts are not successful and the individual is repeatedly and negatively affecting the workplace, more may need to be done. If the Bean Counter is truly interfering with your capacity to move your work forward, it makes sense to try and clarify that for him. Sometimes the presence of a deadline can "snap" him out of his rigid process. "Hey, it is really important for me to get this in on time, and I need your part before I can send in the entire submission." Sometimes he might actually be looking for an external force to drive him into action. Focusing your efforts on helping him make a decision might be particularly useful. "Don't worry about addressing X. I think if your draft focuses on Y, it will be great."

But if you're left truly paralyzed by such a person and he's unresponsive to your pleas, you may eventually need to address the situation with someone even higher up or with HR. The possibilities of more formal interventions for Bean Counters are diverse. Referrals to brief stress management advice, mindfulness-based stress reduction, time-limited cognitive therapy to learn to appropriately assess risk, or long-term psychodynamic therapy focused on relieving underlying insecurity are all options. Luckily, however, the traits of Bean Counters are considered relatively responsive to professional mental health treatment (Mancebo, Eisen, et al. 2005). Of course, as with any therapeutic intervention, the Bean Counter must *want* to change.

Broader workplace interventions may be helpful for Bean Counters as well as other employees, such as providing opportunities for enjoyment and deemphasizing the importance of working long hours. Relocating the individual to a role that involves details, rules, regulations, data, or policy may be very helpful (Furnham 2007; Langan-Fox, Cooper, et al. 2007), as is taking them out of positions that require creativity, experimentation, or spontaneity. A visionary leader might want to pair herself with a Bean Counter to allow herself to continue to dream big without getting caught up in the details. He may do well with tasks like developing protocols or analyzing data, particularly if given specific individual assignments. And if none of this is an option in your workplace and you are truly trapped by a Bean Counter, you may need to think hard about whether your job is really worth it.

Pierre: Part Two

Pierre eventually came to my attention because he found that he couldn't stop thinking about death and was concerned for his own safety. He was adamant that he wasn't suicidal. He had no plan or intent to harm himself. But it was the thought of death and only the thought of death that brought him any relief from swirling rehashing of his mistake. Why? Pierre had built his life on the notion that if he was a careful, attentive, and good man, he could control everything. He made list after list of his goals and plans and carried them out in an organized, stepwise manner. He found comfort in reviewing these lists and seeing that he accomplished the things he wanted to. So he couldn't understand how the mistake had happened. His methods had always worked before, but the incident suddenly made him lose control of his world. He didn't understand what his world had become and where his place in it might be. He didn't know what would happen to him now, and his world was turned upside down.

Of course, Pierre came into therapy really wanting to know why he had made the mistake and wanting to prevent himself from making any future errors. Wanting to become even more perfect was his motive for seeing me. As I carried him through his thought processes, he reviewed decision point after decision point, describing things he used to believe he could manage that he no longer felt he could. He was almost hysterical considering his newly accepted inabilities. He'd come to feel that his life was an illusion; his sense of integrity, a house of cards. Wasn't there anything left that he could control? As it turned out, only in death did he feel these questions could be answered. Only in death could he accept that he was powerless, that there were no more decisions for him to make, that he could finally just rest.

This morbid realization was an epiphany for Pierre because, in discussing it with me, he recognized the absurdity of hanging on to death as a solution for certainty. He realized how much of his life he still wanted to live and how little it made sense to give up on a future for himself and his family. He allowed himself, for a moment, to accept that sometimes you just have to throw your hands up and say "oh well!" and that there are things in life beyond your control. Finally, he began the long but essential process of starting to forgive himself, to let go of things, to always try his best but to let the chips fall as they might. Instead of trying to understand why he had made the mistake, we began to focus on why making the mistake had caused him to spiral into such despair. He came to see the goal of perfection as the illusion that it had been all along. Years later, he would reflect on how he used to "live so hard" and would joke about trying to control the weather. He became more spontaneous and fun, and his personal and work life improved dramatically. He remained an excellent worker, but one with reasonable expectations. We explored his ability to tolerate simply being—instead of always having to accomplish something—and, over time, he was more able to appreciate art, music, and even daydreaming.

Pierre was pushed to a very extreme point before he was able to loosen up. Short of that, the task at hand for those of us working with obsessive, controlling people is to figure out how to help them loosen up on us. The problem is, Bean Counters are everywhere in our offices and, as mentioned, often get promoted beyond their capacity to manage.

A Checklist of Ways to Effectively Deal with a Bean Counter

- Avoid direct challenges or arguments concerning their detail-oriented nature.
- Express appreciation of their dedication while emphasizing your own.
- Document suggested changes made by the Bean Counter, citing them when you represent your "corrected" work.
- Acquiescing to their logic often appeals to the Bean Counter's empathy and helps you achieve the desired result.
- Never promise more than you can deliver. Take responsibility for mistakes, avoiding rationalization or defensiveness.
- Appropriately appealing to supervisors may be beneficial, since Bean Counters are often more receptive to structural changes passed down the hierarchy.
- When evaluating their work, normalize mistakes and point out that perfect can be the enemy of good.
- During periods of increased anxiety, direct reassurance and reality testing may be helpful.
- If possible, direct the Bean Counter's job toward detail-oriented duties and utilize clear directions and deadlines.
- As a last resort or for extreme cases, formal interventions may be required.

The Distracted

In college I had a friend who was strikingly brilliant. He was a bit of a renaissance man: stayed up late playing the drums, wrote endless short stories, had an encyclopedic knowledge of history that he would engagingly detail. But he was also extremely good at procrastinating, not listening during conversations, and losing his keys. His contrasting intelligence and inability to carry through with tasks was fascinating to me, as I wrapped up my assignments and watched him struggle to start his.

THE DISTRACTED'S BASIC TRAITS

Diagnosable inattention has fallen under some scrutiny in recent years for two main reasons: the addictive stimulant medications prescribed to treat it are sometimes misused, and these medications are frequently prescribed to children. Although the current treatment for inattention can be controversial, the problem itself has been recognized by physicians since the eighteenth century (Lange, Reichl, et al. 2010). Two nineteenth-century German tales by the physician Heinrich Hoffmann, the stories of "Fidgety Phil" and "Johnny Look-in-the-Air," have been said to represent stories about problems with attention. With his characteristic restlessness, Fidgety Phil's family wonders "if he is able to sit still for once at table." The story ends with disaster as the table topples over: the mother "did fret and frown," the father "made such a face," and "Philip is in sad disgrace" (Hoffmann 1999). With similarly astute observation and description, the other story details that Johnny Look-in-the-Air is distracted by swallows, watching them until he falls into a river: "Headlong in poor Johnny fell!" Because of their difficulty with concentration, both Phil and Johnny certainly suffer.

What is difficult for these and any distracted individuals is to pay attention: to continuously focus on one thing and not others. Concentration, once described as a moral ability, is now viewed as a partially inherited skill set with some neurobiological underpinnings. The formal psychiatric diagnosis describing impaired functioning of these skills is attention-deficit/hyperactivity disorder, or ADHD. While this was previously considered a short-lived condition of childhood, it is now viewed as often persisting into adult life—typically with more subtle symptoms. In fact, while about 5 to 10 percent of children have ADHD, estimates say about 2 to 5 percent of adults have it as well (Sadock 2000; American Psychiatric Association 2013). The difficulty has been described more commonly in individuals who identify as non-Hispanic Caucasian and who are unemployed and previously married (Kessler, Adler, et al. 2006). Strikingly, ADHD is twice as common in males (American Psychiatric Association 2013). However, even as far back as the 1700s, Alexander Crichton— who posited the first medical description of what later became known as ADHD—noted that everyone can get distracted (Lange, Reichl, et al. 2010). For those we will call the Distracted, however, the ability to maintain attention over time is consistently difficult, and this struggle interferes significantly with their ability to do well.

The Distracted have a frustrating difficulty paying attention. They make careless mistakes, have problems with listening, and find it hard to follow instructions. They struggle with organization and evince a pattern of being late, forgetful, and losing things. As with Fidgety Phil, the Distracted often have difficulty sitting still, being quiet, and waiting their turn. They tend to interrupt others. How these traits appear may change over time, but some evidence of them is persistent beginning in childhood and across various settings, such as work, home, and school.

Mark: Part One

Mark was a creative consultant for a large PR firm who was referred to me after losing several big accounts for the company. He was relatively new to the job and, from the beginning, was impressive. Despite being late to his interview, he had dazzled the partners at the firm with his energetic, sociable way of interacting. After he got the job and began settling into the office, he continued in this mode—often late but always brightening up the room—and landed a couple of contracts right from the get-go. However, it soon became apparent that he just couldn't deliver on his promises, and I was called to see if there was any way to keep him on.

His documents were riddled with typos, he took directions poorly, and he kept an incredibly messy office. It became almost comical to his bosses, the way he would promise to complete something by the end of the day and then forget to even try. He'd often walk out in the evening, leaving a superior flabbergasted by his lack of follow-up. Aware that he wasn't getting much done, he would sit in his office looking at the piles of incomplete work and become completely overwhelmed with anxiety. In not knowing where to begin, he'd usually not begin at all. At other times, he would start one project but, without making any headway, quickly move on to another.

His focus was on sales because these were live performances, in the moment, and he knew he could be rewarded for his charm and energy. Mark would captivate potential clients up front, dazzling them with his big-picture ideas and his confident promises that seemingly anything could be accomplished. Afterward, he would lose them to disorganized presentations, misplaced documents, and missed deadlines. His own reputation started to negatively affect his company, which started to lose clients; people were upset.

What became evident talking with Mark was that he was trying hard, wanted the job, and had great ideas. But as a Distracted, he lacked the fundamental ability to stay on target and thoroughly complete a task. It was something that his parents, teachers, friends, and now—as a young professional—bosses knew to be true about Mark. He also knew it about himself—and felt terrible about it—but didn't know how to change.

HOW DID THE DISTRACTED GET THIS WAY?

While many are quick to blame classroom settings or parenting styles, difficulty with attention is said to be approximately 60 to 98 percent heritable (Sadock 2000). Risk factors also include low birth weight and exposure to cigarette smoking while in the womb (American Psychiatric Association 2013). Oftentimes, there will be hyperactivity present even in toddlerhood, but this can be very difficult to differentiate from normal behavior for this age group. Characteristic distraction usually appears between ages four and twelve (American Psychiatric Association 2013). As children encounter attention-requiring tasks in elementary school, the Distracted have more difficulty than their peers. Over the years, the hyperactive features of being Distracted tend to fade while the difficulty with attention persists.

As Mark entered school, his teachers noticed that he was unusually active and unable to sit still, even when playing games he enjoyed. His homework, which he hated doing and often lost, was riddled with careless mistakes. His parents bought organizers and made lists and reminders for him; they tried to limit the things he would lose or forget and attempted to keep him on task. But it was hard not to become furious with him when, for example, he lost his expensive dental retainer three times. He was also a "motor mouth," constantly interrupting conversations and yelling answers to questions in class when other children were directly asked to respond. People called him the "Energizer Bunny" because he just wouldn't stop—physically or verbally—and of course he couldn't wait in line for anything. He would literally drop a book, game, or project on the floor and move toward whatever caught his fancy at any given moment. People often found his behavior frustrating and annoying.

Over time, some of his behaviors did improve, though he was still a restless and relentless fidgeter. Some teachers felt he was lazy and careless, but others seemed to note his creativity and superior problem-solving abilities. What was coming off as laziness was not a lack of effort but real difficulty focusing. He often felt overwhelmed with unmanageable obligations and bad about his performance.

Mark was terribly frustrated with himself and felt misunderstood by his parents and his teachers. Eventually, these feelings began to impact his self-esteem. He believed that he grasped most everything—objectively, he was very bright—but people only seemed to notice what he couldn't do. Fortunately, he was an affable young man and saw that people uniformly responded well to him socially. He thus put a great deal of energy into developing his interpersonal skills, and his charm began to draw people away from his inability to focus. These skills would allow him to gain entry into schools and jobs before people noticed his inability to follow through. And his inabilities seemed exacerbated by some school and work environments.

DEGREES OF DISTRACTION

Remember that not every Distracted person has ADHD. Many just have trouble with organization, time management, or procrastination. Of course, we are all occasionally vulnerable to distractions—a new love, a family crisis, even a TV show that's on in the neighboring room. When I refer to the Distracted character type, I mean those people for whom distractibility is a relatively chronic state of being.

Interest becomes a major factor in concentration. That is, if I'm fascinated in the topic at hand, I can concentrate on it for long periods and generally get the work done. Of course, the most famous contemporary example is the extraordinary Olympic swimmer Michael Phelps, who won twenty-three gold medals with a diagnosis of ADHD and a history of taking stimulant medications; he surely was able to focus for long hours on his passion of swimming (Baron 2010). However, if a person is not interested in a subject, he may have significantly more difficulty staying attentive.

Most of the Distracted lack a consistent system of organization as a primary problem. Commonly, in the face of a major project, those tasks that are considered small or nonurgent are moved aside, as all available time and concentration must go to getting the big job done. And that big job may in fact be completed on time. The problem is that all the little things have now piled up. The satisfaction of finishing is soon permuted into panic about everything that fell by the wayside. Calls and e-mails have not been returned. Requests that the Distracted considered small are now urgent; the various requestors did not view them as unimportant, and now they're completely pissed off by the long wait. The hundreds of unread e-mails and the scattered papers all over the desk are overwhelming. Where to begin?

Such delay can also occur with the Distracted on a daily basis. Even given repetitive tasks, his inability to organize makes it hard to finish and get out of the office each evening. I recall a particularly tragic medical intern who couldn't ever get out of the hospital before midnight. All of his peers blew out of there before 5 PM, but he just couldn't do it. Even though there were national regulations about how long first years could stay in the hospital, which most interns relished, he still couldn't get out on time and, in effect, broke these rules. He came from an Ivy League school, and his residency training program had been really excited about his arrival. But his great reputation quickly plummeted as patient and staff frustration became the new talk of the town. Requests weren't addressed for hours and hours, unless they were true medical emergencies. And addressing an emergency would throw him off so far that he almost couldn't get back on track.

The assumption was made, because he had such great credentials and managed to get through such esteemed educational programs, that he was a Bean Counter whose perfectionism held him up. But review of his work revealed that it was in fact incredibly sloppy. He'd forget to draw blood for particular lab studies and would have to go back to the same patient to draw blood again, sometimes twice in a day, putting patients at risk with unnecessary needle sticks. Those chart notes that took hours to produce were generally one line long and written in illegible chicken scratch. The only responses to his work from onlookers was, "What is he *doing*?!" and "What was he *thinking*?!"

The Distracted tends to be unrealistic about time and therefore cannot manage it, imagining that tasks will take much less or much more of it than they actually do. Add in the fact that the Distracted tends to lose things, forget things, and derail easily, and he once again ends his day feeling that he accomplished little and will never catch up. Stress exacerbates the distractibility. More disorganization then exacerbates the stress, creating yet another vicious cycle.

In contrast to so many of the types we've discussed, the Distracted doesn't tend to get into direct conflicts as a result of his interactional style. If anything, he is hardest on himself. He is frustrated and frustrates others. So while people may get angry at him, they don't feel much anger from him, likely only guilt and remorse. He may feel angry when pressured to complete tasks on a schedule that he can't manage, but this won't generally lead to major interpersonal problems. At times, however, Distracted people fail to hold in anger and other emotions because they are impulsive and have difficulty with inhibition; however, emotional outbursts aren't a major problem for them, and they often feel bad and apologize afterward.

When disorganization reaches a critical level—I have known people with more than 100,000 e-mails in their in-box—the Distracted might take a dedicated chunk of time just to get his affairs in order. He might use a week of vacation time to sort and file in order to see the top of his desk for the first time in months. This will give him a tremendous sense of satisfaction, and he will vow to maintain order from now on. For a period of time, to-do lists and attempts to act on tasks in a timely manner will improve, but the Distracted won't be able to keep it up as things begin to pile up and he again falls behind.

Some distractibility can be related to the functioning of our bodies. I recall when I was pregnant with my son that I'd walk into a room three or four times before I could remember what I was trying to do. Hormonal shifts, stress, and even simply growing older can all be culprits for increased disorganization. As might be imagined, even during these times, the person with excellent time management and organizational skills will generally suffer less than the individual who is a Distracted at baseline.

WHEN THE SCHMUCK IN THE OFFICE IS DISTRACTED

Research shows that the Distracted can have significant problems in the workplace, including frustration and disappointment for themselves as well as their coworkers (Mao, Brams, et al. 2011). Regrettably, they are often seen as lazy and irresponsible (American Psychiatric Association 2013). A Distracted individual is likely to have more frequent occupational accidents and injuries, including motor vehicle crashes, than the average worker (Lyon, Baker, et al. 2009; Küpper, Haavik, et al. 2012). From an organization's perspective, it is important to note that these individuals often have higher medical costs as well as more absences than other workers (Secnik, Swensen, et al. 2005). The Distracted are also more likely to quit or be fired and often have numerous job changes (Harpin 2005; Secnik, Swensen, et al. 2005). In addition, the Distracted may have intellectual potential but underachieve at work. They are less likely to go after promotions or new opportunities, even if they're perfectly capable of succeeding, because they are all too aware of their shortcomings and assume they will fail.

It is important to note, however, that these individuals have been characterized as good at jobs that involve creativity and spontaneity instead of recurring tasks (Küpper, Haavik, et al. 2012). They can be great "idea people." So, interestingly, some Distracted individuals may do better in think tanks or higher-level positions when they have administrative or secretarial assistants to help with some tasks (Adamou, Arif, et al. 2013). They will obviously have more difficulty if, in addition to being distracted, they have other cognitive or intellectual difficulties.

HOW TO DEAL WITH THE DISTRACTED

Remember that the Distracted often feels incredibly helpless and frustrated with himself. He's not acting distracted to make your life harder—he's living hard himself. I have a friend who is both brilliant and entrepreneurial and yet remains essentially unemployed. He didn't do particularly well in his classes because, although he clearly understood the material with far greater depth than just about anyone, he was always late on his projects and papers. By handing in whatever unfinished product he could before the lateness became absurd, he couldn't demonstrate his talent to his professors. After graduation, he landed great jobs but then either couldn't deliver or delivered so slowly that opportunities passed right by him. He has had more billion-dollar ideas than is imaginable and yet can't follow through on any of them past the basic plan. Even his supporters have stopped investing in him—they may still encourage his ventures but are no longer willing to lose their money to his disorganization. I remember him calling me once in tears, aware that he was about to get fired from a job he really, really loved because of his slow and low productivity. Eventually, he landed a Web development job where his only deliverable was the occasional contract gig to support himself. This job represents devastating underemployment for him—and is painful to see. As a friend, I have always been around to comfort him but have never been in the position to force him into changing his ways. Instead, I have stood by and listened and offered strategies and interventions, but he's never been able to make change on his own.

But in an employment setting, there are a lot of techniques that managers and coworkers can use to foster a workable environment for the Distracted. Giving them the best opportunities for success is simply a matter of making sure they're directed to tasks that appropriately draw on their skills, coupled with some basic frameworks for enhancing organization. It is important to give them small tasks that they can achieve and feel good about: for example, breaking down a project and assigning it step by step can be incredibly helpful. Also, providing some assignments that require inventiveness can inspire them to keep engaged with the task. Depending on their position, offering assistants can be helpful to keep them from getting swamped and sidetracked by more tedious jobs.

With respect to managing such a character type interpersonally, supervisors who are overcritical can often worsen disorganization by increasing anxiety, as can micromanagers who might further overwhelm the individual with details (Nadeau 2005). The Distracted feels bad enough about his productivity without added pressure. A general approach is to be clear, patient, and predictable. Regular meetings scheduled for the purpose of helpful feedback can provide some overarching structure. If the meetings are habitually scheduled for the same time and day of the week, the employee is less likely to be late, which can be an important strategy for helping them learn to be on time.

Sometimes clear, task-oriented, written instructions can be useful, particularly when they lay out goals and the steps to attain them on a timeline. It's helpful, too, for a manager to describe the process of how he or she decided to prioritize the steps. This is a great modeling exercise for the Distracted, who should be encouraged to emulate a similar approach next time, with supervision. And, in general, it's important to keep the Distracted individual from overcommitting himself and from trying to completely finish one task before beginning the next. He may be overambitious and need gentle guidance in breaking down projects into assignments that are achievable in a given time frame. It is imperative to discuss steps in tangible, measurable, constructive, and attainable terms (Kooij 2012). At other times, the Distracted may be overambitious because they want to make up for past failures and avoid disappointing others. As such, it is important to let them know that breaking up a project is not punishment and that they can still have ownership of the larger project (and its future success). Encourage the Distracted to let others know in an honest conversation what help he may need (e.g., someone to check in on the progress weekly). He might also benefit from help determining how to delegate parts of projects or reassign older tasks when taking on new ones.

Even the setup of the physical environment can be important in limiting distractions by optimizing space, light, and temperature and reducing interruptions like television, radio, or neighboring conversation. The work station should be in a quiet place if possible, facing away from hallways or other distractions. Desk accessories such as color-coding systems, folders, binders with labeled dividers, and nearby wastebaskets can be helpful with organizing clutter. Even having a regularly scheduled "declutter hour," perhaps at the end of the week, can assist with keeping the Distracted individual focused while working during the rest of the week. Sometimes simple interventions like white noise machines, noise-canceling headphones, timers, alarms, planners, and apps can be useful (Nadeau 1997; Adamou, Arif, et al. 2013). Desk and wall organizers can help the Distracted develop routines. For example, a simple wall hook near a desk to hang one's keys can save the daily frantic hunt for the lost ones. Asking them what environmental changes they might find helpful can be a productive and cost-saving intervention.

By helping the Distracted automate routine actions and processes, you will help him achieve organizational "victories" that will allow him to move forward. Baby steps that give the Distracted even the smallest sense of efficiency and accomplishment can really go a long way toward making him want to build on the progress. The Distracted are used to having structure represent something they can't be successful with: deadlines and appointments signify a potential for lateness, for example. After multiple failures, the Distracted person avoids even attempting to implement organization. Once they experience the good feelings associated with timely task accomplishment, however, they may be more motivated to focus their efforts. And we can assist our coworkers, managers, and direct reports by quietly modeling organized behavior. In letting the Distracted develop interest in learning more about these skills at his own pace, you're more likely to see sustained change. So referral to training in time management, planning, and organization for the Distracted who is ready to make some changes can have a real impact (Solanto, Marks, et al. 2008).

Seeing a physician for possible stimulant medication is another option for affected individuals who cannot self-correct and have the personal awareness to seek treatment. While stimulant medications are by no means always a panacea, when prescribed by a qualified physician in a properly diagnosed individual who uses them appropriately, the results can be significant: better success with retaining employment, for example (Halmøy, Fasmer, et al. 2009).

In general, if an employer can find a way to "capture the good," that is, take advantage of the Distracted's strengths without allowing him to get mired in all the things he can't do, or can't do fast enough, there's real hope of having a satisfying work relationship. Of course, it isn't always possible to arrange the work environment or expectations just so, and if the accommodations described have no impact, then the Distracted might eventually require transfer to a different position or may want to look elsewhere for employment. But clearly communicated empathy, flexibility, structure, modeling, and customizing a job to the Distracted's often ample abilities can have tremendous results. As mentioned, the Distracted responds to victories, and he can progress when he feels good about himself and the fruits of his labor. Then everybody wins.

Mark: Part Two

Meeting Mark, I understood that his current and past problems indicated a possible diagnosis of ADHD, so I sent him for a full psychological and psychiatric assessment. This evaluation included a computer test during which Mark was connected to a motion tracking system, which monitored how well he could sit still and pay attention to tasks on the screen. Indeed, after the psychological testing and a clinical evaluation with another physician, his diagnosis was determined to be ADHD. He accepted a medication intervention and, though still on the scattered side, was subsequently able to function significantly better both at work and at home.

Medication combined with some of the strategies outlined below made a significant impact on his ability to be productive, and Mark found his work to be much more enjoyable and fulfilling with this help. The medication allowed him to *concentrate* better, but at first he still struggled because he had no organizational skills.

Thankfully, his company was willing to invest a bit of time and energy in his success, and that made all the difference. Mark's boss sat down with him and described a few sample tasks, to hear from Mark how he might approach them. It became evident pretty quickly where Mark was losing his way. They began with three relatively small and circumscribed projects and agreed on a due date. Then, they sat together and broke them down into digestible, measurable steps. Mark's boss went so far as to create a daily to-do list with Mark that was realistic and achievable. At first, Mark took offense because the list looked so rudimentary, but his boss reminded him that Mark had already demonstrated his inability to finish even a rudimentary set of tasks.

Mark's boss also scheduled two to three "midday checks" with Mark to see how he was progressing on his to-do lists. His improved concentration combined with these defined quanta of work allowed Mark to regularly achieve his daily goals. Soon he began to learn the little tricks that helped him do repetitive tasks the same way each time he completed them. This improved his proficiency and allowed him to feel a sense of mastery. Mark's boss slowly backed off on the oversight as Mark's confidence improved. Mark learned, slowly but surely, how to be more productive.

When Mark would become overwhelmed, at the beginning of this process, his boss would work with him to dissect what had happened. With time, Mark became fully independent. He began to feel better about himself and his abilities, and, as he did so, his performance improved. While his boss's initial input was effortful, it was time well spent, as Mark became a truly valuable contributor to the company.

A Checklist of Ways to Effectively Deal with the Distracted

- Enhance productivity by assigning small, achievable projects with step-by-step tasks.
- Increase engagement in the job by having imaginative and creative components.
- The preferred management style is clear, patient, and predictable, without overbearing micromanagement.
- Encourage the Distracted not to overcommit themselves, to finish one task before starting on the next, and to seek out help or delegate work as needed.

- Minimize distractions in the workplace and employ aids for organization.
- Implement trainings in time management, planning, and organization.
- Therapy and/or medication assistance may be helpful for severe distractibility.

Mr. Hyde

I have seen people do some of the most ridiculous and heartbreaking things because of an addiction. As a medical student, I once observed a treatment group for doctors with addictions—there were people stealing medicine from patients, using medical equipment to give themselves vodka rectally, and even stealing clean urine to pass drug tests. I've had patients give up everything—careers, homes, families—for their drug of choice. This chapter's title alludes to the story of Dr. Jekyll and Mr. Hyde because of the extreme changes in behavior typical of this character type. Unfortunately, since addiction is common, almost everyone has known someone affected by its heartless reaches.

Recognizing and managing addiction is a field of study unto itself, and I am no expert. As one learns early on in psychiatry, substance intoxications can mimic almost any psychiatric disorder, so there are myriad manifestations. A person who appears paranoid may be an addict, a distracted person may be an addict, an angry person having a tantrum may be an addict, and so on. There are characteristics that seem to render a person more prone to addiction, as we will see, but there is no single addiction-associated way that Mr. (or Ms.) Hyde appears. In fact, in psychiatry it's generally impossible to make a diagnosis of mental illness without first determining that it is not, in fact, the result of substance use.

For these reasons, I address addiction in general terms and simply attempt to help you determine when it may be a factor, or the factor, causing difficulty. I offer some strategies for intervention and referral but encourage you to undertake a more in-depth review of this vast topic if you are contending with it.

To begin with some background information: the history of using mind-altering substances varies with time and place and has been associated with everything from enlightenment to disease, debauchery to religion, pleasure to pain, and habit to choice. Archaeologists have found that humans were drinking wine during Neolithic times (Berkowitz 1996) and that prehistoric Grecians were using opium as early as the fifteenth century BC (Askitopoulou, Ramoutsaki, et al. 2002). In contemporary times, wine is still important in the Catholic Mass, and certain religious groups are allowed to use the hallucinogenic plant ayahuasca. Yet in the United States, we had over a decade of alcohol prohibition and outlawed cocaine, which at one time was recommended by Sigmund Freud.

In the United States, thinking about addiction as harmful began with alcohol in the late eighteenth century. Around this time, Native Americans started forming sobriety circles, and Dr. Benjamin Rush and temperance crusaders called for the creation of sober houses (White 2007). Simultaneously, addiction began to be associated with having weak willpower. Then at the turn of the twentieth century, drug use was perceived to be associated with ethnic and racial minorities and individuals in the lower socioeconomic class (Shaffer, LaPlante, et al. 2012). Later, during the 1970s through 1990s, various pieces of legislation, such as the Drug-Free Workplace Act, formalized concern for addiction in the office (Mack, Kahn, et al. 2005). The War on Drugs led to people being arrested and imprisoned for substance use, one factor in the mass incarceration of minority ethnic and racial groups. Now, however, there is a growing trend toward more sympathetic and treatment-oriented approaches to addiction. Also, categories of addiction have expanded—according to some—to include behaviors like eating, having sex, and using the Internet.

HYDE'S BASIC TRAITS

There is no single picture of Hyde. However, there are general characteristics more likely to be found in Dr. Jekyll (that is, Hyde before he starts using drugs or alcohol) than in other people. One is a predisposition toward feeling negative emotions. Someone who is an addict is also less likely to be inhibited when it comes to making choices and acting out, and as such they may take more risks. These people have been characterized as being somewhat antagonistic and tend to feel like they lack purpose (Frone 2013). Some of these personality features might make individuals more likely to use drugs and become attached to them. These individuals are also more likely to seek new experiences and to be somewhat more aggressive (Shaffer, LaPlante, et al. 2012). They also may have difficulties with mastering relationships with other people, feeling good about themselves, and controlling their own emotions. On the other hand, once and after someone becomes Hyde, he may additionally seem to be manipulative, deceitful, selfish, or uncaring because the drive that they have to use the drug is so strong that it barrels over responsibilities and relationships.

No matter the drug considered—alcohol, cigarettes, heroin, cocaine—the essence of addiction is use despite significant problems in one's life. There is craving or compulsion to use the drug when the person just can't get it out of their mind. They lose control over their behavior and spend lots of time seeking and using the drug. Once someone is Hyde, he will continue to use the drug regardless of whatever negative consequences it is having for him or those around him. Addiction ends up affecting the way someone feels, thinks, and acts.

While simply having an occasional drink might not be harmful for some people, true addiction potentially affects life at home and work as well as one's physical health. According to estimates, about 25 million people in the United States have a drug-use disorder, and this number does not even include cigarette smoking (Sadock 2000). This figure means that about 8–10 percent of the population over age twelve has a drug addiction (Kaye, Vadivelu, et al. 2014; Rastegar and Fingerhood 2015). Such diagnoses are more common in men, those of younger age and lower socioeconomic status, Native Americans, and Caucasians (Kaye, Vadivelu, et al. 2014). At the same time, not everyone that uses a substance has the problem of addiction: approximately 10 percent of drinkers, 15 percent of cannabis users, 25 percent of cocaine users, and 50 percent of heroin users have an addiction that negatively affects their life (Sadock 2000). Mr. Hyde does not just use, he lacks control so that responsibilities are forgotten and dangerous consequences are encountered. This pattern of consumption is often associated with significant shame and guilt because of the disruption it causes in Hyde's own life and the lives around him.

The inner world of Hyde often contrasts sharply with a seemingly unsympathetic exterior. He may feel worthless because of his behavior and completely hopeless about his situation. Even as Hyde goes to extreme lengths to get intoxicated, he may try to resist but feel helpless to the allure. Hydes may want the love and support of the very same people they seem to be pushing away. At the same time, they often tell themselves, "I can stop. I'm in control. Just one more time."

Depending on what drug Mr. Hyde is using and how often, his issues can appear in a multitude of ways in the office. What is consistent among these presentations, however, is a change in behavior from the way the person used to act at work. He will now start failing to meet obligations; he will be late or miss a day, two, or more with poor and unverifiable excuses. His performance is likely to become erratic, and those around him might notice he is getting into arguments or having accidents. Other new behaviors might include borrowing money and complaining about physical symptoms like nausea and headaches. The overall picture might be one of changes in the person's energy and mood, as well (Carruth, Wright, et al. 2014). The person might also look different and have changes in their pupil size, poorer hygiene, and a more disheveled appearance; you might also see them sweating, yawning, or breathing differently. The coworker, boss, or employee finds herself thinking, Who is this? or What is going on here? This change is the transformation into Hyde: one of the most common reasons for declining work performance over time.

The above description is the primary point of this chapter. It is the *change* in behavior that is key. It is likely, at least initially, to be intermittent with return to the usual, baseline behavior between episodes. Many are described as "Jekyll and Hyde" because the behavioral changes are so palpable. As addiction takes hold, the problems worsen and become more frequent until the person may truly seem to be someone else.

Myles: Part One

Myles was an architect who was found in his office one morning, asleep on the floor in a puddle of vomit wearing his clothes from the day before. There he was, with an empty bottle of whiskey lying across smeared construction plans. This grotesque discovery was only the final straw, however, in Myles's disruptive behavior at work, which had gone from commendable to appalling in just a couple of years.

One morning, his boss noted a strong smell of alcohol on his breath. He called Myles aside to ask about it. His boss framed the conversation well. He was nonaccusatory, and simply told Myles that, while he seemed fine, the odor was significant and might raise questions among his peers, particularly the trainees on the job. Myles expressed profound embarrassment and admitted that he'd been out with college buddies from out of town the evening before. He said he was appalled that so many hours later it was still perceptible. Myles thanked his boss for the heads up and assured him this wouldn't happen again.

But it did happen again, a few months later, and again Myles expressed horror at the recognition. At this point, his boss gently warned him that he was concerned a pattern might be forming and that, were Myles to come to work smelling of alcohol once more, or appearing intoxicated, he would need to take action.

Myles started making more mistakes in his work and being less productive than normal. He began to have problems with keeping appointments and meeting deadlines. Once, at a meeting, Myles addressed the group, and it was hard not to notice his deeply flushed cheeks and the marked tremor in his hands as he spoke. Myles became irritable and angry when at work. He would not admit that there was anything unusual about his behavior, and he started cutting ties with coworkers he had been close with when they attempted to engage him. He began to look more and more unkempt—sometimes as if he hadn't showered in days. Soon, Myles was missing from work for hours at a time, and eventually he just started missing days altogether. It was at this point that I got a call from his boss, asking what to do about the situation. He wasn't sure exactly what was going on, but he said that people speculated that Miles might have a drinking problem. I met with his boss to discuss strategies for how to intervene when Myles came back to work.

HOW DID MR. HYDE GET THIS WAY?

Biology, family upbringing, gender expectations, personality features, and other factors, including specific considerations of different drugs, make some people more susceptible to developing addiction than others. People who grow up in a household with substance-using family members are more likely to develop their own habits, both by being exposed to it and for genetic reasons. In fact, inherited reasons for drug-use problems are said to contribute about 50 percent of the reasons why people become Hydes, while experiences in life provide the other 50 percent (Frone 2013). In homes with a parental Hyde, there might also be neglect, abuse, or chaos, further increasing an any individual's predisposed genetic chance of becoming Hyde. Children and teens who have difficulty tolerating stress are at increased risk of developing a problem, as well. Of course, the desire or pressure to fit into a peer group can often drive initial use in adolescence. By the time someone is of high school graduation age, 90 percent have drunk alcohol, 80 percent have gotten drunk, and 60 percent have used illicit drugs (Shaffer, LaPlante, et al. 2012), but those numbers do not reflect any necessarily problematic patterns of behavior. The age of the most drug and alcohol use is at twenty-one, and the amount people use tends to decline in the population at large after that age. However, for some individuals, use does not fall off, and they develop or continue a substance-use disorder.

At some point, as the addiction took hold, Myles had lost a degree of power over his behavior. With addiction, an initial feeling—to feel good, to escape from pain, even to feel more productive or strong—becomes important to the user. Depending on the drug, he might want to feel calm or energized, normal or blissful, awake or dazed, warm or connected. Mr. Hyde starts using more of the drug to achieve his goal, but usually this endpoint becomes increasingly difficult to reach as the mind and body get used to the drug. This pattern of increasing use is called developing tolerance. There is an underlying denial about the problems that using causes for the person, which allows him to keep taking the substance. He really does not feel there is a problem.

Myles had switched from occasional social drinking to chasing the bottle after his fiancée had ended their engagement. He wanted to drink to forget what had happened, and initially it felt good to do so. On the advice of a bar friend, he started taking pills that made him feel like he was drunk without having to smell like alcohol at work. Myles's increasing addiction to alcohol and prescription pills exactly mirrored his decline in work functioning. He had begun to take more and more drinks and pills, and he spent a large amount of time drunk, high, or recovering from both. Over time, he developed cravings to use more and more and eventually started using at work and even before driving his car.

By the time someone becomes Hyde, their brain has actually changed in significant ways. No matter what type of mind or mood alteration a specific drug is associated with, an addictive drug is associated with gratification. Parts of the brain that regulate pleasure seeking become disrupted by the patterns of seeking more and more and more. Individuals find things less fun or enjoyable over time—both the drug and past pursuits and hobbies—and instead may use in order to feel stable, different, or to just not feel the sickness of withdrawal.

THE DIFFERENT OUTFITS OF HYDE

I am reticent to define particular types of Hydes because I yet again want to reinforce the notion that addictions can look like just about anything. As with other groups discussed in this book, some of the Hyde clan may manifest as hyper or aggressive while others may become more withdrawn. A single Hyde might become activated with one substance and sedated on another, and thus the primary difficulty at work may be erratic behavior. Then there are Hydes who only use on weekends. They might start the week off slowly, recovering from a hangover. Alternatively, they might become more irritable and short-tempered as the days pass and they impatiently wait until they can use once more. Or maybe they do both. There are also Hydes who use every day. They may use so regularly that you only ever see them while intoxicated and, as such, any decline in performance may be imperceptibly slow. Maybe another Hyde uses so frequently that, as tolerance builds and they use more and more, the decline is readily visible.

The point, again, is that it is the *change* in behavior—change over time, change in a day, whatever, however—that must be considered. Once revealed, the degree to which Mr. Hyde accepts his difficulty and is willing to make change determines the course of intervention.

WHEN THE SCHMUCK IN THE OFFICE IS HYDE

Hyde has significant problems in the workplace. Because the defining characteristic of addiction is that it affects one's obligations, one's work can be significantly disrupted. This relationship has huge economic and interpersonal effects on the workplace, as about 60 to 70 percent of persons with addiction are employed full-time (Aldworth 2009; Frone 2013). Some of these individuals primarily use after work, some before, some during breaks, as well as some during and even at work. In a recent year, a national company that runs laboratory testing on urine drug screens reported that approximately 3 percent of samples tested positive for illicit drugs (Frone 2013).

Being intoxicated can interfere with job fulfillment, of course, but so can related things like hangovers, crashes, distracted time spent thinking about or obtaining the drug, and trouble one gets into while intoxicated but not working. Employees who use drugs take twice as much time off and are involved in three times more accidents at work (Roberts and Fallon, Jr., 2001). Annual productivity losses for drugs in the American workplace are estimated to be around 80 billion dollars, and most are related to alcohol consumption (Roberts and Fallon, Jr., 2001). Organizations can suffer from decreased productivity as well as increased turnover of staff leaving or being fired from their jobs. Companies are also liable for on-the-job accidents as well as potential medical and insurance costs related to drug addiction (Schifano 2005). For example, there is a strong correlation between alcohol use and workers' compensation claims (Mack, Kahn, et al. 2005).

Certain professions, such as pilots, musicians, artists, and athletes, may invite use of so-called "performance-enhancing" drugs for desirable effects on working. Some of these individuals might use for perceived help with staying awake, getting stronger, or improving creativity, though use of such substances may also evolve into full-blown addiction. In addition, certain workplace environments may be more likely to have a Hyde as an employee, such as those with more permissiveness or high-stress atmospheres (Mack, Kahn, et al. 2005). The food service and construction industries are noted to have the most Hydes in them (Slavit, Reagin, et al. 2009), as do arts and entertainment, sales, hospitality maintenance, and transportation (Frone 2013). There are also relationships between specific jobs and use of particular, easily available drugs, such as anesthesiologists using pain medications or wait staff using alcohol (Frone 2013).

In the contemporary workplace, with so much work performed on the computer and online, the idea of access and availability to habit-forming substances and behaviors brings up issues about Internet addiction. A recent survey indicated that when individuals are on the Internet at work, they spend 40 percent of their time shopping, e-mailing, watching pornography, or engaging in other activities not related to their job description (Griffiths 2010). Even while it remains unclear whether this is a veritable addiction as occurs with drugs and alcohol, it nonetheless represents problematic, compulsive behavior that may interfere with work efficiency. Of course, this does not apply to jobs that actually require constant Internet browsing—this is about activities that are not related to work at all. In fact, in 2004 it was estimated that non-work-related Internet use was responsible for about $54 billion dollars in lost productivity (Young and Case 2004). Though more organizations have Internet monitoring applications that limit some usage, the omnipresence of smartphones adds another wrinkle to this problem.

There is general consensus that stressful job conditions and roles can increase drug and alcohol use in employees, particularly when work is felt to interfere with home and family life (Frone 2013). In addition, such stresses have been shown to be related to problematic Internet use in employees at work (Chen, Gau, et al. 2014). Various employment characteristics, such as jobs being demanding, underpaid, and not challenging are correlated with worker substance use, as is exposure to harassment or violence in the workplace (Frone 2013).

Interestingly, however, having a job is one of the best predictors of someone's being able to stop their Mr. Hyde behaviors (Kaye, Vadivelu, et al. 2014), and addiction interventions implemented at work are among the most successful. Even very short one-on-one counseling sessions delivered to employees who have Hyde-like tendencies can reduce their amount of drinking, for example, and potentially save organizational costs (Watson, Godfrey, et al. 2015). Also more elaborate and specific at-work treatments for heavy users have been investigated. Recent research has even shown that using Internet-based workplaces that train individuals in computer skills and pay them when urine drug testing is negative can be effective in treating chronic addiction. At the same time, it helps with unemployment (Silverman, Wong, et al. 2005). In addition, the workplace can be a good space in which to help with recovery from addictions that may not directly impact the individual's present work abilities, such as cigarette smoking; here, help in the form of counseling or reduced health insurance for quitting can help with behavioral change (Cahill and Lancaster 2013).

HOW TO DEAL WITH HYDE

If you suspect that someone is Hyde and want to help him, the best approach is to be direct yet caring as you begin to address the problem. You can straightforwardly state your suspicions and reasoning for them. The most effective time for a discussion is immediately following an obvious problematic event that is likely related to substance use, as we saw above with Myles. You are quite likely to get excuses and deflected answers, but that doesn't mean you cannot challenge them in a friendly and understanding way, such as, "How do you explain such and such then, because what I see is X, Y, and Z. I'm willing to hear your point of view or how you think this can be changed." If your questions are asked in a gentle manner, even if Hyde does not agree at the time, he might eventually come back to you for help figuring out his situation. Remember, in addition to denial, there is often significant guilt and shame, so Hyde might be looking for someone who can offer advice without being overcritical or judgmental. Even if the person walks away seemingly upset after a minute or two, your approach may have been helpful. And, yes, no matter how compassionately you try, they will often be downright hostile in response to your questions. Remember that change for Hyde, like everyone else, really depends on the desire to implement it.

If you are able to engage the person in conversation about his use, be clear about the need for change (Rastegar and Fingerhood 2015). With a workplace relationship, the focus of the conversation should be on the job itself instead of the substance, though it is, of course, related. It can be important to point out specific examples of the way that performance has affected Hyde's life. Use compassion when encouraging treatment while still being firm about its necessity. As a supervisor, it can be beneficial to bring along straightforward evidence of slipping work performance, with specific comparison to previous periods of time, if possible. Despite how obviously the drug may have affected—or even destroyed—Mr. Hyde's work, he might not be as aware of this as you are. Convey that Hyde is responsible for making his behavior better but that you are willing to help. For example, you can offer assistance with finding treatment, securing leave for appointments or rehabilitation, or providing general encouragement and support. Have a referral resource in place to follow any conversations; whether it be with employee assistance or a professional outside the organization, don't lose the opportunity for Hyde to immediately engage in the process of change.

Some employers have robust drug-free workplace policies that identify indicators of substance use. They permit "for-cause" drug and alcohol testing when there is reason to believe the employee is using. In such cases, users may be required to participate in some form of rehabilitation as a condition of continued employment and to sign an agreement upon return that allows for monitoring and random testing as well as employment ramifications should there be future use. Such policies must conform to legal requirements and should be prepared with assistance from knowledgeable human resource professionals.

Be prepared to deal with your own anger as you confront possible distortion, lying, and deception from Hyde. Remember that he is so good at misleading that he often has tricked herself into thinking he does not have a problem; you're fair game as well.

Hyde is driven by an extremely strong urge to continue or return to using, and thus his deception is not an active choice. You may need to be firm with limits and consequences and write down conversations and stated understandings. Hydes often need strict agreements in place—both about not using and about logistical factors such as attendance, tardiness, and leaving early, even beyond what the standard employee may agree to. "For-cause" (as opposed to random) drug and alcohol testing can be used to confirm suspicions of drug or alcohol use, limit the lying and manipulation, and further compel treatment.

If you are the employer, you may be able to directly leverage the job into getting Hyde to seek help. The person must understand that he is at serious and potentially immediate jeopardy of losing his job. Of note: a Hyde who is compelled into treatment by an employer is more likely to recover from his problems than someone without such a reason to get help (Weisner, Lu, et al. 2015). Many people who seek out mental health treatment—in fact, nearly 50 percent of such patients—often have problems with addiction (Stern, Rosenbaum, et al. 2008). However, a number of them are seeking help with feeling down or worried and not directly with being a Hyde. Because of the denial about negative consequences inherent to addiction, it can be difficult to get Mr. Hyde to change the pattern of using substances. However, there are a number of effective therapies, and a good time to use them is when addiction is first uncovered at work, using the desire to keep the job to force quitting (Miller and Flaherty 2000).

There are various types and levels of treatment available depending on individual needs, including medications, twelve-step and other self- or mutual-help programs (like Alcoholics Anonymous), after-work programs (specifically designed for employed substance users), individual or group therapy, and inpatient rehabilitation stays. Some have even found help from relaxation strategies, acupuncture, and hypnosis. It is important to know that not all drugs can be stopped immediately without medical assistance, since people can have seizures or die from withdrawals associated with drugs like alcohol and certain pills like Xanax. In addition, unlike some of the other workplace problems, individuals can significantly benefit from prescribed medications, such as methadone or suboxone, to help keep them away from their drug of choice and able to work and fulfill obligations. Indeed, some people may benefit from being on such medications indefinitely, and appropriate use with physician oversight should be supported in employees.

Many people slip up or completely relapse while they are attempting to stop or cut back on their using. During these periods, people often want to avoid negative emotions and feel excessive social pressures, and relapses are known to occur around holidays, vacations, and trips or following painful losses such as death, divorce, or unemployment (Rastegar and Fingerhood 2015). Another common time for someone to relapse is after incentives for not using drugs or alcohol end, such as the end of close monitoring at work (Silverman, DeFulio, et al. 2012). Even a brief return to using can cause Hydes to quickly slip back into old patterns as they deny the problem or feel hopeless when they realize what they're doing.

A final note on prevention is also important. Having explicit "no drug or alcohol" possession, use, or intoxication policies may be useful and should be drafted with regard to specifics of the workplace environment and local laws and regulations, as mentioned above. On the other hand, drug testing has not necessarily been shown to reduce use or improve productivity in employees

(Frone 2013; Pidd and Roche 2014). Perhaps more important and accepting are interventions to reduce stress in the office through education, support, and programming focused on employee assistance, workplace health, and harassment and violence.

Myles: Part Two

The day Myles was found passed out in his vomit at work, his boss asked him to go home to sleep and to come back the next morning to talk about what happened. He ordered him a cab and told him that they would figure things out when they met. The next day, Myles acknowledged that he'd lost control. His boss remained understanding and gentle, and Myles divulged that he'd been waiting for this day for months, the day that his boss would fire him. But that's not what his boss was doing at all—his boss just wanted him to go get help. Myles admitted to his excessive alcohol usage and that he was ready for help. Thankfully, his workplace was ready to help him.

Myles had avoided seeking treatment for some time. He had no intention of stopping on his own but when his boss expressed how much his work was being affected, he considered change. I advised his boss to bring in a list of unfinished projects over the last couple of years to show the decline in Myles's performance. His boss sought to avoid implicating anyone directly but knew that Myles's colleagues were complaining about the way he looked, acted, and sometimes even smelled at work. Sitting down, as per my recommendations, Myles and his boss went through the hard data as well as some of the personal—albeit anonymous—reactions to his change in the office. His boss explicitly referred to the warning that Myles had been given: that he could never again come to work affected by alcohol. It worked. Myles was willing to hear the information, admit that he had lost control, and seek treatment.

So he made it quite easy for the company. All that his boss had to do was approve his time for medical leave and off he went. He confirmed his insurance coverage and addressed the other financial implications of taking this much-needed time to invest in his health and recovery.

A few months later, he was back at work; though he struggled, he slowly made progress. He voluntarily engaged in a monitoring program, and this helped keep him on track. He had a few setbacks over the first year or two but had the support in place to get himself back on course quickly. It's been several years now, and Myles is doing great.

A Checklist of Ways to Effectively Deal with Hyde

- Confront assertively but empathically, ideally closely following trouble at work.
- Be prepared to provide direct examples of increasing problematic behavior over time.
- Although the individual is responsible for behavioral change, reinforce that you are there to help.
- Document conversations and agreed-on plans to avoid future distortions.
- Be firm with limits and consequences, potentially using the employee's job as leverage to encourage them to enter treatment in concert with HR and/or legal.
- Be familiar with different treatment plans (twelve-step programs, individual or group counseling, medication assistance, inpatient rehabilitation, alternative therapies) and have resources and referrals available.

- Recognize that recovery can be punctuated by setbacks and that they should not always be viewed as "failure."
- Steps toward prevention may be helpful, such as implementing alcohol- and drug-free policies, employee assistance programs, and stress-reduction initiatives.

The Lost

America is aging in unprecedented ways. While the population of the United States slowly grows, the population of elderly Americans is increasing at a much greater rate. The average life span went from around fifty years of age in 1900 to more than seventy years of age for men and eighty years of age for women by the year 2000 (Berkman and D'Ambruoso 2006). Between the years 2000 and 2030, the number of individuals aged sixty-five or older is set to have doubled and will have grown from approximately 12 percent to 19 percent of the overall populace. With growth at such a dramatic rate, dementia and cognitive slippage have become prevalent issues. The definition of *dementia* is an impairment in cognitive functioning that becomes chronic and progresses over time. By 2050, it is expected that there will be upward of 80 million people with dementia (Sadock 2000). Many of these individuals may still be employed for at least part of their illness.

THE LOST'S BASIC TRAITS

As early as 2000 BC the Egyptians had figured out that age was a risk factor for developing dementia, as did later Greek and Roman thinkers. Cicero correctly concluded that not all elderly persons acquired dementia (Boller and Forbes 1998). Over time, dementia has variably been called *dotage*, *lethargy*, *organic brain syndrome*, and *senility* (Boller and Forbes 1998). The term *dementia* itself is derived from the Latin—*de mens*—meaning "out of mind" (Berkman and D'Ambruoso 2006). With a poetic turn of hand, a French psychiatrist of the early nineteenth century described the disorder using phrases such as "a demented man has lost the goods he used to enjoy; he is a wealthy person turned poor" (Boller and Forbes 1998). In 1907, Alois Alzheimer noted his first case of the form of dementia named after him (Stern, Rosenbaum, et al. 2008).

The primary problem in any dementia is broad difficulty with using one's previous intelligence. It may begin to show itself as trouble understanding, remembering, paying attention, or thinking (Sadock 2000). To be considered true dementia, a person is required to have deficits in memory that worsen over time and lead to increasing difficulty in various aspects of life. All of this change can be extremely frustrating and frightening for an individual as he or she notices the problems.

Another group of people have a simpler set of memory difficulties—more like a cognitive slippage. These people have greater problems with memory than is typical for normal aging but less than occur with full-blown dementia. Individuals with cognitive slippage will notice some difficulties but will not experience major life problems. However, half of people with this mild cognitive impairment will end up having some form of dementia within five years, and there are no treatments to prevent the worsening of symptoms (Robertson, Kirkpatrick, et al. 2015). There is some debate over how different dementia and cognitive slippage truly are from the normal processes of getting older (Huppert, Brayne, et al. 1994; Merskey 1995). For the Lost, just as for other character types in this book, there is a spectrum of associated behavior, but what is most important to understand is how to address the problems at work.

There are many different dementias, which vary with regard to how quickly they worsen and the specific symptoms. All types of dementia, however, cause a decline in functioning related to thinking. In addition to difficulty remembering skills and facts, those with dementia can also have significant changes in the way they act. An individual's skills, judgment, language, mood, personality, and motivation can all be affected. Dementia eventually progresses to death as the brain deteriorates in such extreme ways that it is no longer able to support basic life functions like swallowing and breathing. It is important to know that although age is a risk factor, dementia does not appear exclusively in the elderly. Younger-onset dementias affect approximately 640,000 Americans under age sixty-five at present, making up about 2 to 10 percent of all dementia diagnoses (Alzheimer's Association; Robertson and Evans 2015).

Marjorie: Part One

Marjorie was a bank teller who came to me after she learned that a number of customers had complained about her work performance. She had been employed there for some time and had never encountered any difficulties before. In fact, she was well liked and was a feature of the office, the go-to person for just about everything. She was especially appreciated for the home-baked cookies and other tasty treats she would bring in on Monday mornings. Now, people were complaining that she, among other things, was trying to cheat them out of money on withdrawals, making change, and other transactions.

The differences in her behavior had been slow to accumulate so that no one could exactly put their finger on what had changed. But people she had worked with for years knew she was making mistakes that were not typical for her. She missed a couple of days of work, reporting that she thought the weekdays were Sundays, days when the branch was closed. She began to sometimes have difficulty coming up with words in conversations. "Silly me!" she would say and brush off simple mistakes with a shrug of the shoulders. She forgot certain procedures at work, like how to instruct customers to make deposits, and had to ask other tellers for help. They felt uncomfortable showing her how to do things that she should have been able to do and awkward about pointing out the difficulties she was having. "She's just getting old," they would think, "or is having a bad day."

All of this bothered Marjorie, and she found herself wondering—"How can this be? I used to know how to do this!" At first she hid the mistakes from everyone, including her husband, unless she absolutely needed help. She was embarrassed and worried about what the pattern might mean. By the time she came to see me, however, she knew that something was wrong and had been aware of it for quite some time. In fact, she noted that she had been feeling increasingly depressed and stressed lately because of how much trouble she was having.

At this stage, I was able to characterize Marjorie's change in behavior as related to a progressing cognitive slippage, to see her as one of the Lost. There was evidence that her learning and memory had steadily become more impaired over time and that she was having trouble doing things that she would have previously been able to complete with ease.

HOW DID THE LOST GET THIS WAY?

Dementia may be caused by a very wide variety of factors, and among the most common dementias are two called Alzheimer's disease and vascular dementia. Each type of cognitive decline has its own risk factors. For example, risk factors for Alzheimer's disease, which accounts for between 60 and 80 percent of dementias, include being born female, having family members with the disease, and having experienced head trauma (Stern, Rosenbaum, et al. 2008). Some people with Alzheimer's—especially young individuals—have inherited a specific gene called *ApoE4*. When the brains of people who died of Alzheimer's disease are examined under a microscope, pathologists can see specific markings inside of the brain cells. These are called *plaques* and *tangles*, and they contribute to DNA damage and problems with communication among various parts of the brain, which in turn contribute to the dementia. On the other hand, vascular dementia, or dementia that develops after strokes or ministrokes when parts of the brain don't get enough blood, is associated with high blood pressure and heart disease. Having diabetes is associated with an increased risk of having Alzheimer's disease as well as vascular and other dementias (Robertson, Kirkpatrick, et al. 2015).

TYPES OF DEMENTIA

Among the various dementias, there are some unique features. Fronto-temporal dementia may be associated with new hypersexual behaviors, while Lewy Body dementia has a high frequency of very detailed visual hallucinations. People with Parkinson's disease will move slower and with a tremor, while someone with progressive supranuclear palsy will fall frequently and have difficulty moving his eyes upward. What is important is not to remember all of the specific differences between how people may become one of the Lost but to recognize how many different types and associated features there really are. In one of the rarest—Creutzfeldt-Jakob disease—people may die very quickly; this type may be inherited or, believe it or not, acquired through cannibalism. Yes, cannibalism.

The behavior of the Lost can take many forms. If the person has dementia, that behavior will depend on which dementia they have. However the way in which the individual disrupts the office is often related to how the person reacts to noticing or being corrected after a given mistake. Just as with many other characters I've discussed in this book, there are different subtypes, one more active and the other more withdrawn.

The Full-of-Excuses Lost

The Full-of-Excuses Lost struggles with mistakes by fighting back and creating stories to cover noted deficits. A scientist caught in a mathematical error may bark angrily at her research assistant and insist that something he did distracted her and caused her to get sloppy. A salesperson who doesn't recognize a client might create a fantastic story about where they met, then announce that—oh gosh!—she was mixing the client up with someone completely different. In so doing, she buys herself more time to try to remember who the client really is. Such coping strategies can progress to what's termed *confabulation*, the fabrication of imaginary stories and experiences to compensate for memory loss. She will come off as intermittently angry, confused, aggressive, and nonsensical compared with how she might have seemed in the past. She may angrily argue back when others point out her mistakes and is quick to try to turn the tables. Instead of having specific critiques of another's errors, however, she might just bring up something from the past, insult someone in broad strokes, or question the person's authority to evaluate her work.

There was a very famous and very brilliant researcher at the company of one of my friends from business school. She was the "big name" attached to the company and its work and was a revered fixture there. My friend was up for promotion, and the company's process was to sit before senior management for a group interview. My friend knew, or knew of, everyone at the table, but it was still a rather nerve-wracking experience. All was going well until my friend's work in a more controversial area of the field came up. The work he did was standard and accepted, but the mode was still considered unusual by some of the older executives. The famous researcher began to dress him down, attack his character, even scream at him in an escalating monologue that was nothing short of shocking. My friend didn't say a word, and no one intervened. And, after the diatribe, there was deafening silence that seemed to go on for hours, until another executive thanked my friend for the interview and sent him on his way.

It was a very curious explosion. It came seemingly out of the blue, and when it was over, the researcher looked around at her peers, who acted as though nothing had happened. All that was ever conveyed to my friend was a side comment the next day from a member of the senior team, who said, "She's just not who she used to be."

It seems that she had been raging at people for the past several years, more and more frequently, attempting to blame others for her mistakes, which hadn't happened earlier in her career. People thought that perhaps she was unduly stressed, that maybe there were problems at home. The researcher's behavior worsened so significantly that by year's end she could not manage a single project, even with supervision. Explosions were frequent, and she was even moved to aggression at times, throwing objects at other scientists. She retired soon thereafter. About three years later, my friend saw the researcher in a restaurant with his grandson. She was "reading" the menu upside down, mumbling to herself, and was spoon-fed her entire meal.

Lost Under the Radar

On the other hand, the more withdrawn Lost Under the Radar still has changes in memory, but they lead the afflicted person to feel quietly embarrassed. The Lost Under the Radar individual may start by gently apologizing for mistakes and at first seek help for small tasks. But soon she may begin to spend more and more time alone in her office checking and double-checking her work in an effort to cover up what is starting to happen. She is ashamed about her difficulties and is often struggling to figure out what is going on. She will brush aside critiques, shrug her shoulders, mumble excuses. She may seem to disappear as she moves from hiding her mistakes to hiding herself.

A beloved teacher at a well-known boarding school was one of the most charismatic educators in his field. His method to engage students was compelling and fun, and his class was considered the highlight of senior year. There was always a waiting list to get in, and he won at least one teaching award almost every year. As the years passed, he continued to enjoy a fine career at the school and lived on campus among his students, and all were happy with the arrangement.

He stayed well past retirement age but was such a fixture at the school that no one wanted him to leave. He taught less often but still lived among the students as a dormitory advisor. Eventually, in his nineties, he only "taught" one class, and, in fact, all he did was play a video of himself teaching the class as a younger man. Students still attended because he was a very, very relaxed grader. He spent the entirety of each day alone in his office, door closed, but insisted to all who asked that he was "working."

But when it came to the school administration's attention that his ability to care for himself personally was decreasing and that he was asking the students in his dorm to help, trouble started. He had students shopping for him, cooking for him, and even handling his finances. The students felt responsible for his welfare and too torn to say anything to anyone. By the time the school addressed the situation, he was truly unable to manage his daily life. He was transferred to a local nursing home, where students continued to check in on him with regularity.

WHEN THE LOST IS AT WORK

When employed, the Lost's difficulties are often first noted at work. They might be having new memory problems and forget facts or how to complete once-familiar tasks. Or there may be a more specific problem at first like difficulty with math. Some might first show trouble with planning or organization. They might start misplacing things and, of course, may end up getting actually lost.

As this all begins to happen, the individual may notice their own difficulties before those around them have any sense that something is changing, sometimes by years (Öhman, Nygård, et al. 2001). Some of the Lost may try to develop strategies to make up for their difficulties or to retain a sense of control, and some such strategies may indeed be successful for a while (Nygård 2004). Cognitive slippage is most likely to be noticed when persons are employed in settings that require mentally complex activities because it is harder to hide the mistakes. However, there has also been research that associates having a job in the blue-collar, technical, service, and skill trades with having higher rates of dementia, even when considering educational background (Bonaiuto, Rocca, et al. 1995). So if you're at an intellectually tough job, the difficulties might be noticed early because the tasks are so difficult, but someone in a less complex job might actually have a higher overall risk of becoming one of the Lost. It is thought that educational and professional success may decrease the risk of certain dementias by either allowing individuals to better figure out how to hide problems or by having a greater reserve of cognitive skills to begin with before any decline begins (Bonaiuto, Rocca, et al. 1995). Some even hypothesize that work itself, when it is mentally stimulating, may help to prevent becoming one of the Lost, perhaps by exercising the brain over time; this may be particularly true in jobs that are challenging but in which the worker nonetheless feels she has some control over circumstances and outcomes (Seidler, Nienhaus, et al. 2004; Robertson, Kirkpatrick, et al. 2015). In fact, eating healthily and getting adequate physical exercise over the course of one's life can also decrease chances of becoming one of the Lost (Robertson, Kirkpatrick, et al. 2015). Similarly, having friends, participating in hobbies, and living with someone all also lower one's chance of dementia (Seidler, Nienhaus, et al. 2004). On the other hand, exposure to environmental toxins that may exist at certain jobs could also effect development of cognitive slippage, though this relation has never been proven (Seidler, Nienhaus, et al. 2004).

Some of the Lost, particularly those who are younger, may continue to work after diagnosis of dementia and most certainly after any initial difficulties begin to develop. One survey showed that 18 percent of individuals between the ages of forty-one and sixty-five in the United States continue to work after a diagnosis of Alzheimer's disease as well as 10 percent of persons with the diagnosis between sixty-five and sixty-nine years of age (Alzheimer's Society, UK. 2016). When retirement age for the country is raised, this will also increase the number of the Lost in the workplace. And not only are more people getting diagnosed with dementia, but they are living longer—sometimes a decade or two—after the first symptoms develop.

When cognitive difficulties are uncovered, individuals are often encouraged to retire or are otherwise moved out of the workplace. But it is in fact possible to assign the Lost to work in a new role with different expectations (Cox and Pardasani 2013). And many of the Lost may want to work. In fact, some individuals are actually able to learn new skills allowing them to adequately fulfill job requirements even after a diagnosis of actual dementia (Robertson and Evans 2015). Appropriate workplace experience has been positively associated with self-esteem and life satisfaction in persons with dementia, since employment status affects personal and social identity; younger people with dementia identify employment as contributing to their sense of happiness, engagement, and purpose (Cox and Pardasani 2013; Robertson and Evans 2015).

HOW TO HELP THE LOST

In speaking with the Lost, the approach depends on how much trouble the person is having and how aware they are of their difficulties. A supportive conversation pointing out some of their struggles may truly help the Lost. She may not be aware of how she is changing and may need someone to hold a mirror up to how her skills have changed over time. As conversations deepen and open, the person may need to discuss not only the job role and expectations but also figure out finances, retirement, benefits, and other logistics before such planning becomes more difficult or even impossible.

A person's abilities should match their job obligations, and how potential errors might affect workplace safety should be considered. The Lost person will also need a protected environment—for example, a safe method of transportation to and from work. Often, memory prompts such as to-do lists, Post-its, and calendars can be helpful, and various technological aids are available if the person has the ability to use them. Sometimes the work space itself can be modified to allow for easier completion of tasks in a safer manner, such as moving away from hazardous items or areas. Routine, structure, and simple instruction may go a long way; for example, having the same task list each day or scheduling meetings at a regular time.

Communication should be simple and clear—and spoken loudly enough (without distracting background noise) that if the person also has hearing impairment, they have a fair shot at making out what is being said. Depending on family resources and wishes, social workers or occupational therapists can often help assist with a thorough evaluation of what someone is able to do and what accommodations may need to be made to help them achieve this. Of course, functioning will likely worsen over time.

When the Lost is no longer able to work, the individual should be supported in this decision and transitioning to life after employment. This evolution can be a particularly stressful and difficult time for the Lost and their families, particularly with regard to finances. Engagement in modified volunteer roles or day programs can help sustain some of the benefits that the individual derived from work, like structure, social interaction, and goal attainment. Sometimes volunteering at a place of previous employment can be comforting. A supervisor might initiate a conversation, perhaps including someone from HR, to discuss options. Consider whether you would be able to transfer her to any other positions. Ask the individual if she has an expectation for the time that she would like to stop working. Also ask if the individual's physician needs any information about the job's description and abilities if a disability claim is being pursued. Putting forth a supportive and encouraging space to have these conversations is extremely important, as is acknowledging the opportunity to continue the conversation in the future.

Initiating the retirement or role-change discussion can be extremely difficult and met with tremendous resistance. Some people are so wrapped up in their work identity that the idea of leaving seems incomprehensible. This can be true for most anyone but is particularly tricky when dealing with the Lost because her resistance to considering change can eventually prove dangerous depending on the manner of work involved. I have seen many a senior executive whose limitations in work function have become apparent but whose gravitas and glorious past history make interventions very difficult. Many were so high functioning as younger people that, when tested, they may still score well above the average functional range. But the score still represents tremendously decreased function *for them*. It thus becomes difficult to convince them that they are functioning less well when they are still seemingly doing better than others.

When concern begins to develop that the Lost is no longer safe to perform certain functions, and she is resistant to make changes or accommodations, a medical evaluation may be required to determine fitness for duty. Such referrals would certainly involve human resources and/or the legal department. When addressing the possibility that someone in the workplace may be the Lost, it is important that he or she sees a physician so that simple tests can exclude possibly treatable causes, such as low vitamin B_{12} levels or hypothyroidism. Certain medications may be slowing someone down so they look like one of the Lost when, in fact, symptoms disappear when the prescriptions are adjusted. Sometimes the doctor will order scans of the brain to see if there are other causes of the difficulties—like a tumor or fluid collecting around the brain. But many other causes of cognitive slippage are currently not reversible, even though some available medications may help slow the progression of decline. Of the dementias, Alzheimer's disease is by far the most common, representing more than half of all cases, and it is not able to be cured. The medications prescribed to someone with dementia may help slow worsening of the disease but are not known to be very effective and do not work in many people.

Friends and family members who care for the Lost during their declines may also have difficulty in the workplace. Though this will not be explored in this chapter, it is worth mentioning that taking care of the Lost can be a very time-consuming, labor-intensive, and emotionally draining job that can undoubtedly affect someone's job performance and mental health overall. Often, the person will have extensive responsibility for the Lost on top of their day job—and the emotional impact of seeing their loved one's health decline in such profound ways. It is important as an employer or colleague to be aware of this stressful caregiver role and its many effects.

Marjorie: Part Two

Things at work started to get worse for Marjorie. She was initially able to hide most of her mistakes—she'd correct any errors with upset customers and would generally ask the younger tellers to help her out with things she couldn't do. But soon those who'd known her longer began to see problems as well. Their first reaction was frequently anger. They'd come to rely on Marjorie and not need to check her work, so when she made a mistake, it put them in an awkward spot. "What's going on with her," they began to ask one another. Some hypothesized that she was drinking too much. Others worried that she had cancer or some other illness with treatments that were making her spacy. Eventually, some coworkers came to angrily confront her, but stared back, like a deer in headlights, scared and apologetic.

So Marjorie became a topic of water-cooler speculation, and people started to avoid her out of discomfort. They would happily talk about her, but not to her, and though Marjorie had her own things to worry about, she noticed the change and began to feel marginalized.

A phone call between Marjorie and a colleague about a problem at work eventually turned the tide. Her coworker learned firsthand how lost Marjorie was and how much distress this was causing her. Instead of dismissing her difficulties, the coworker started to listen to just what Marjorie was going through. Working through the problem "together," she noticed Marjorie was unable to hold on to thoughts, to complete simple tasks, to follow multiple steps. How she struggled! She'd whisper to herself, repeating sentences over and over to forget them, have endless pauses as she tried to add numbers, to delete an item, or to remember to save her work on the computer. Listening to the tortured monologue of uncertainty, fear, and vacancy was almost too much for her colleague to bear.

Anger swiftly turned to concern, and as this exchange was shared among the staff, people really started to worry. The team approached leadership stating that they thought Marjorie might need some help, and Marjorie's boss called her in to talk about it. Now that he had more information, he started the conversation by offering to help figure out and assist with whatever was going on.

Fortunately, she was simultaneously discussing the situation in treatment with me. In our discussions, she initially resisted divulging that her mother suffered from fronto-temporal dementia and that for years she had lived in fear that it would afflict her, too. Her denial was so dense that, when symptoms began, she sought any other possible explanation she could fathom. But when she found that she was having trouble controlling her impulses— yelling more at home, feeling totally overwhelmed by her inabilities—she knew where things were headed and sought diagnostic clarity from a neurologist.

In the meeting with her boss, she explained what was going on. They came up with a plan to allow Marjorie to work fewer hours for a period of time, not as a bank teller but in the same branch location. Her task was to be a greeter and to make sure the pamphlets and other materials were stocked up front. Marjorie was asked to discuss this—and its financial impact—with her husband, who was supportive and also agreed to make sure she had transport each day. They also agreed to have regular conversations as performance worsened, and they established a retirement plan for when the time came.

With the plan in place and Marjorie feeling more comfortable about the recognition, acceptance, and support of her condition by coworkers and loved ones, her irritability dampened for some time. She was glad that she was able to contribute something to the company she had been at for so long. After about six months, things began to further deteriorate. She wasn't standing her post, wasn't refilling the pamphlets, and was starting to wander around much more. Marjorie's assigned daily supervisor approached her and asked her to speak with the boss, who called her husband in.

At this time, it was decided that Marjorie would leave the company with the support and kindness she deserved after a fine career there. Her farewell party was better than she could have imagined, with love and appreciation showered upon her for her years of warm collegiality and her many contributions to the work team at the bank. Because of the conversations already in place, her husband had set up a day program for her to enter into with other seniors.

Tragically, within a few years of the initial conversations, she was already in need of total care and was moved to a nursing home. She was unable to recognize her family and lost most of her ability to communicate. She died soon after transfer. Her family was understandably upset by their loss, but they were comforted that they had enacted a plan that they knew Marjorie had agreed to as she began her decline. They also were extremely appreciative for the support of the company and acknowledged their thanks in many conversations with the community.

A Checklist of Ways to Effectively Deal with the Lost

- Have a supportive conversation to help the Lost recognize difficulties they are having and how these difficulties are impacting their life and work performance.
- Safety is a primary concern, and the Lost's job responsibilities and workplace environment should be carefully considered.
- Use memory prompts and technological aids and assign tasks that are structured without much day-to-day variability.
- Use clear and simple language spoken slowly and loudly.
- With input from HR and the legal department, consider referral for medical evaluation.

PART IV

Can't Put a Finger on It?

Cultural Sensitivity

In my last year of business school, I took a job in an emergency room on nights and weekends to help pay my tuition. It was a wonderful, active, friendly environment, staffed by great people with whom I'm still very friendly. Early on, I learned something about the group that I found unusual. Whenever there was an extended period of downtime, literally everyone there would open a Bible and read quietly. It was understood that all chatting would stop and that this would be personal time for everyone. Initially, I didn't understand this at all, and I think I was pretty disruptive to the group. I'd tease them, tell jokes, and generally distract their attention from their serious task at hand. I'd wonder aloud why they had to study right then, when we'd finally finished seeing all the patients in the emergency room and could play! In retrospect, I was incredibly offensive, and I'm lucky that they were so kind to me. I was gently redirected, and redirected, until I stopped. I learned to bring a textbook and do my own brand of studying while they did theirs. And, in fact, it felt good to take those "time outs" and calm down amid the insanity of an active ER. I learned a lot from them, and they appreciated that I became respectful of their practices.

Any time one makes judgments about another individual, and particularly when deciding about how "normal" someone's behavior is, it is important to consider the context of the judgment. In using this book and in deciding what behaviors are disruptive and what to do about them, one should also consider background factors about a given individual and the surrounding context, including the workplace environment itself.

Part IV looks at disruptive individuals who may be difficult to understand because the person may seem odd, weird, or somehow different. When faced with this type of disruption, it is important to recognize that mere differences in opinion, culture, and values are not themselves significant or indicative of a problem. As such, we need to assess our own biases, stereotypes, and prejudices—both conscious ones and those of which we might not be readily aware. It requires us to look, once again, at our own possible contributions to workplace dysfunction.

An individual's background, including ethnicity, religion, spirituality, stage of life, family structure, and customs, is often comprised of differences to be appreciated rather than labeled *disruptive* or in any way *abnormal*. Certain cultures may be more competitive, more individualistic, more outgoing, or may have more social interaction or physical contact than others. The customs of one culture may vary widely from those of another and must be considered when contemplating a person's behavior. An average American worker, for example, visiting another country such as Spain may be thought strange for not napping during the business day, whereas someone who napped during a workday may be seen as unproductive in the United States, despite short daytime naps being important potential promoters of alertness and health (Dhand and Sohal 2006; Ficca, Axelsson, et al. 2010).

Psychiatrists must take the same care when they consider diagnosing patients professionally. Even as psychiatric diagnoses become more precise and accurate, they nonetheless implicate values and norms in determining what qualifies as mental illness and health (Sisti, Young, et al. 2013). Mental health professionals consider the cultural identity of an individual and potential differences between the cultures of patient and provider when making diagnoses so as not to misdiagnose an individual based on a mere lack of understanding. For example, in Jamaican culture it may be considered normal to communicate with duppies, or ghosts, whereas within other worldviews this may be seen as impossible and indicative of abnormal mental processes such as psychosis (Miller 2005). Thinking about cultural factors may include understanding whether someone identifies with being in a specific ethnic community or faith group and the practices that accompany such an association. Even someone's generation or subculture can be important. Where someone is from, where he has lived, what language(s) she speaks, what religion(s) he practices, as well as a person's sexual orientation, gender identity, race, and relationships with family and friends can all set different standards for the way a person is expected to act (American Psychiatric Association 2013).

In the following section, we will see individuals who struggle in the workplace because of difficulties understanding other people (the Robotic), strange beliefs (the Eccentric), and paranoia (the Suspicious). However, it is important to know that strange beliefs, paranoia, and social differences by themselves may not be disruptive or even abnormal in a specific context. What makes any of these or other character types deviant is a pattern of consistent behavior that leads to impaired functioning in various contexts and is not consistent with any specific cultural worldview.

The Robotic

I was once referred a civil engineer who was working, serendipitously, in a position he never expected to end up in. His wife was a successful researcher, and he had initially been hired as part of her recruitment package. On his own, he wouldn't have made it past the interview because of his poor interpersonal skills. He related in an oddly aloof manner, looking through people as though he was speaking instead to someone behind them. Twenty years later, still in the exact same position, he was lonely, unhappy, frustrated, and absolutely hated by everyone in the workplace. He was dissatisfied with the quality of everyone's work but his own and determined that his company was beneath him: "a circus full of clowns." His colleagues in the lab thought that he was odd and arrogant and thus the actual problem. He'd routinely hurl loud insults at his team members and supervisees about issues that were easily solvable with a bit of understanding and teamwork on his part. He never considered offering either, because he felt he never made mistakes and couldn't tolerate them in others. And, despite feeling incredibly angry, miserable, and underemployed in the job, his narrow-mindedness, rigidity, and commitment to routine were so entrenched that it had not even crossed his mind to make a switch.

The basis of disruptive behavior in the Robotic lies primarily in his or her inflexibility and difficulty communicating with and understanding others. In the workplace, being flexible goes a long way with coworkers, employees, and bosses. The Robotic can be so inflexible in routine, morality, or conversation that others often come to despise him. The environment needs the Robotic to be able to adapt and communicate, and she simply can't.

THE ROBOTIC'S BASIC TRAITS

When referring to the Robotic in the workplace, this book does not refer to people with true autism spectrum disorder as a diagnosis. It is helpful to use that diagnosis as a lens, however, for understanding this rigid coworker type and what can be done to compassionately help the Robotic. Those with autism are often loved and respected and can love and respect others, but understanding more about rigidity in this diagnosis can be useful in assisting coworkers to interact with them, and those with similar traits, more successfully.

Around the beginning of the twentieth century, the Austrian psychiatrist Leo Kanner described eleven patients with "early infantile autism" as having problems in communication alongside special abilities and behavioral problems. He also noticed that they responded to the environment differently from their peers—often appearing especially sensitive to some things while simply not noticing others. The following year, the Austrian pediatrician Hans Asperger described "autistic psychopathy" as impaired speech, social interactions, coordination, and skills (Scott and De Barona 2007). Eventually, autism and the renamed Asperger's syndrome became regarded as separate, though related, conditions of childhood. Asperger's syndrome was generally considered a less severe syndrome that lacked difficulties in language and intelligence. That distinction remained until 2013, when revisions to the *Diagnostic and Statistical Manual of Mental Disorders* again collapsed autism and Asperger's into the newly named autism spectrum disorder (American Psychiatric Association 2013), a change that has sparked considerable controversy. For one, many individuals with Asperger's, and their family members, have argued for having a separate diagnosis because they feel that those with Asperger's differ from individuals with more severe autism. Tied to this change is a debate about how financial and other resources are divvied up among the populations.

The two skill sets affected in those with autism spectrum disorder are impaired social interactions and rigidity. Individuals have a restricted set of interests and routines. The diagnosis does not currently identify impairment in a person's intelligence, but there is a lack of social skills with a particular interest in the inanimate environment: think trains over people. These individuals are often very sensitive to sensory stimuli, including loud sounds, certain sights, or irritating physical sensations. They also have strong allegiance to habits, schedules, and preferences and often choose to do the same things over and over at the same times. Some individuals will also have unique displays of repetitive body motions, such as flapping their hands, rocking back and forth, or walking on their toes.

Of course, problems usually arise because of difficulties interacting with other people. The problems in social settings may be numerous and diverse, such as difficulty listening to others and taking turns in conversations, often dwelling on certain topics of conversation for too long. They may speak with different pitch and rhythm and often make less eye contact. Overall, there is a difficulty perceiving emotions and understanding sarcasm, metaphors, social cues, or other nuances of language (White, Keonig, et al. 2007). At the same time, such individuals may have a desire for social interactions, and they may feel lonely and really want friendships or romance. This combination of desire for social connections alongside a lack of the appropriate skills to navigate them may erupt into frustration and anger. Even as adults, they are known to throw tantrums, largely trying to express their difficulty with understanding the world around them. Irritation of their physical senses can also often cause, or worsen, their anger and frustration. In addition, many of these individuals experience significant anxiety, and sometimes the tantrums are related to feeling overwhelmed by worry.

Brody: Part One

Brody was a new postdoctoral researcher in mechanical engineering who came to see me soon after the academic year began. The undergraduate students he taught began to complain about how he treated them. He was seen as extremely smart, albeit arrogant, but without common sense or social grace. Brody had little ability to see others' perspective and failed to realize how he came off to others. He would point out errors in students' work to the whole class, saying, "So and so did *terrible* work here." When first approached by his supervisor about one such incident, he said—in his somewhat monotonous voice—"Well, that doesn't make sense. He's wrong. And I know the right answer—he just needs to learn it and accept it."

He was overly direct in the worst possible way. His supervisor suggested that he approach a student whom he'd insulted terribly, and he again responded with, "But she was wrong. Why would I apologize just because she can't get the answer right?" He was advised that this rigidity would lead to poor evaluations from students and difficult relationships at work, but he met this information with a blank stare. What did one thing have to do with the other? he thought. Why was being "right" now being labeled "rigid"? He would ponder, alone, the fact that people seemed to overlook his positive attributes—his intelligence, the quality of his work, his vast knowledge of classical music, and his sincere desire to be a friend to someone, a partner to someone. People were focusing on the wrong things, and those things were simply not up for discussion. Fact is fact. How could no one else see this?

During one lab, he said to his students, "If you can't get this assignment right, you will never have a career. This will be the end of your chance at engineering, like it or not." He often explained concepts at a level that was far more advanced than what was being taught in the class, and it left his students feeling anxious and lost. When his students didn't answer his questions, he'd stand in the middle of the classroom yelling. When particularly frustrated with their "stupidity," he'd use vitriolic expletives and even throw papers at them. These behaviors also translated into similar patterns in his interactions with other postdoctoral students and even the more senior researchers. He became overtly disliked, even hated. Yet in the midst of this, he didn't understand why he didn't have friends and often seemed aggressive at his attempts for companionship. "Did you know I got the grant?

I'd love to show you my submission if you'd want to see how I did it because it obviously went over very well."

I understood Brody's behavior as being one of the Robotic types as opposed to just being arrogant or uncouth. When I met him, there were nonverbal difficulties that came across, like poor eye contact, uncoordinated facial expressions, and very little spontaneous movement. In my waiting room, he rose and stood uncomfortably close to me. His voice was loud and monotonous. In our first conversation, I could see that he clearly had difficulty in his ability to engage with other people and was not able to understand relationships. Even his engineering interests were very particular and circumscribed, perhaps not totally unusual for a researcher, but he was unable to speak about other topics (except music, his other great focus). Even during our meeting, he went on and on and on—and became upset when I tried to change the subject or provide any commentary or feedback.

Though he logically recognized that his behaviors were affecting his perceived work performance—indeed, he came to me to discuss them—he seemed entirely unemotional and even uninterested in the topic. He thought that he would simply look for a new university if he had to. There was nothing to change; the issues leading to his referral were fact-based conflicts, and he was right. Brody described himself as "brilliant," boasted about his IQ, and insisted that he had many ideas that would soon be patented. He would start his own company and then he would be the boss, so dealing with people's hurt feelings would not be an issue. Their feelings shouldn't be hurt, anyway! For now, he just needed a forum to complete his postdoctoral work so that he could move on to his larger goals in an arena more suited to his strengths. He didn't particularly care where he went, by the way. He relayed that he, of course, deserved to have gone to MIT, but he would succeed in his field no matter what, because he had studied and mastered the "formula" to do so.

He truly didn't understand why he was so reviled and why it rendered him so alone when he desperately wanted friends and a romantic relationship. Although, conceptually, a grown man asking such vulnerable questions would usually rouse tremendous empathy within me, I found Brody hard to like. There was no reciprocity to our conversation, and the internal conflicts with which he struggled only rose to the fore on occasion. When I'd attempt to follow these themes (they were, of course, the ones that I found interesting!), he would simply talk over me and move on to the more concrete topics. He sat, robotic and unemotional, and talked *at* me for nearly the full assessment. He lectured about his engineering and classical music interests and noted his vast, if not unparalleled, knowledge base. He assumed that his command of facts would be astounding to all and that this would buy him a position of tremendous respect. He was frustrated that it did not. He was so hungry for companionship that I couldn't even discern the gender(s) of his romantic interest—it seemed he just wanted somebody, anybody—and despite his belief that he tried hard and often to attain it, he really did nothing manifestly to do so.

HOW DID THE ROBOTIC GET THIS WAY?

For individuals with an actual diagnosis of autism, awareness of problems in behavior typically begins before two years of age and almost always before age three. Parents often notice that their child does not interact like other children of the same age and sometimes worry that he or she might be deaf. Early on, the child may have difficulties with playing games, imitating others, or otherwise sharing in interactions. There is a vast range of individuals who are diagnosed with autism—thus the term *autism spectrum disorder*—ranging from those who hold steady jobs and relationships to people who are entirely unable to speak verbal language.

The potential causes of autism spectrum disorder have been among the most controversial of the mental health problems in recent decades, particularly as divided camps have sought to causally link or separate immunization as a risk factor for diagnosis. Most scientific evidence does not support this association. However, risk factors do include having an older father, low birth weight, and male gender (at a striking 4 to 1 ratio) (American Psychiatric Association 2013). Autism is generally considered one of the most genetically determined of the psychiatric conditions (Sadock 2000). A linked medical diagnosis, such as fragile X syndrome or tuberous sclerosis, is only found to explain the autism in approximately 5 to 15 percent of cases, though individuals are also known to have higher rates of seizures (Sadock 2000; Stern, Rosenbaum, et al. 2008; Howe, Palumbo, et al. 2016).

There is a sociopolitical movement for respecting neurodiversity, and many individuals with autism (and their advocates) feel that their atypical neurological functioning may be equally valid, if different, from the presumed norm. Another controversial aspect of autism has been the rapidly expanding number of individuals diagnosed over several decades. Some estimates pointing to an increase from 1 in 4,000 to 1 in 68–100 individuals being labeled as on the autism spectrum (Stern, Rosenbaum, et al. 2008; Christensen 2016).

If you asked Brody, he'd say he didn't "get this way." He'd say he started this way, and I'd tend to agree. Brody was incredibly intelligent but always had relational difficulties. As a small child, he developed an interest in trains, and it was all-consuming. He studied trains throughout history and could speak fluently about the evolution of engines, fuel types, train manufacturers, and rail lines. He collected model trains and built many of them himself, spending countless hours on the most minute details. His frustration was explosive if he made any mistakes. He was not an overtly affectionate boy despite having very loving parents. They couldn't really engage him on any other topics and soon learned that, to connect with him, they had to sit quietly and hear him lecture, yet again, about the trains of the world, the trains in his collection, trains, trains, trains. He had no friends, but the few other boys who had some interest in trains (never as great as his) would play with trains near him but never *with* him. Others often bullied him for being "weird." His parents sought counsel from his teachers, who noticed his poor social skills, exceptional academic performance, and lack of behavioral acting out in the classroom, characteristics that unfortunately made them reassure Brody's parents rather than suggest intervention.

As the years passed, Brody's interest in trains didn't particularly wane, but it did evolve. He became more and more specifically interested in how trains ran and how their engines worked. He was consumed with the notion that he could perfect the engine. He believed that his novel ideas could redefine motor efficiency. He wondered at times whether he could be the one to create a perpetual motion machine.

These preoccupations led quite naturally to an interest in engineering and, more specifically, mechanical engineering. Throughout childhood and adolescence, he remained friendless, home every night reading, writing equations, and building models, and seemingly quite content. Kids at school would either ignore him or try to get a rise out of him because they couldn't understand his indifference to the social goings-on. He was seen as a strange and annoying mystery.

By the time I saw Brody, he was living alone, supporting himself with scholarship funds and help from his parents, listening to music a lot, and designing his superengine. Sadly, our sessions were the lion's share of his human interaction outside the classroom.

TYPES OF ROBOTICS

Two types of robots seem to exist in the workplace, and they, once again, represent different sides of the same coin. As we've seen in other character types, one side is more explosive, and the other more internally focused. But rigidity, repetition, anxiety, and frustration are features of both. Indeed, even as I write about the Robotic, I find myself curiously mirroring him, repeating the same information, trying to drive the same points home over and over by writing about the Robotic in only slightly different ways, frustrated that I may not be fully conveying my thoughts. The emotional constriction associated with the Robotic conundrum is palpable and maddening.

The Circuit Overloader

Brody falls squarely into the first of the two types of Robots, the Circuit Overloader. This type is full of opinions and has no ability to filter what should be said when or to whom. He focuses on single topics and is perseverative in his viewpoint. There is no

sensitivity to office culture or politics. His thoughts are conveyed bluntly, dogmatically, aggressively, and repeatedly. Personal opinions are considered *fact*—correct and carved in stone. No other perspective is valid, and he considers other positions to be wrong or dumb. There is only one way to think about things, and that's his way. He thinks that if he asserts his position again and again, people will have to understand.

The Circuit Overloader offends constantly but has no sensitivity around doing so. He has no understanding of how his style of interacting might make others feel. He can be loud, doesn't modulate his tone, and—combined with his poor sense of interpersonal boundaries—can seem menacing and strange. He can't be reasoned with, and this is deeply off-putting. When this lack of understanding progresses to unbridled anger and uncontrolled tantrums (i.e., overloading), it can be downright scary. It's almost impossible to relate the tremendous anxiety the Circuit Overloader is experiencing during these interactions, which is a shame, because doing so might help others find empathy for him. Instead, a hornet's nest of confused and uncomfortable feelings on both sides prevents any chance of a viable, reciprocal exchange.

The Failed Igniter

Whereas the Circuit Overloader has no problem getting in your face and your space, however oddly, the Failed Igniter can't look you in the eye, stands too far away, and often avoids you altogether. Even small talk seems to be too much for him. He appears cold, emotionally restricted, and distant. He is withdrawn and deeply socially avoidant. The Circuit Overloader is prone to

e-mail from behind a closed door rather than have face-to-face interactions. He is less given to tantrums, but they do indeed occur, and when they do, they happen for the same reasons as those of the Circuit Overloader. Anxiety is prominent. The Failed Igniter may even quit a job if he perceives intense feelings from others, such as a boss's being upset with him. He utterly fails to understand what is going on and fears having to deal with this incomprehensible intensity. The Failed Igniter won't attempt to be a part of his coworker group—you won't see him at the office holiday party—and he will always choose the passive, aloof, avoidant response to any perceived emotion. If you make the mistake of hoping for some reaction from him, you're sure to be frustrated, confounded, and disappointed. The Failed Igniter would never respond well to your telling him you're upset, you're not feeling well, you're attracted to him, whatever. He is likely to stare back at you, cold and impassive, and say nothing. Inside, he may be swimming in anxiety about all that he doesn't understand, but you'd never know. Don't even expect an "I'm fine. How are you?" when you ask how he is in the morning. He won't seem to care about you in the slightest. When overwhelmed, he may be prone to suddenly disappearing—either absent for days or resigning completely—rather than face what is going on.

Someone in business school told me about a very successful vice president in a software company. He was absolutely brilliant, and his intelligence was never in question. Before holding the vice president appointment, his interactions tended to go okay, but they were always one-on-one. His approach was to convince whomever he was meeting with to stop talking to him verbally and, instead, walk over to his chalkboard and "talk" to him in words, symbols, charts, and algorithms; in his mind, this caused everything to go just fine. When issues were dissected in this way,

people left his office satisfied, with their questions answered. But when he moved into a leadership role, problems arose.

He studied the leadership literature obsessively and took every relevant seminar he could find. He had a sense of his shortcomings interpersonally and hired an executive coach—then another, and another. He practiced hand movements and took voice lessons to feign spontaneity while speaking. He studied men's fashion magazines and dressed to the nines. He developed, with one of his coaches, a leadership "platform" and presented it, over and over, as his strategic vision. Even as his jobs changed over time, he presented this same basic visionary framework, but he was so unwaveringly committed to it that people miraculously didn't seem to notice that he was a one-trick pony. He was even able to find a partner during this period of coached evolution. Though his partner soon began to complain bitterly about the lack of emotional connection between them, he felt satisfied because he had someone. He rose and rose and rose until he became VP of this enormous global enterprise.

Even brand new in the job, he refused to meet anyone but the closest members of his team, and he refused to take more than one meeting in a day. In that first year, he met lots of senior members of the company but connected with none of them. His right-hand advisor did all of the "emotional work" for him, but eventually he too grew tired of the VP's robotic style and the lack of any connection or feedback. He'd appear for polished public speeches but then disappear as soon as they were done.

As the years passed, conflicts were ignored and sticky issues were referred to his advisor. It appeared that his advisor was making all of the big human capital company decisions. People couldn't get the VP, physically or emotionally, and they began to accuse him of being completely ineffectual. He remained holed up in his office, demanding of others but offering nothing in return and terrified of anything that smelled of confrontation. His senior staff grew to hate him, and as they became more emotional about him he appeared to become even more passive and aloof. They'd joke that a blow-up doll was living in the VP office pretending to run things. Complaints eventually reached the CEO and the ever-increasing groundswell of animosity led to the VP's ejection. The entire organization was exasperated when he left, but the VP just walked out with his strategic leadership platform and his practiced hand motions and went on his way to another big job. This is the story of a Failed Igniter.

WHEN THE SCHMUCK IN THE OFFICE IS THE ROBOTIC

Most of the studies cited here consider individuals with a diagnosis of autism spectrum disorder and not the Robotic character type of the workplace. In the literature, only the most high-functioning persons with autism are likely to be successfully employed independently. In fact, only 25 to 50 percent of people with true autism spectrum disorder are employed in any capacity (Hendricks 2010). Of those who are employed, many need support such as one-to-one supervision. Others may be too impaired to live on their own, and some individuals do not have any verbal language.

The Robotic character type found at work may still have difficulty keeping jobs, leaving them intermittently employed without consistent career development or financial security. They are drawn to the fields of science, technology, engineering, and mathematics (Wei, Wagner, et al. 2012) and are less inclined to work in areas involving customer service. In 2013, a German software company announced its intent to recruit a certain percentage of employees with autism, saying that such individuals may have uniquely beneficial skill sets, including attention to detail and problem-solving abilities (Wolde). As we've seen, the Robotic employee is often perceived as skillful at the tasks of his job but unskilled with other people (Schall 2010), and this can present a variety of problems. Unfortunately, data shows that when they are successfully employed, they often feel bullied, unsupported, excluded, and not understood (Richards 2012) and often find jobs to be boring and unfulfilling (Baldwin, Costley, et al. 2014). These individuals are often characterized by others as having short tempers and being conceited (Richards 2012). The Robotic will have difficulty holding a job because he is often seen as weird and not likable, mainly because of his problems in social communication. They similarly cause difficulty learning new skills from coworkers and managing the difficult interpersonal relationships of the workplace. As employees, the Robotic may either overtly challenge authority or have significant difficulty being assertive. The Robotic will often avoid the social aspects of the workplace, like team-building events, happy hours, or holiday parties; he might eat by himself during lunch breaks, even as others gather in a designated room.

Given the propensity for sticking to strict routines and problems with accepting change, any disruption to the regular flow of work may be very difficult to handle. They will have particular problems with personnel turnover, scheduling changes, new policies, or even something like an unexpected fire drill. The Robotic may have real difficulty with organization and planning. Given sensitivity to various sounds and sights, the Robotic may be particularly prone to distractions. Fluorescent lights, a colleague with a cough, or the hum of a fan can throw him completely off course. He may occasionally manage stress through repetitive movement, such as rocking back and forth or banging on a desk. Tantrums or property destruction may also occur (Hendricks 2010). On the other hand, strengths of the Robotic in the workplace may include dedication, efficiency, unique perspectives, strong visual learning skills, detail-oriented thinking, honesty, and a commitment to logic and rationality (Simone and Grandin 2010; Baldwin, Costley, et al. 2014).

HOW TO DEAL WITH THE ROBOTIC

The general approach to interacting with the Robotic in the workplace is to aim for utter clarity in your own communications. Be explicit. Be upfront. Be concrete. The individual will only be able to listen to the literal meaning of what you are saying and may have difficulty understanding nuances. Do not rely on any subtle implications. A helpful approach is to write down directions or feedback, as the written word relies less on subtlety, interpretation of voice modulation, or body language. The general aim is to make sure both of you (or the group at large) have the same understanding of the message being conveyed. Let nothing be lost in translation. Avoid nuance, metaphor, and sarcasm. Never anticipate that they understand the unwritten rules of a workplace. When verbal information is provided, it is best exchanged in one-to-one, rather than group, interactions and with sufficient time to process the meaning. If there is a meeting, letting the individual submit thoughts or ideas in writing beforehand can be helpful to letting their ideas be heard and understood.

In addition, workplaces may be modified to minimize distractions to which a given individual is sensitive; this might include any repetitive sounds or sights like buzzing, humming, or flickering. Earplugs, music, white noise machines, or tinted glasses can be helpful for the individual, as can placement of a desk in a low-traffic, naturally lit area (Grandin and Duffy 2008). Building a workplace environment in which employees have some access to private space can be helpful—for the Robotic and other individuals. The Robotic employee often has very clear preferences about what would help him function better in the workplace, so it can be elucidating to straightforwardly ask.

In addition to being explicit, it is important to be predictable. The Robotic in the workplace will appreciate concrete plans—often written or otherwise visually displayed. Your efforts should aim to make him feel grounded and structured. Tasks may need to be clearly and concretely defined, and the Robotic may benefit from very consistent schedules and timelines as well as the use of aids for organization (calendars, checklists, etc.) (Hendricks 2010). This straightforward portrayal also applies to the overarching job description, employee expectations, and any hierarchical structure of the workplace. Workplaces with rigid routines or concrete steps to success can be most comfortable for the Robotic. A career built around special interest areas—like Brody and his trains—is most likely to hold attention and motivate good performance. We might find the Robotic type working as a computer programmer who largely works alone, a statistician, an archivist, a librarian with circumscribed human interaction. As a side note, I'm aware of one Robotic who applied rigid formulas to the field of sales, the most counterintuitive career choice I could have imagined for him given its reliance on social skills and interpersonal interactions. He carefully studied sales strategy books and guides to field interactions. He kept a book of prompts as a guide—if a person says X, you say Y. He learned, for example, that if you write things down while people are speaking to you, they feel you are listening to them. He had no emotional or intuitive connection to any of these strategies, but he studied them and was incredibly successful. Go figure.

Remember that the Robotic's style of interacting—whether overloading or failing to ignite—might not feel natural to you. In fact, it might be totally off-putting, frustrating, upsetting, or infuriating. Try to understand that this isn't necessarily about you. He may have a given style, and that's just what it is—a style. It may seem cold or uncaring, but in the end it is a unique way of processing the world that has less focus on interpersonal skills and interactions. When he says he doesn't like your outfit, remember that you probably don't like others' outfits either; it's just that you understand not to make such a comment. At the same time, remember that the Robotic may want connection, and in fact feel excluded, but that they often don't have deep understanding of what relationships involve. You may be able to develop a connection with them, but it will often feel like "going through the motions." One approach, however, to bridge an attachment would be to ask about their particular area of interest, be it bugs, bridges, or electricity; you may find yourself learning something new. Maybe even let them pick the next company event and attend whatever interesting happening they choose, which may feel out of the norm for you or other coworkers.

Some of the most difficult interactions with the Robotic at work can happen when they have tantrums. This disruption often stems from being anxious and overwhelmed by someone trying to communicate a message they don't understand. To help prevent this reaction, present any feedback in a calm and concrete way: "This is the issue, and this is what you can do about it."

If, however, they begin to have a tantrum, they have often passed the point of being able to have a rational conversation. If you are in any position of authority—or can find someone who is—it will be an extremely important time to set limits. He may need to take some quiet time to calm down; this should occur in a place without significant potential for overwhelming sensory distraction (i.e., without flickering lights or noise). Most important, do not try to engage the Robotic on matters of importance during one of these upsets.

The Robotic tends to be rule bound, and thus a strategy to help contain their tantrums is to deliver concrete, written limits (something like, "Rule 7: no screaming at junior staff members"). Of course, these need to be provided when they are calm rather than in the middle of an outburst. Rules tend to work for them. In fact, it is often the breaking of rules by others that can be extremely overwhelming and anxiety-producing for the Robotic. So use the Robotic's interest in rules to your advantage in delineating what is and is not appropriate in the workplace.

Another technique to help minimize tantrums or egregious social errors is to simply point out that they may have hurt someone's feelings. Remember, the Robotic's difficulty comes not from intending to harm anyone but from not understanding interactions. Often, they may not even know that their behavior or language has been hurtful. By pointing it out, you may help tap into their conscience, which can encourage behavioral changes. If you are a manager who observes distress associated with social impairment, you may be able to take the Robotic aside and give straightforward instructional feedback about interacting with others. This approach might include suggestions that they ask coworkers if they need help and say "hello" in the morning or more formal guidance on how to respond to feedback ("Thank you, I will try to work on that"), give feedback ("Good job, but I think you could improve by . . ."), or even take turns in a conversation. Such on-the-job training may use role-play scenarios or modeling of negotiation techniques. As disconnected as they feel, these individuals may greatly appreciate pointers on how to navigate the workplace. There are also a number of workbooks and self-help guides that individuals can use to improve their interpersonal skill sets—some even have a particular focus on the workplace.

Nonetheless, the Robotic will often need formal training in communication and interpersonal skills in order to succeed or even adapt. Such treatment is generally less focused on talking about, experiencing, or processing emotions than is treatment for other character types. Social-skills training can often be very specific— with explicit tips on and making and reading eye contact, modulating facial expression and tone of voice, and implementing changes in body language and mannerisms. Interventions that take broader approaches aim to improve relationships and general social functioning and even to encourage understanding of how others think and feel. Teaching may involve games, role-playing, and team building, sometimes with feedback using videos of sessions (Howlin and Yates 1999). Related instruction may cover stress management, problem solving, and assertiveness. In addition, training often focuses on understanding and operating in specific contexts, such as job interviews or dining experiences.

The focus is usually on skill development—whether social skills or coping skills—in individual treatment or in groups. There is generally no need for medication unless there is an overlying anxiety or depressive disorder.

Brody: Part Two

The good news about Brody was that he really, really wanted a social life, and he knew that his behavior was not helping him attain one. As I have mentioned repeatedly in this book, the person who really wants to change is likely to be able to do it. Brody accepted referrals from me to group therapy based on cognitive behavioral techniques as well as to a social-skills training group. He continued to have no interest whatsoever in changing or improving his work interactions. Those issues were separate, and he was just right, end of story, so he insisted that we just stop talking about them. However, by allowing him to call the shots and focus on his "social life" interactions, he was able to learn strategies that mitigated many of his work conflicts. His rigidity, perseveration, and lack of frustration tolerance were unchanged, but he learned methods for conveying his positions on school matters that seemed to upset people less. The feedback he received from his peers and his therapists in the two groups he joined, and to which he was very committed, helped him feel less confused about peoples' responses to him. Though new approaches never came naturally to him, role-playing and the interpersonal group interactions allowed him to start to figure out what seemed to work when dealing with others. He was able to keep his position and finish his postdoc and, though his final career was quite similar to the one he'd envisioned for himself, he did also form a little social circle and felt decidedly happier in his life.

A Checklist of Ways to Effectively Deal with the Robotic

- Effective communication is clear and concrete; written instructions may be preferred to verbal; one-on-one meetings are preferred over group meetings.
- Minimize distractions in the environment; provide access to private space.
- Rigid, predictable schedules and explicitly defined tasks are ideal.
- Incorporating tasks related to specialized interests may help motivate the Robotic.
- Avoid behavioral outbursts or tantrums by communicating feedback in a calm and concrete manner; during a tantrum, have an authority figure employ limit-setting strategies.
- The Robotic has a propensity for rule following; use this to your advantage in delineating what is appropriate behavior in the workplace.
- Helping the Robotic recognize how their behavior may impact the feelings of others may be beneficial; training sessions that use role-playing scenarios can also be implemented.
- Specialized interventions focusing on skill development may be considered.

The Eccentric

I once knew a doctor who thought every single health problem was related to lead poisoning. She was a functioning physician, treated patients, had a steady income. But, according to her, each and every medical illness led back to lead poisoning—excess lead levels were the cause of everything that could go wrong in a human body. She did more blood work for lead levels and talked about lead more than any other doctor I had ever met. Colleagues thought she was odd, of course, and although her beliefs were unusual, she didn't cause many problems. She would treat other possibilities for illness as well but still couldn't seem to let go of the fact that lead *really* was always the underlying cause.

There was another physician, whose work received no complaints, barely spoke, mostly looked at his shoes, and always seemed to be mumbling something to himself. When engaged, he interacted like anyone else. But his hair was overgrown, and it was clear he'd cut it himself, and, even then, only when it got in his eyes. His clothes were many sizes too big. In fact, his pants were so long that he'd tread all over the cuffs, so that shreds of filthy fabric would trail behind him as he walked. His oversize belt was pulled tight to keep his huge pants up, and this left at least a foot of leather hanging awkwardly in front of him. It was as though he were stranded on an island, naked and without options, and happened upon a much larger man's suitcase full of clothes that he simply had to wear to stay warm and covered. No one ever asked him about it and he functioned well in the hospital.

THE ECCENTRIC'S BASIC TRAITS

How do we understand such individuals? More than a century ago, doctors began thinking about a group of people who, in some ways, were similar to patients with schizophrenia. People with schizophrenia have genuine psychosis—they lose contact with other's vision of reality. This new group of patients was somewhat similar to people with schizophrenia but didn't seem as out of touch with the world around them. In addition, individuals in this group often had family members—mothers, fathers, brothers, sisters, children—with actual schizophrenia. Then came a scientific study in 1975 that looked at a class of people considered to have "borderline schizophrenia." This study led the groundwork for understanding people who eventually became known, in 1980, as having schizotypal personality disorder (Kendler 1985). This personality disorder is still sometimes considered to be related to schizophrenia, though not as directly as originally thought.

The underpinning of this personality is a pattern of difficulty relating to other people because of some particularly unique ways of seeing the world, often tied to magic or the paranormal. Individuals with this personality type may have seemingly strange beliefs, act in odd ways, be difficult to understand, and have experiences that seem quite different from other people. If you see someone like this, they often appear detached, isolated, and aloof. When interacting, the things that they say and believe often seem irrational. You may find yourself thinking, "What, really?! I can't even believe . . ."

Such a pattern always needs to be considered in the context of a given person's religion and culture. This is not just a creative person, someone different, or a nonconformist. We don't judge someone for those characteristics and give them a diagnosis—even if they seem really different from others. Instead, the people in this category have a really hard time living life and are distressed because of the way they experience the world and relate to those around them. Studies show that schizotypal personality disorder affects between 2 and 6 percent of the population (Sadock 2000).

Wayne: Part One

Wayne was a veterinary assistant who came to me when his boss told him that some of his behaviors were making people feel uncomfortable. The veterinarian had approached Wayne after learning about some of his odd interactions with customers. The vet learned that Wayne had been gluing crystals to the collars of many of the animals before sending them home to their families. When approached about the crystals, Wayne initially responded that they were to help the animals heal. He did not stop applying them, even after being asked. With further questioning, Wayne also revealed that he thought the crystals helped him communicate with the pets.

Even before the vet found out about these ideas, he had felt that there was something odd about Wayne. At first, he had suspected that Wayne was just nervous about his new job, but his awkwardness did not let up over time. He ate by himself, even when the office paid for a staff lunch. He rarely laughed or smiled and often did confusing things, like tapping his feet or hands in odd patterns. When others had conversations with him, however limited, he spoke in vague metaphors. "The sun rises as such to the beat, my friend, I must return to work." The vet told Wayne that he was worried about the effect of some of Wayne's behaviors on the business, because other employees and several pet owners complained about them. For the most part the vet liked Wayne. He also wondered if Wayne might have schizophrenia.

Upon meeting Wayne, I agreed that Wayne was incredibly odd, but after spending some time with him, I understood that he was not psychotic but, rather, an Eccentric. He appeared strange and wore stained clothing; as we met, he did not make eye contact and had significant difficulty conversing with me. He seemed uncomfortable. He had a variety of odd, superstitious, and unusual beliefs, though he saw some validity in arguments against them. He did not insist that they were absolutely true for every individual but held that they were the way that he personally saw and experienced the world. He felt unfairly mocked and criticized about his ideas but continued to believe in them.

Wayne revealed during our meeting that he, too, wore crystals to stay healthy and to enhance his abilities. At baseline, he believed he had a special connection with animals. Supplemented by crystals, he felt downright enmeshed with them. The crystals conveyed a certain positive energy that brought out the best in him and in his animal friends. The energy allowed them to feel more hopeful and, he insisted, could help beat any illness. The crystals also connected those who wore them together, into a powerful positive-energy micro-universe. He explained that these connections were invisible to the naked eye, like radio waves, but that they were almost as powerful as the sun. Animals have the power to bring and spread happiness, but animals wearing crystals could triple that power.

The crystals didn't particularly help with human relations, though. He acknowledged that they were a challenge for him and that, for all of his thirty-two years, he was very happy living alone with his mom.

In any case, he was distressed by the complaints and certainly never intended to make anyone uncomfortable. But he struggled with wanting to do what he felt was both best for his animals and himself. He didn't want to stop the important work he was doing to spread positive energy and unbridled hope. It was incredibly interesting to me that he spoke of these bright, expansive themes but was himself diminutive, reserved, and flat. He could hardly connect with me at all. Talk about still water that runs deep. His gray exterior was like a shroud covering the marching bands, rainbows, and fireworks within—a complete disconnect.

HOW DID THE ECCENTRIC GET THAT WAY?

I found out that Wayne had a sister with schizophrenia, which is not uncommon for the Eccentric, indicating a possible genetic component to the pattern of behavior. However, there is not much actually known about the roots of true schizotypal personality disorder. There is some speculation that these individuals have an underlying difficulty with understanding the negative emotions of other people, such as frustration, dislike, shame, or fear (Ripoll, Zaki, et al. 2013). This trouble disconnects them from others and sets them spinning in their own self-contained worlds. They also tend to jump to quick conclusions about ideas and causes. However, researchers don't know much about the causes or even underlying experiences of such individuals. This lack of information may be related to the fact that less than 2 percent of psychiatric patients have the diagnosis of schizotypal personality disorder, so that mental health practitioners interact with such individuals less frequently than they do those with other diagnoses. However, some experiences that have been linked with the development of schizotypal eccentricity are child abuse and trauma. Though, unfortunately, many types of patients have had such pasts, these individuals tend to have higher rates of such adverse experiences than other groups of psychiatric patients (Raine 2006). One well-known finding is the association of schizotypal personality disorder with fragile X syndrome (Raine 2006), a somewhat common inherited form of intellectual disability. Associations may also occur between schizotypal personality disorder and pregnancy, including both the flu and stress in pregnant mothers, as well as complications of birth and delivery. Another linkage is found with marijuana use in early adolescence (Raine 2006; Gabbard 2007).

Wayne couldn't tell me much about his sister. She was quite a bit older and became ill right after college. So she was already away for several years before her first admission to a psychiatric hospital and had a rather rocky course with multiple antipsychotic medication trials and inpatient stays until things became more stable for her. His mother's reaction was to hold on tight to Wayne. Going away to college wouldn't be an option for him; maybe, she wondered, that was where she went wrong with his sister. His father died when Wayne was quite young, and his mother brought pet after pet home to try and fill the void. His sister was always a loner, and his mother was overprotective and depressed. And he was never the most popular boy at school. So Wayne would run home each day to his animals and to the wonderful micro-universe they created together, and in a very sweet way he did find happiness and hope there. Albeit oddly and without other humans.

FLAVORS IN THE ECCENTRICITY STEW

The two physicians described at the beginning of the chapter give us a sense of the two main types of Eccentric. One has ideas or perceptions that are magical or unusual, and the other just sort of stands out because of the way he or she acts or relates.

The Sorcerer

The Sorcerer has a big idea, and she's not afraid to share it. Maybe she can read minds or tell the future. She knows she can't *really* do these things, but she's also confident that she is more connected to this higher, powerful consciousness than the average Joe. So if you want some supernatural intel, she's your go-to. Initially, she may seem fun in a wacky, party-trick kind of way, but when these magical themes pervade everything she has to say, it eventually grows tired.

I have a close friend whose college roommate was a Sorcerer. She was very beautiful and very extroverted. She was married to a successful but very awkward, nerdy tax attorney who loved that she was so "out there." He felt she brought the excitement to their personal and external relationships and, superficially, was thrilled to have such a good-looking woman on his arm. She finished college but never worked, and, luckily for her, her husband was in a position to support her various interests.

Whenever she would visit my friend's home, she'd blast through the door and literally sniff around the house like a hound, to get a sense of the energy. Once assessed, she'd produce volumes of sage, which she'd light up like a torch, and then go on a "purification" rampage until the house was just right. Only then would she stop to say hello—like she hadn't noticed anyone before—and settle in.

Every visit began with a reading, whether we wanted one or not. Initially, this was great fun. She'd pull out her fancy tarot set and lay out intricate patterns that apparently held our past, present, and future. She'd turn cards over, and we'd hang on her expressions and interpretations. "What will happen to me?" I'd wonder. Of course, rationally, I didn't believe it held any meaning. But it was so different for me to suspend reality for a bit and hear what she had to say that I simply enjoyed it. And it seemed I'd always get many of the "major arcana," and this caused her to label me "magical." I just loved being perceived as magical by her (see "Narcissus," in part II!), and I enjoyed seeing whether I stayed special with each reading.

But sometimes we didn't want our cards read. And sometimes my friend didn't feel comfortable having the house sniffed or a big open flame brandished near her flammable textiles. Sometimes we wanted to talk about other things besides dead relatives and medicine wheels. No go when she was around.

With time, we both lost patience with the required routine and had less and less interest in seeing her. I managed to trust that my "magic" was secure without regular readings, and we made a point of only seeing her in public spaces, where she'd usually suppress her need to purify the area, and for more limited engagements. This was a bright and appealing person, but her insistence on dominating all interactions with her routines and preoccupations made it too hard for us to maintain the relationship.

The Sorcerer is so referential that everything must trickle back down to her overvalued ideas. She's not necessarily trying to convince you of them, and she's not on a crusade to convert you over to her side. She just believes them so wholly and so pervasively that they are the lens through which she views the world. When you interact with her, they are her reference point, and even if she trains herself to suppress them in mixed company, they're always right there under the surface.

The Sore Thumb

The second doctor I described in the introduction stuck out like the Sore Thumb type that he was. He wasn't *doing* anything bizarre, or thinking anything odd, as far as I could tell. But he dressed in tatters, like a hobo in a 1930s movie. He had no insight into the effect of his appearance on others. When he was passed over for, say, opportunities to address a medical school class for teaching, he complained and tried to defend himself and his abilities. Indeed, he was bright and certainly had the requisite credentials. But no one would ever stand him up in front of a group of students as a representative member of the field. And, of course, we can say that appearance shouldn't matter or isn't everything, but he really had no idea that there should be a mere modicum of professional decorum and that even trying just a little would help him out.

He chose a particular part of medicine where his interactions were individual and generally long-term, with little potential for emergencies. This worked best for him. He found a group of patients who were comfortable with his overall package, and they stayed with him for many years. Had he chosen a field like surgery, for example, where teamwork and communication are essential, I suspect he would not have succeeded.

It seems he lived with his mother, just as Wayne did, and never left home for school or residency. And it seems they were entangled in fixed routines since his youth. She, for example, always cut his hair. When she died, he stayed in the family home and attempted to continue their routines; among them was cutting his own hair. And I can only imagine that the clothes he wore may have fit him at one time, many, many years ago, and he never thought to refresh them. He simply lacked that connection to the world and to his effect upon people. And it was so odd given his technical acumen.

The Sore Thumb may stand out for a number of reasons, not just the way they look. They may have odd inter-relational styles or habits. They may have odd beliefs or ideas, but be less likely than the Sorcerer to make them known. They just seem weird, and it can be a bit harder to sort out exactly why.

WHEN THE SCHMUCK IN THE OFFICE IS THE ECCENTRIC

In the workplace, the Eccentric may initially be seen as "creative" or "innovative" (Burch and Foo 2010). He may have an exciting initial appeal that makes you want to know him. However, if the individual also has more impulsive characteristics, she may begin to act in an alarming or offensive manner. The Eccentric's inability to outwardly control himself leads to problems in the workplace. Otherwise, for the most part, the Eccentric doesn't cause too much trouble.

In general, these individuals are often labeled "odd" by co-workers and spend time by themselves. However, it may be important for organizations to learn how to harness some of the Eccentric's creativity into productive ideas. The research shows that the Eccentric is often not as disruptive as other difficult types of workers (Kemelgor, Sussman, et al. 2011). At the same time, however, they often have difficulty finishing education and maintaining employment.

When they are found in the workplace, the Eccentric is more likely to be a subordinate than a supervisor (Kemelgor, Sussman, et al. 2011). For perhaps obvious reasons, they are not usually found at jobs requiring much interaction with customers (Rosell, Futterman, et al. 2014) and may not do well in group learning or on collaborative projects. However, when the individual does express useful, creative ideas, it is important to provide her with a safe space to do so without inhibiting other employees. It may be helpful to let such individuals engage in what has been termed *nominal brainstorming*, asking them to generate creative ideas by themselves to later bring to a superior or group (Burch 2006). As such, the Eccentric may do well in research and development or in artistic positions.

HOW TO DEAL WITH THE ECCENTRIC

Overall, the approach to working with such individuals is to let them be themselves and to recognize that, for the most part, they don't cause too much trouble. They may be best suited to an environment that caters to their specific interests. Let's take the doctor who attributes everything to lead poisoning: she may have been most comfortable working for a project such as the Centers for Disease Control and Prevention's Lead Poisoning Program. Career counseling can be helpful for such persons. If there are specific, odd beliefs that do not incorporate well into a current setting, the individual may just need to be gently instructed to avoid overasserting their personal beliefs in the workplace and to avoid forcing them on others. It may be helpful for coworkers to give the Eccentric some personal space, as well.

It's important to reinforce that, regardless of the Eccentric's beliefs or oddities, she is still responsible for the same deliverables. The physician preoccupied with lead poisoning still needs to offer the appropriate standard of care to her patients. So does the disheveled physician. But my Sorcerer friend was clearly unable to do that. For example, she was physically uncomfortable when unable to purify her environment with each change. Presumably, she might have functioned in an office where she could perform her rituals each morning and then get down to business. But she was so compelled to interact with others by reading the energy in the office, advising people about what might happen to them, and so on that she was unproductive and very distracting. After a few failed attempts after college, she stopped even trying to look for paid work and spent time honing her sorcerer skills in a variety of self-help, alternative settings. Which seems to be what she enjoyed.

Because a significant number of Eccentrics are also depressed, they may seek or be encouraged to seek clinical treatment, which can also address personality difficulties. Significant anxiety or depression may be addressed with medication, though many of the primary, underlying issues may not be alleviated with prescriptions alone. Therapy may be helpful, as with so many of the personalities we have discussed, but the Eccentric is generally one of the least likely to seek treatment of all the character types. One goal of such talk treatment would be to enable more adaptive personal relationships, allowing them to connect better to other people.

Functionally, the same advice that has dominated this book remains true: be gently direct. When the disheveled physician asked if he could address the medical school class, that might have been an opportunity to say something like, "Well, you certainly have a great deal to offer, and I'm sure you would be a fine teacher. But my expectation would be that you dress the part of the physician role model for our students. Is that something you'd be willing to do?" The reaction could range from embarrassment to anger and indignation to complete oblivion. But it's a reality check that lets him know that he's losing out on something he wants because of his actions. This could start the ball rolling to increase his awareness of his effect and impression on the outside world. If he were to repeatedly hear these messages, he might attempt to address the concern.

Similarly, we tried this with our Sorcerer friend, but failed. We said, very directly, that while we really enjoyed our readings and hearing about her alternative teachings, we also wanted to do some other things together—go shopping, see a movie, talk about current events. She just couldn't hear us. When anything did penetrate, she would begin to insult us, telling us that we were just avoiding learning the truth about our fate and that we needed to stop being so fearful. Given such perseveration on talking about only her own interests, we eventually just began to stop seeing the Sorcerer. It seemed she couldn't function in any environment that wasn't utterly permissive or directly engaged in her areas of interest.

The best of both worlds is for the Eccentric to seek a work environment that caters to her special interest and to limit exclamations of the odd beliefs. That's why Wayne's choice to work at a veterinary practice made so much sense. But it's also why his crystal intrusions caused trouble.

Wayne: Part Two

Wayne was really fearful about harming his animals or getting sick himself were he to decrease or limit his crystal usage. He understood that not gluing a crystal onto a collar wouldn't actively hurt an animal, but he felt certain that it would slow or decrease the capacity for recovery. We spent a great deal of time discussing the conundrum of the Western medicine physician who is trained in and believes wholeheartedly in alternative medicine. He or she may be forced to practice the Western standard and choke down alternative solutions if his patients or his practice setting are unsupportive. We discussed the concept of nonmaleficence and the Latin phrase *primum non nocere,* or "first, do no harm."

Through our conversations, Wayne began to realize that a customer who left the practice because of his personal behavior meant an animal who would then have no exposure whatsoever to the positive energy. He thus slowly became more comfortable with the idea that not every animal needed a crystal to survive. He began to realize that the positive-energy micro-universe could be additive but not essential if he were relegated to an imperfect world. And he acknowledged that the world, and his world, was indeed imperfect but that we all make our way through it nonetheless.

He tried to become more discerning about who absolutely needed a crystal and to understand that, for some, a crystal was simply an augmentation. And when he felt a crystal was really important for an animal to have, he'd ask the animals' owners for permission to glue on the crystal and underplayed its meaning by suggesting that he believed it was "good luck." Framed in this manner, most people said "Sure, why not?" He did ramp up his own crystal wearing, though. He all but sparkled beneath his clothes and imagined that his "healing touch" was exponentially increased. The ups and downs that ensued were now focused on how many crystals Wayne really needed to wear for ultimate healing capacity. That's the thing about magical ideas—they tend to be fixed. But the conflicts were now wholly internal to Wayne. He could spend time and energy on this personal optimization and didn't need to share it with anyone.

It wasn't perfect, but it was the best he could do for now, for his animals. The complaints from customers decreased sharply (his coworkers still thought Wayne was strange, but endearingly so, and nonthreatening), and all seemed to stabilize. This is our hope for the Eccentric in the office.

A Checklist of Ways to Effectively Deal with the Eccentric

- Where possible, employ the Eccentric in an environment that caters to their special interests; when not appropriate, gently remind them that their personal beliefs should not be forced onto others.
- Reinforce that they are held to the same standard of work quality and quantity as other employees.
- Be gently direct with addressing odd or inappropriate behavior, using reality testing to showcase limitations they bring upon themselves.

The Suspicious

A conspiracy theory is defined as a belief that an event was intentionally caused by a secret or evil plot, often by powerful people (Swami, Chamorro-Premuzic, et al. 2010), and a great number of people believe in them. For example, a 1992 survey by the *New York Times* indicated that more than 75 percent of Americans believed that other people were involved in Lee Harvey Oswald's assassination of President John F. Kennedy, despite official reports to the contrary, (Goertzel 1994), and nearly 50 percent of New York City residents believed that the United States government knew about the 9/11 attacks and intentionally chose not to intervene (Sunstein and Vermeule 2009). Common themes of conspiracy theories are assassinations, government plans, and secret technology. The basic tenet of a conspiracy theory is the suspected hidden existence of an underhanded and malicious endeavor. A paranoid person is a person who tends to view the entire world around them in a suspicious way, where everything is viewed as having a possible secret and evil plot behind it. The Suspicious are walking conspiracy theorists—finding underlying meaning in newsworthy events, like the ones described above, but also in the most minute interactions with others in their lives.

BASIC TRAITS OF THE SUSPICIOUS

Just as they did with schizotypal persons, psychiatrists started thinking about paranoid persons in relation to people with schizophrenia. Of note, people with schizophrenia are individuals who will usually have unusual experiences in addition to the paranoia of the Suspicious, such as hearing voices, having elaborate and bizarre beliefs that most people think could not be true, showing disorganized behavior, and speaking nonsensically. They are generally more impaired and have much clearer breaks with reality than the Suspicious. In early studies, psychiatrists observed that some family members of individuals with schizophrenia exhibit "paranoid traits," self-consciousness, and jealousness; often misinterpret comments; and make accusations (Kendler 1985). Precursors of the eventual diagnosis that we now call "paranoid personality disorder" included *fragile personality, contentious psychopathy*, and *self-insecure personality* (Akhtar 1990). Interestingly, Freud described the essential dynamic as related to suppressed homosexual urges—remember that he related most everything to sex—wherein the individual turned his attraction toward another male into the idea that the other person was instead attracted to him (Stone 1993). "It's *him* who is out to get *me!*"

Individuals of the Suspicious type are always on the lookout for harm, exploitation, and deception. Their relationships are judged in terms of their degrees of loyalty and trust. They tend to avoid sharing information and hold frequent, lengthy grudges. They tend to think that there is foreboding meaning behind things that others would find to be neutral and are quick to perceive character attacks by others (American Psychiatric Association 2013). Ambiguity is extremely difficult for them to tolerate, and they feel as if they can see underlying truths that others cannot. The Suspicious view their thinking as "rational," however, and value their methods as informed and intelligent. In actuality, they tend to oversimplify things and jump to conclusions based on limited evidence (Stone 1993).

While at times it may be important to question commonly accepted truths, such as that the sun circles the earth, or to be suspicious about someone with true malintent, paranoia becomes problematic when it causes widespread distrust of the world. In some situations, being distrustful can be helpful or even adaptive, since it helps the individual be alert to danger. At these times, assumptions about potential threat can help save a person from harm. The problem is that when everything is viewed as unsafe, there is no way to differentiate what is truly threatening from what is harmless. Clinical paranoid personality disorder—or such widespread and engrained distrust—is estimated to exist in 0.5 to 4.5 percent of the American population (Sadock 2000; American Psychiatric Association 2013). It is also a disorder more commonly found in males and among prisoners, refugees, the elderly, and those with hearing impairment (Bernstein, Useda, et al. 1995).

Alvin: Part One

Alvin, an information security officer, was referred to me after he made a comment at a job-training exercise in which he indicated that he joined the company so that he could protect Americans against "ultra-liberal Democrats" with whatever means necessary.

He had made this comment in front of a supervisor, who stated that his wife was in local government and that both of them were committed Democrats, but Alvin just stared at his supervisor silently, intently, and without a reassuring response. "I meant what I said," he eventually stated. This incident led to people feeling uncomfortable and unsafe, and I was asked to evaluate the officer. He began our session by excessively asking about me, inquiring about the purpose of each question that I asked, and attempting to deflect divulging any information about himself. My conversation with Alvin was marked by paranoia with regard to "liberal" persons; in addition, Alvin had clear suspiciousness about most others in the world around him. For example, he stated that he knew that the government controlled all news media and that he had to find "underground radio" to get "the real story." He felt that even being referred to me was an attempt by colleagues to keep him from getting a deserved promotion. In our meeting, he later stated that he knew that the government had a file on all citizens from wiretapping their phone lines and that information from our conversation could very likely be added to that file "because it happens everywhere." He was polite and even personable, but he kept asking me to divulge my ethnic and religious background. I gently asked why he felt it so important to know this information, and he focused on its absolute necessity. I did not provide the information, which visibly frustrated him, but I urged him to stay in order to discuss his job if he wanted to be able to return. When talking about anyone at work, he seemed to have a grudge. He was fixated on the fact that no one at work could be trusted. Alvin told me countless examples of how he knew others were against him, using stories about seating arrangements at lunch, task assignment, and almost every other part of his job being used against him. Before the event that sent him to me, he'd considered filing a grievance with Human Resources and was ready to sue for discrimination if they didn't help him. He even had a private lockbox in which he stored documents that he felt may be helpful in later proving his suspicions about the intent of those around him.

In his mind, almost no one could be trusted—except his wife and his dogs. He had a veritable fleet of Dobermans at home. When I asked why and how he had decided that his wife was safe, he seemed unable to articulate any reasoning, stating, "She just is." Raised in a busy city, Alvin moved to a lazy, bucolic town where he could buy tons of acreage cheaply. He liked to shoot his many guns to work on his target accuracy, and it was really important to him that he not have to "deal" with neighbors, or even see them, because he felt that they would collect information about his personal business to somehow use it against him. He and his wife had no friends, all of which was just fine for him. He felt as safe as he could be, immersed in their relationship, his dogs, and the expanse of his land.

His job as an information security officer afforded him early access to information about local nefarious activity. He needed and wanted to know things "to be ready." He dreaded the notion of having "the rug pulled from under" him if he were blindsided. But much of his thought was focused on the greater evils of the world at large, of cultures he feared and didn't understand.

I saw that Alvin's primary way of interpreting the world around him was through suspicion. He was able to acknowledge that his beliefs were extreme, and maybe even overstated, but this helped him feel prepared for the worst, even though he knew that the worst was not necessarily guaranteed to occur. That grain of reality testing, and his general societal functioning, were what differentiated his paranoia from that seen in someone with the illness of schizophrenia. As the Suspicious, though, he saw everyone as malicious and hostile and believed they were taking advantage of him. Alvin was always the victim and had difficulty understanding how anyone could see otherwise. He interpreted conversations and events with unjustified mistrust. His suspiciousness made him appear unforgiving and hostile, and everything was used as evidence to support his paranoid ideas. He thought a lot about power—the power that he felt others had—and about what he could do to feel more powerful and protect himself from these people. He was always on alert for how others would try to hurt him.

HOW DID THE SUSPICIOUS GET THIS WAY?

The Suspicious, who view the world apprehensively, tend to have childhoods marked by varying degrees of social isolation, anxiety, poor relationships, and sensitivity to criticism. This group of children often includes those who experienced sexual and verbal abuse (Cohen, Crawford, et al. 2005). They very often have experienced shame and humiliation while growing up, leading them to expect more of these emotions over time—always waiting for the next attack (Force and Association 2006). Repeat experiences lead to the belief that depending on others is dangerous and that the world is full of possibilities for being attacked.

Alvin was raised by overprotective parents in a high-rise apartment building. Though his family lived in the same place for decades, they never spoke to their neighbors. It was a common family practice to wait at the apartment door until any neighbors who happened to be in the hall would disappear down the elevators. They gleaned little bits of information about some of the neighbors over the years, but whatever they learned was twisted into something negative and scary, and just made them redouble their efforts to stay away.

Alvin didn't have many friends growing up, partly because they almost eventually betrayed or disappointed him in some way, but also because his parents would interrogate him each night about his school interactions and warn him of their various pitfalls. He was taught to walk in the middle of smaller streets whenever possible so no one could pull him into an alley and mug him. He was taught never to make eye contact on the streets and never, ever to say hello to a stranger. The only safe place was in the fold of his loving family; he was made to feel that it was them against the world. And this was a real challenge, because the world presented seemingly endless dangers.

Whatever leads to the development of such widespread suspicion about the world, the mind of the Suspicious seems to be a master of misinterpretation. Some think that this trait stems from a sense of personal inadequacy, which tries to protect self-esteem by viewing the outside world as the cause of all negative experiences. Some theorists trace the mental pattern to paying far too much attention to misunderstood social cues. The Suspicious interpret everything as being influenced by malevolent people in order to protect themselves from thinking it is their own fault if something bad happens or they are unable to achieve success. It may be easier, for example, to think that there is a plot to keep you from getting promoted than to think that you are not worthy of a promotion on your own merit. In a sense, it seems easier to blame others as being out to get you than to think you may be truly undeserving.

DEGREES OF SUSPICION

Of course, these problems frequently extend into the workplace. While I don't believe there are significant categorical subtypes of the Suspicious, as we saw with other types, there are those among the Suspicious who suffer more silently and those who manage their anxiety through confrontation with those around them. The internally focused Suspicious who spend more time alone in their thoughts can hold it together most of the time but have flares of paranoia related to events or comments at the office that make her feel unsafe. This worsening of fear will typically occur when something unexpected happens, such as the firing of a coworker. The most healthy of the Suspicious will feel safe enough to "check out" his feelings in a reasonable way—that is, reality test—and hopefully, after review and explanation, feel better and calm down. Unfortunately, though, most paranoid individuals will just ruminate and spiral into deeper and deeper thinking about the plots of others out to get them. And then there are those among the Suspicious for whom nearly everything is misinterpreted— the flares can occur on a daily basis—and their tendency is to self-protect by frequent accusation and confrontation. It is very easy to feel afraid of interacting with this type of the Suspicious.

Many of us have had the experience of being called to a meeting or asked a question without context or explanation, and we know that can make us feel a little paranoid about what's going to happen. Or perhaps we learned secondhand about staffing changes that make us wonder if we are the next in line for termination. Our minds can wander pretty quickly into tangled webs, piecing little bits of data together to support our worst fears of what is to come. And, depending on who we are, we may walk right up to the person in charge and say, "Am I in trouble?" or stew alone in our office twirling ourselves into an anxious, paranoid frenzy, wondering what's next for us. "Am I getting fired?" This is where the anxious and the paranoid meet, as I mentioned with the Bean Counter. Those who isolate during these times will generally wait silently for a verdict, recalling conversations or endlessly reviewing e-mails and voice messages, collecting "the evidence" to support their theories.

The difference between "us" and the Suspicious is the frequency with which these fears arise. The Suspicious experiences these events constantly. It represents his worldview. The individual who is rarely suspicious usually gets rolled eyes and laughter in response to, "Am I in trouble?" whereas the same question from the Suspicious leads to annoyance and frustration: "For the hundredth time . . . NO, you're not in trouble!!!" And the Suspicious who so frequently isolates when afraid may well marginalize himself by withdrawing too much from the office community and creating some of the very situations he fears.

Whether the usual tack is withdrawal or confrontation, violence remains a risk, albeit usually a remote one. It's important to pay attention to the concerns that the Suspicious rouses in others, since these feelings are a big clue about possible violence. This, of course, was the fear with Alvin. His comment made people uncomfortable, as did his cold stare, and, combined with his general, ever-vigilant manner, everyone was afraid he'd go get one of his guns and come back to work to do something dangerous and dramatic. It's easy to see how the confrontational sort can get into an escalating conflict and become aggressive.

But sometimes the Suspicious who withdraws and ruminates can get so worked up as to become violent, too. This is the disgruntled employee who is released from a company, seemingly without incident, and then expresses homicidal feelings toward the boss after a few weeks spent at home going over everything that transpired.

One can't always predict these internally driven scenarios and so, again, it's important to use the tactics described and to be aware of how the individual makes the office tone change. Paying attention in this way and communicating clearly, directly, and concisely are your best bets.

WHEN THE SCHMUCK IN THE OFFICE IS SUSPICIOUS

Possibly hiding a fragile self-esteem, the Suspicious at work may evince a sense of superiority. In addition, such individuals are often seen as cold, unemotional, rigid, stubborn, lacking a sense of humor, and scary; they often have difficulty with jealousy, anger, and bitterness. These traits tend to push people away, which compounds the Suspicious's sense that others are distant and hostile. They tend to receive any feedback about job performance as disapproving. They spend lots of time trying to figure out the meaning behind things—impairing productivity. If it's not obvious already, working on group projects with the Suspicious may be particularly difficult. However, at times the Suspicious does form interpersonal groups with people who have similar patterns of thoughts or even shared cult or conspiracy-theory beliefs. The Internet allows the Suspicious to connect with other people who share ideas. In the office, the Suspicious tends to form "circles of trust" with insiders and outsiders. When moving between positions, he may bring along his own people instead of try to work with others. Work spaces populated by the Suspicious tend to become mills for gossip and rumors about what things "really mean."

However, in comparison to some other disruptive types, the Suspicious are often able to have a job, at times successfully. The way the Suspicious constantly views every angle and possible outcome in a given situation makes him ready for most anything. People may use suspicious traits effectively as security personnel, investigative reporters, private investigators, or critics; people with paranoia have also been said to do well in competitive roles against other businesses as "enemies" (Miller 2003). They also do better when working in relatively solitary positions (Boxer 1993). The difficulties that the Suspicious has interpreting authority and power makes this type better suited to jobs with more independence and less hierarchy (Sperry 1997). As bosses, the Suspicious type tends to run their organizations through closed-door decision making. It's also not uncommon for the Suspicious to be involved in legal disputes.

When the Suspicious is fired or otherwise feels threatened or under attack, the most serious concern is violence in the workplace. This risk is elevated if the individual is a male, has an addiction, or has any past violence (Bensimon 1994). The profile is often a middle-aged Caucasian male whose identity is extremely wrapped up in a job that he is at risk of losing. This danger is particularly elevated after a termination, so it is absolutely necessary to take any threats extremely seriously, particularly during such a time period. Most states have specific laws against terroristic threats that can be evoked in these circumstances. Even something vague such as "You'll regret this" could be a marker for violence. It is also important to note the responsibility that the company takes for creating an environment that does not provoke violence; this would include attempts to limit a toxic workplace—one that is high stress, understaffed, and run by an authoritarian leadership style (Johnson and Indvik 1996).

HOW TO DEAL WITH THE SUSPICIOUS

Having the Suspicious in your office can be pretty tough. This individual always seems aggressive, blames others for his own problems, and thinks that everyone else is causing the mess. Because of his constant misinterpretations of words and actions, it becomes very easy to misstep and get into conflict with him. The office can begin to feel like a minefield with everyone held hostage by the fear of setting him off. As people tiptoe around the Suspicious, their communication becomes stilted and clipped—or, worse, indirect—and this alone can make him feel mistrustful. As opposed to the Venus Flytrap or Narcissus, walking on eggshells around Suspicious involves fear in addition to the simple dread of setting someone off. It's really hard to know how far the Suspicious will take his anger, and we can begin to feel paranoid ourselves.

When the Suspicious feels acutely threatened, it can lead to some pretty uncomfortable scenes. The more confrontational Suspicious may call you out with accusations that seem to come from far left field. Your surprise and confusion can look like evasion and provide more evidence for the Suspicious that you're guilty as charged. The more silent Suspicious will not directly confront you but, instead, will communicate with leading questions and intimations to trap you in perceived "lies."

In working with such individuals, it is important to be as clear and straightforward as possible in order to leave minimal room for paranoid misunderstanding about your true intents. It is important to provide matter-of-fact, rational explanations for task assignments and other decisions. Attempt to provide simple but helpful reality checks with direct terminology and logical explanations. For example, when introducing a new assignment, one might say, "Here are the facts: I have decided to assign you to this project because I feel your ability to do X will be useful for our goal." Another helpful strategy is to attempt to offer control when it is possible; often, this can happen through providing a list of available reasonable choices. Say "Would you like to do X or do Y?" instead of "What would you like to do?" Remember that your honesty and loyalty will be tested every step of the way. In an effort to decrease paranoia in an individual—or organization at large—it is important to share information on a regular basis. Keeping people updated—about neutral, good, and bad news—is an important tactic for minimizing unfounded gossip and fears.

Being straightforward can be surprisingly tough. Our natural tendency is to "package" our words during more difficult conversations—to couch whatever harsh or uncomfortable thing we may need to say in more pleasant thoughts. In fact, we directed you to do just that with Narcissus, but it can really backfire with the Suspicious. I've seen this quite a bit in the physician leadership population. An intimidating, powerful, acting-out doctor may be called into his chairman's office after an incident. Often, the chairman is so anxious about having to redirect this guy that he starts and ends the conversation with compliments and kudos, with a limp sentence or two about the bad behavior shoved in the middle. "John, I called you in here to tell you what a great job you're doing and how much this department values you. Your productivity and high-quality work are simply unparalleled. I really don't know how we'd run without you. I heard something about you throwing a phone at a medical student today—I'm sure a misunderstanding. So anyway, thank you—great job, as always."

This can go quite well with Narcissus, as the chairman can slip the difficult message in without angering the physician. But, clearly, this interpersonal tactic really, really won't work with the Suspicious. The Suspicious always smells a rat. Every word you say will be reimagined, reconsidered, and dissected. Why is he complimenting me? Does he mean it? What's he really saying? Is it only the department that values me? Does that mean that hospital administration does not? How is he "sure it's a misunderstanding?" How did he find out about this in the first place? Does he know what the medical student did to ME? Are they ganging up on me? And on and on it goes.

This is a situation where less is truly more. Use fewer, but well-directed, words. Take out the fluff. Tie your simple statements with simple explanations. "Alvin, your comment about Democrats scared us, and we feel too uncomfortable to continue to work with you." End of story.

Overall, it's a good idea to try to facilitate confidence while being firm but nonjudgmental. Without a sense of trust, any blunt confrontation to a worker's conspiracy thoughts (e.g., "Obviously, no one is against you! How could you think that?!") may only cause further distrust, alienation, and paranoia. The idea is to be concise and direct but not confrontational. Instead of openly challenging their beliefs, be straightforward and clear about your own intentions. One technique that can be helpful is to agree with the possibility of the person's assertion ("There is no way that I can prove they don't like you") while at the same time offering alternative possibilities ("But it may be more likely that their comments really were meant to describe how the whole team is doing and wasn't anything about you in particular. In fact, management said the same thing to me just yesterday"). Of course, in the tricky world of the Suspicious, anything—even compliments, particularly when excessive—can be misinterpreted as part of a grander plot against them. They may wonder why a nice person is "acting" so nice because—in a world of hostile intent—any warmth may be seen as necessarily fake. In the same vein, they are inclined to refuse offers of help because of suspecting the underlying motives.

I cannot stress the power of concise and direct communication enough (I believe that we should almost always communicate in this way, with everyone), particularly as it relates to the Suspicious. Even if the Suspicious becomes acutely threatened and causes a scene, mirroring back what he is doing and clarifying why it is a misinterpretation will be helpful and appreciated.

I am at an unfair advantage where the Suspicious is concerned because of my decades of work with acutely paranoid schizophrenics at an inpatient unit of a psychiatric hospital. Again, by using an extreme example of working with even more impaired individuals as a psychiatrist, I hope to drive home just how important direct communication is in working with anyone who is paranoid. With these individuals, I've been able to see the positive impact of relating concisely and directly versus beating around the bush. I recall this most poignantly in the case of a young man with whom I worked in both in- and outpatient settings for many years. He had fixed delusions about the FBI observing and following him. He had generally accepted treatment recommendations and was quite stable—with a small group of friends and a quiet job in a tailor shop. The FBI fears were omnipresent but, with the support of our sessions and medication, usually contained to his thoughts and did not affect his ability to live in the world. And even though he firmly believed that the FBI was monitoring him, he was usually able to at least entertain my assertions that his fears were somewhat ungrounded.

Occasionally, "real life" would interfere with his stability. Maybe a world terrorist event would hit the news and prove to him that conspiracies do happen, or he would read a story about a spy. Such news would unnerve him, and, depending on the intensity of his reaction, he might not respond to reassurance, becoming more and more paranoid. At these times, he would require hospitalization to offer heightened support until he'd return to feeling like himself.

But imagine being this guy. Untrusting even when feeling well, he's now at his worst and he's hearing me propose that he let me lock him up and play around with his medication. That I draw his blood and test it. Am I part of the plot? Will I use his blood for evil experiments? Instead of drawing blood, will I in fact inject something while he's not looking? Will I poison him with unfamiliar pills? Once he's admitted, will I ever let him out? Pure terror.

So I remember one such event, literally standing with him (a pretty big guy) at the door of the psychiatric unit, listening to his paranoid debate about whether or not he should trust me and go in. I recall watching his eyes narrow with anger and suspicion and how this would alternate with a softened expression as he'd recall the realities of our relationship and the fact that I'd never steered him wrong before. And all the while I'd be saying, "This is all related to your illness, which you know causes you to feel suspicious and unsafe. I see how uncomfortable you are, and we both know you want to feel better. I will admit you to my unit, I will visit with you every day, I will draw blood and get you a physical exam to be sure you aren't medically sick, and I will adjust your medication if we both agree that these are the right things to do. And once you are feeling safer and we both agree that you're ready, I will open the door and send you home. That's all we are doing here." I'd meet his assertions that I was part of "the plot" by reminding him there was no evidence to support that fear and by asking him to recall all of our years together. In the midst of his desperation, he trusted me and went in. And he was better in no time.

The point is, of course, that by establishing yourself as a "straight shooter," you will have a tremendously easier time with the Suspicious, just as I have had with my schizophrenic patients. Interactions with him may feel like tightrope walking over a shark tank, but patience and tenacity will usually pay off.

Referrals to a professional may also help engage someone in a therapy that can work on minimizing hostility while improving feelings of self-efficacy, feelings of control, social skills, and reality testing. Medications may be used if the person also has symptoms of anxiety or depression. A useful time to make a referral can actually be when the individual is making a complaint about how someone else is treating them—framing the intervention as a way to help deal with the stress of conflict. Of course, because of the difficulty that the Suspicious has trusting others, it can be difficult for the person to see the benefit of speaking to a professional.

A very serious reminder: make sure that such people do not want to retaliate against any individuals for perceived mistreatment (Resnick and Kausch 1995). Any statements about retaliation should be taken seriously and referred to a psychiatrist and/or legal authorities for an evaluation of risk of violence. There are some of the Suspicious that you just do not want to try to help in the office, particularly when threats or any statements about violence have been made. The risk is just too high. And remember that the company can be held legally at fault if violence occurs.

If someone is fired, it should be done with care and caution, and every attempt should be made to preserve the individual's self-esteem. Avoid public displays that could worsen anger or humiliation. Your communication with the Suspicious should be direct, clear, and concise about why he is being terminated. At the same time, in an effort to cool down angry feelings and lessen the possibility of retaliation, one can be kind with tying up loose ends and figuring out the details of the termination negotiations. Remember, the person might be suspicious about excessive sugar coating, so aim for straightforward but compassionate communications.

Alvin: Part Two

The hostile and paranoid perspectives about others cost Alvin his job: I recommended that he be terminated, since I believed that he posed a risk of violence. The aggressive comment in front of his supervisor along with his general suspicious and defensive attitude made too many people at the company uncomfortable. His hostile relationships at work, his suspiciousness, his focus on firearms, and his large personal collection of weapons added up to too much risk, and, in the end, he was fired. His boss was clear that these were the reasons for termination, and nothing else. He also offered to help Alvin submit unemployment paperwork and proposed that he could still take an online programming training course at the company's expense.

There was a great deal of anxiety by coworkers after that decision since many people worried he'd show up at the office and just open fire. But that never happened, and no one in the company ever heard from him again since he likely went further into isolation after this incident. This setup was perfect in my mind, since the only type of work he should have been doing was alone, perhaps with his dogs.

After Alvin's departure, the company itself implemented clearer strategies on workplace threats and violence. Staff received training on warning signs of violence and what to do if someone feels unsafe in the office, including specific reporting protocols and how to involve security. There were also trainings on the non-discrimination policies, as well as re-education about the zero-tolerance policy for threats and violence. At the same time, the management recognized that, although nothing violent had happened, everyone was under a great deal of stress thinking about the possibilities. A staff retreat was held where everyone was able to relax but also contribute to a discussion on how to make improvements to the workplace, helping them feel more at ease but also valued.

A Checklist of Ways to Effectively Deal with the Suspicious

- Be clear and direct with communication and provide transparent rationale for decisions.
- Offering a choice between alternatives can help the Suspicious feel more in control.
- When addressing inappropriate behavior, use simple statements

with simple explanations, taking out the fluff or extraneous information, without being confrontational.

- With HR's input, consider referral to psychiatric services.
- Safety of everyone in the workplace is the most important consideration; treat any threats or implications of violence with the utmost gravity and engage the appropriate authorities.

PART V

Conclusion

Am I the Schmuck in My Office?

Although this book is about understanding different types of difficult behavior, it is important to recognize how much of creating a healthy environment lies with each of us. When someone's behavior bothers us, we have to ask ourselves, Why is this behavior affecting me in this way? Why am I bothered by it, and is there something about me that I can look at to understand another person's behavior?

When having interpersonal difficulties, you must always ask yourself what, if any, contribution you may be making to the situation. If in workplace after workplace, you can't get along with your colleagues, something is wrong. Maybe it's the office culture, maybe it's the field itself, but whatever it is, you'd better take a look inward. Perhaps you feel you get along with people just fine, but coworker after coworker complains about an inability to get along with you. Go get the mirror. Hurry.

A trick of my trade boils down to this: if someone chronically gets under your skin, get away from the situation, sit down, and take a look inside yourself. The intensity of your emotion is a hint you can use to realize that it's time to do this—something about this person is rousing something very personal in you. If you can be honest and thoughtful, it works every time. Maybe some of his traits remind you of your mother or your father? Do you notice that you can't stand it when you feel some of the emotions that seem to make him act out? Is it possible that you don't like this about yourself, either?

No one of us is perfect. We all struggle with things. Certain situations, interactions, and types of people rouse feelings in us that the person next to us might not feel. Take clues from your surroundings to learn about yourself. The better you know yourself, the better chance you have to find the right job, the right partner, the right social circle.

Early in my career, I had a lot of trouble treating deeply egocentric patients in psychotherapy—until I looked inside myself. When I did this in response to a patient I felt I simply couldn't treat, I realized that some of his behaviors reminded me of similar behaviors in some members of my family and, worst of all, behaviors that I myself had taken on despite my distaste for them. The feeling of vexation moved squarely onto me as I realized that, in some way, I was guilty of the very things I reviled in my patient. Indeed, I suddenly felt I had a window into his feelings, I found empathy for his distress, and we developed a fruitful working relationship.

In my career, as I continued to work on learning about myself in my own psychotherapy, traits in others bothered me less and less. When their behaviors did bother me, I learned to call them out in the moment or soon thereafter, directly and honestly, telling them what they did, why I thought it was wrong, and how it made me feel. I've found that the directness of my communication leaves little room for argument—you agree with me or you don't, but you most certainly know my position on the matter and you learn something about me. In understanding myself and in understanding others, in embracing them, and in finding empathic strategies to work with them, I have helped propagate my own success and happiness through better relationships.

We all have the responsibility to be honest. Workplace relationships are just another type of relationship between people, and they need to be built on openness and communication. We need to be honest with ourselves and with others.

Workplace Philosophies

Throughout my career consulting with disruptive behavior, and as a psychiatrist in general, I have been in awe of the fact that interventions really do work and often in profound ways. If someone wants to change, they can. It might require commitment and effort, but in the end they are able to do it. When behavior is disruptive, early intervention is key, and coworkers need to be clear in calling out what they see and how they feel about it. Communications should be concise and direct and have the goal of supportive change.

I recently received a letter from someone who had been referred to me in the past for disruptive behavior. In the preceding months, he had been up for reappointment, and, because of previous disruption, he was required to write an explanatory letter. The essay that he wrote was really quite poignant and expressed that he didn't have the tools to know how to do better before, even though his heart had been in the right place. He knew he wanted to change but felt that all of his behaviors—and their unfortunate consequences—had to be accepted as permanent parts of him and his life. It was only when coworkers started refusing to work with him, and subordinates brought up complaints about the way they were treated, that a desire to really and truly figure out how to change ignited.

In the end, this book aims to make a better workplace environment. While it is important to address disruptive behavior, the overall goal is not to homogenize different personalities but to make work a productive yet comfortable atmosphere where people are valued and supported.

Take the early-morning meeting. Everyone looks so miserable, but then when we laugh and interact and brighten the mood, our entire outlook changes for the day. The workplace does not have to be a sustained riot of overwhelming fun, but it can be a place that does not feel oppressive. Work can be a place that people enjoy, a place where they can accomplish tasks but also get to appreciate the people around them.

In figuring out disruptive behavior, solutions should be able to help everyone, including the person labeled as *disruptive*. We can remember that people do not set out to be disruptive, and often the person is a victim of her own conduct. Interventions that help the workplace can help the individual feel more at ease in doing her job and in interacting with others. From subtle adjustments to overhauling interventions, these methods should have positive aims; they may very well allow someone to live a happier life.

How we function at work, in our primary relationships, and in our social life is all largely dependent on how well we interact with other people. The solution is in the interactions themselves, the bravery to have difficult conversations, and the manner in which we elect to approach them. We must talk to one another, listen to one another and notice one another. We must find language and tone that helps connect us. We must give direct feedback with the intention of solving problems and helping us coexist comfortably. By giving people the tools and opportunities to function better in the workplace, this book aims to give them the ability to have more fulfillment and, then, a more satisfying life overall.

ACKNOWLEDGMENTS

Jody

Many thanks to the following:

Michelle Joy, who appeared like manna from heaven to share her undeniable brilliance.

Eric Lupfer, for finding me and asking that we write this book.

Michael Flamini and St. Martins Press for seeing the value in our message.

Drs. Amy Gutmann, Caryn Lerman, Ted Brodkin, Lib Hembree, Adrian Raine, Reed Goldstein, Mahendra Bhati, Scott Campbell, Juliette Galbraith, Cecilia Livesey, Frances Jensen, and Ms. Vicki Mulhern for their incredible kindness and wise counsel.

Scott Sill and Michael Haugen for their unerring support and generous friendship.

My wonderful niece Sophia for her ongoing enthusiasm and a thoughtful and comprehensive edit.

My late and deeply beloved parents, Essie (who was horrified by the title of this book) and Hal (who thought it was funny), and brothers, Michael and Rafe, all of whom I miss, so sharply.

My sisters, Stacy and Tamar, for being here and keeping our inexplicably tiny family together.

My Abbe, my gentle powerhouse, my compass, my love.

Michelle

I want to echo Jody's appreciation to everyone who helped out along the way at William Morris, St. Martin's, and Penn.

And thank you for this opportunity, Jody, for believing in me and working alongside me these last years.

We've made quite a team.

Lastly, a huge and sincere thank-you to Cecilia, Jessica, Andrew, and Jon for their support and encouragement throughout this process. Each of you helped in the ways you do best, and for this I am grateful, now and always.

BIBLIOGRAPHY

Adamou, M., M. Arif, et al. (2013). "Occupational issues of adults with ADHD." *BMC Psychiatry* 13(1): 59.

"Aging Statistics." http://www.aoa.acl.gov/Aging_Statistics/index.aspx.

Akhtar, S. (1990). "Paranoid personality disorder: A synthesis of developmental, dynamic and descriptive features." *American Journal of Psychotherapy* 44(1): 5–25.

Aldworth, J. (2009). *Results from the 2007 national survey on drug use and health: National findings.* DIANE Publishing.

Alzheimer's Association. "Early Onset Dementia: A National Challenge, a Future Crisis." https://www.alz.org/national/documents/report_earlyonset _summary.pdf.

Alzheimer's Society, UK (2016). "Employment and Dementia." http://www .alzheimers.org.uk/site/scripts/documents_info.php?documentID=1836.

American Psychiatric Association (2013). *Diagnostic and Statistical Manual of Mental Disorders.*

Arciniegas, D. B., C. A. Anderson, et al. (2013). *Behavioral neurology and neuropsychiatry.* Cambridge University Press.

Arrigo, B. A., and S. Shipley (2001). "The confusion over psychopathy (I): Historical considerations." *International Journal of Offender Therapy and Comparative Criminology* 45(3): 325–344.

Askitopoulou, H., I. A. Ramoutsaki, et al. (2002). *Archaeological evidence on the use of opium in the Minoan world.* International Congress Series, Elsevier.

Babiak, P. (1995). "When psychopaths go to work: A case study of an industrial psychopath." *Applied Psychology* 44(2): 171–188.

Babiak, P., and R. D. Hare (2009). *Snakes in suits: When psychopaths go to work.* HarperCollins.

Baldwin, S., D. Costley, et al. (2014). "Employment activities and experiences of adults with high-functioning autism and Asperger's disorder." *Journal of Autism and Developmental Disorders* 44(10): 2440–2449.

Baron, D. A. (2010). "The gold medal face of ADHD." *Journal of Attention Disorders* 13(4): 323.

Beattie, R. (2005). *Nightmare in Wichita: The hunt for the BTK strangler.* Penguin.

Bensimon, H. F. (1994). "Violence in the workplace." *Training and Development* 48(1): 26–32.

Berkman, B., and S. D'Ambruoso (2006). *Handbook of social work in health and aging.* Oxford University Press.

Berkowitz, M. (1996). "World's earliest wine." *Archaeology* 49(5): 26

Bernstein, D. D. P., D. D. Useda, et al. (1995). "Paranoid personality disorder." *The DSM-IV personality disorders.* 45–57.

Bird, A. (2005). *Blood brother: 33 reasons my brother Scott Peterson is guilty.* Regan Books.

Blaney, P. H., and T. Millon (2008). *Oxford textbook of psychopathology.* Oxford University Press.

Boddy, C. R. (2011). "The corporate psychopaths theory of the global financial crisis." *Journal of Business Ethics* 102(2): 255–259.

Boddy, C. R., R. K. Ladyshewsky, et al. (2010). "The influence of corporate psychopaths on corporate social responsibility and organizational commitment to employees." *Journal of Business Ethics* 97(1): 1–19.

Boller, F., and M. M. Forbes (1998). "History of dementia and dementia in history: An overview." *Journal of the Neurological Sciences* 158(2): 125–133.

Bonaiuto, S., W. Rocca, et al. (1995). "Education and occupation as risk factors for dementia: A population-based case-control study." *Neuroepidemiology* 14(3): 101–109.

Boxer, P. A. (1993). "Assessment of potential violence in the paranoid worker." *Journal of Occupational and Environmental Medicine* 35(2): 127–131.

Burch, G. S. J. (2006). "The 'creative-schizotype': Help or hindrance to team-level innovation." *The University of Auckland Business Review* 8(1): 43–50.

Burch, G. S. J., and G. Foo (2010). "Schizotypal and dependent personality characteristics and managerial performance." *Australian Psychologist* 45(4): 290–298.

Cahill, K., and T. Lancaster (2013). "Is the workplace an effective setting for helping people to stop smoking." *Health.*

Campbell, W. K., B. J. Hoffman, S. M. Campbell, and G. Marchisio (2011). Narcissism in organizational contexts. *Human Resource Management Review*, 21(4), 268–284.

Carey, B. (2011). "Expert on mental illness reveals her own fight." *New York Times*.

Carruth, B., D. G. Wright, et al. (2014). *Addiction intervention: Strategies to motivate treatment-seeking behavior*. Routledge.

Chen, S.-W., S. S.-F. Gau, et al. (2014). "Work stress and subsequent risk of Internet addiction among information technology engineers in Taiwan." *Cyberpsychology, Behavior, and Social Networking* 17(8): 542–550.

Christensen, D. L. (2016). "Prevalence and characteristics of autism spectrum disorder among children aged 8 years—autism and developmental disabilities monitoring network, 11 sites, United States, 2012." *MMWR. Surveillance Summaries* 65(47).

Clarke, J. (2005). *Working with Monsters: How to identify and protect yourself from the workplace psychopath*. Read How You Want.

Cohen, P., T. N. Crawford, et al. (2005). "The children in the community study of developmental course of personality disorder." *Journal of Personality Disorders* 19(5): 466–486.

Corr, P. J., and G. Matthews (2009). *The Cambridge Handbook of Personality Psychology*. Cambridge University Press.

Cox, C. B., and M. Pardasani (2013). "Alzheimer's in the Workplace: A Challenge for Social Work." *Journal of Gerontological Social Work* 56(8): 643–656.

Curtis, R. C. (1991). *The Relational Self: Theoretical convergences in psychoanalysis and social psychology*. Guilford Press.

DeCovny, S. (2012). "The financial psychopath next door." *CFA Magazine* 23(2): 34–35.

Dennis Rader-Bind, Torture and Kill-Serial Killer Documentary. *Crime Prison Serial Killers Documentaries*. http://www.dailymotion.com/video/xvflze _dennis-rader-btk-bind-torture-kill-documentary-shortfilms.

Dhand, R., and H. Sohal (2006). "Good sleep, bad sleep! The role of daytime naps in healthy adults." *Current opinion in pulmonary medicine* 12(6): 379–382.

Dimaggio, G. (2012). Narcissistic personality disorder: Rethinking what we know. *Psychiatric Times*, 29(17), 2179–2192.

Eskedal, G. A., and J. M. Demetri (2006). "Etiology and treatment of Cluster C personality disorders." *Journal of Mental Health Counseling* 28(1): 1–17.

Ficca, G., J. Axelsson, et al. (2010). "Naps, cognition and performance." *Sleep Medicine Reviews* 14(4): 249–258.

Force, P. T., and A. P. Association (2006). *Psychodynamic Diagnostic Manual*. Alliance of Psychoanalytic Organizations.

Fox, J. A., and J. Levin (1994). "Firing back: The growing threat of workplace homicide." *The Annals of the American Academy of Political and Social Science* 536(1): 16–30.

Frone, M. R. (2013). *Alcohol and Illicit Drug Use in the Workforce and Workplace.* American Psychological Association.

Furnham, A. (2007). "2 Personality disorders and derailment at work: The paradoxical positive influence of pathology in the workplace." *Research Companion to the Dysfunctional Workplace: Management Challenges and Symptoms* 22.

Gabbard, G. O. (2007). *Gabbard's Treatments of Psychiatric Disorders.* American Psychiatric Publishing.

Garfinkel, P. (1989). "How nursing staff respond to the label "borderline personality disorder." *Hospital and Community Psychiatry* 40(8): 815.

Giblin, E. J. (1981). "Bureaupathology: the denigration of competence." *Human Resource Management* 20(4): 22–25.

Goertzel, T. (1994). "Belief in conspiracy theories." *Political Psychology* 15(4): 731–742.

Gordon, R. M. (2010). Psychodynamic Diagnostic Manual. *Corsini Encyclopedia of Psychology.* John Wiley and Sons.

Grandin, T., and K. Duffy (2008). *Developing Talents: Careers for Individuals with Asperger Syndrome and High-Functioning Autism.* AAPC Publishing.

Griffiths, M. (2010). "Internet abuse and internet addiction in the workplace." *Journal of Workplace Learning* 22(7): 463–472.

Gunderson, J. G. (2009). *Borderline Personality Disorder: A Clinical Guide.* American Psychiatric Pub.

Halmøy, A., O. B. Fasmer, et al. (2009). "Occupational outcome in adult ADHD: Impact of symptom profile, comorbid psychiatric problems, and treatment: A cross-sectional study of 414 clinically diagnosed adult ADHD patients." *Journal of Attention Disorders* 13(2): 175–187.

Harper, R. G. "Paranoid Personality Disorder." *Corsini Encyclopedia of Psychology.* John Wiley and Sons.

Harpin, V. A. (2005). "The effect of ADHD on the life of an individual, their family, and community from preschool to adult life." *Archives of Disease in Childhood* 90(supplement 1): i2–i7.

Hendricks, D. (2010). "Employment and adults with autism spectrum disorders: Challenges and strategies for success." *Journal of Vocational Rehabilitation* 32(2): 125–134.

Hepper, E. G., Hart, C. M., and Sedikides, C. (2014). Moving Narcissus Can Narcissists Be Empathic?, Personality and Social Psychology Bulletin, 0146167214535812.

Hickson, G. B., J. W. Pichert, et al. (2007). "A complementary approach to promoting professionalism: identifying, measuring, and addressing unprofessional behaviors." *Academic Medicine* 82(11): 1040–1048.

Hilgard, E. R., D. J. Bem, et al. (2000). *Hilgard's Introduction to Psychology.* Harcourt College Publishers.

Hoffmann, Heinrich. (1999). "19th Century German Stories." http://germanstories.vcu.edu/struwwel/philipp_e.html.

Howe, Y., M. L. Palumbo, et al. (2016). "5 medical evaluation of patients with autism spectrum disorder." *Autism Spectrum Disorder.* Oxford University Press.

Howlin, P., and P. Yates (1999). "The potential effectiveness of social skills groups for adults with autism." *Autism* 3(3): 299–307.

Huppert, F. A., C. Brayne, et al. (1994). *Dementia and normal aging.* Cambridge University Press.

Johnson, P. R., and J. Indvik (1994). "Workplace violence: An issue of the nineties." *Public Personnel Management* 23(4): 515–523.

Johnson, P. R., and J. Indvik (1996). "Stress and workplace violence: It takes two to tango." *Journal of Managerial Psychology* 11(6): 18–27.

Kaye, A. D., N. Vadivelu, et al. (2014). *Substance Abuse: Inpatient and Outpatient Management for Every Clinician.* Springer.

Kemelgor, B., L. Sussman, et al. (2011). "Who are the difficult employees? Psychopathological attributions of their co-workers." *Journal of Business and Economics Research (JBER)* 5(10).

Kendler, K. S. (1985). "Diagnostic approaches to schizotypal personality disorder: A historical perspective." *Schizophrenia Bulletin* 11(4): 538.

Kessler, R. C., L. Adler, et al. (2006). "The prevalence and correlates of adult ADHD in the United States: Results from the National Comorbidity Survey Replication." *The American Journal of Psychiatry* 163(4): 716–723.

Ketola, T. (2006). "From CR-psychopaths to responsible corporations: Waking up the inner Sleeping Beauty of companies." *Corporate Social Responsibility and Environmental Management* 13(2): 98–107.

Kooij, J. S. (2012). *Adult ADHD: Diagnostic Assessment and Treatment.* Springer Science and Business Media.

Küpper, T., J. Haavik, et al. (2012). "The negative impact of attention-deficit/hyperactivity disorder on occupational health in adults and adolescents." *International Archives of Occupational and Environmental Health* 85(8): 837–847.

Langan-Fox, J., C. L. Cooper, et al. (2007). *Research Companion to the Dysfunctional Workplace: Management Challenges and Symptoms.* Edward Elgar Publishing.

Lange, K. W., S. Reichl, et al. (2010). "The history of attention deficit hyperactivity disorder." *ADHD Attention Deficit and Hyperactivity Disorders* 2(4): 241–255.

Linehan, M. M. (1993). *Cognitive-Behavioral Treatment of Borderline Personality Disorder.* Guilford Press.

Linehan, M. M. (1993). *Skills Training Manual for Treating Borderline Personality Disorder.* Guilford Press.

Looper, K. J., and J. Paris (2000). "What dimensions underlie cluster B personality disorders?" *Comprehensive Psychiatry* 41(6): 432–437.

Lyon, J., R. Baker, et al. (2009). "Attention deficit hyperactivity disorder and increased risk of injury." *Advances in Medical Sciences* 54(1): 20–26.

Mack, A. H., J. P. Kahn, et al. (2005). "Addictions in the workplace." *Clinical Textbook of Addictive Disorders* 3. Guilford Press.

Mancebo, M. C., J. L. Eisen, et al. (2005). "Obsessive compulsive personality disorder and obsessive compulsive disorder: Clinical characteristics, diagnostic difficulties, and treatment." *Annals of Clinical Psychiatry* 17(4): 197–204.

Mao, A. R., M. Brams, et al. (2011). "A physician's guide to helping patients with ADHD find success in the workplace." *Postgraduate Medicine* 123(5): 60.

Martin, W. F. (2008). "Is your hospital safe? Disruptive behavior and workplace bullying." *Hospital Topics* 86(3): 21–28.

McWilliams, N. (2011). *Psychoanalytic Diagnosis: Understanding Personality Structure in the Clinical Process.* Guilford Press.

Merskey, H. (1995). "Dementia and normal aging." *Journal of Psychiatry and Neuroscience* 20(4): 313.

Miller, D. (2005). "An introduction to Jamaican culture for rehabilitation service providers." *Multicultural Aspects of Counseling Series* 21: 87.

Miller, L. (2003). "Personalities at work: Understanding and managing human nature on the job." *Public Personnel Management* 32(3): 419–434.

Miller, N. S., and J. A. Flaherty (2000). "Effectiveness of coerced addiction treatment (alternative consequences): A review of the clinical research." *Journal of Substance Abuse Treatment* 18(1): 9–16.

Millon, T., C. M. Millon, et al. (2012). *Personality Disorders in Modern Life.* John Wiley and Sons.

Millon, T., E. Simonsen, et al. (1998). "Historical conceptions of psychopathy in the United States and Europe." *Psychopathy: Antisocial, Criminal, and Violent Behavior.* Guilford Press.

Mitchell, S. A., and M. J. Black (1995). *Freud and Beyond: A History of Modern Psychoanalytic Thought.* Basic Books.

Mudrack, P. E. (2004). "Job involvement, obsessive-compulsive personality traits, and workaholic behavioral tendencies." *Journal of Organizational Change Management* 17(5): 490–508.

Murley, J. (2008). *The Rise of True Crime: Twentieth Century Murder and American Popular Culture.* ABC-CLIO.

Nadeau, K. G. (1997). *ADHD in the Workplace.* Brunner/Mazel.

Nadeau, K. G. (2005). "Career choices and workplace challenges for individuals with ADHD." *Journal of Clinical Psychology* 61(5): 549–563.

Nevicka, B., F. S. Ten Velden, A. H. De Hoogh, and A. E. Van Vianen (2011). Reality at odds with perceptions narcisstic leaders and group performance. Psychological Science, 0956797611417259.

Nygård, L. (2004). "Responses of persons with dementia to challenges in daily activities: A synthesis of findings from empirical studies." *American Journal of Occupational Therapy* 58(4): 435–445.

O'Driscoll, K., and J. P. Leach (1998). " 'No longer Gage': An iron bar through the head." *BMJ* 317(7174): 1673–1674.

Öhman, A., L. Nygård, et al. (2001). "The vocational situation in cases of memory deficits or younger-onset dementia." *Scandinavian Journal of Caring Sciences* 15(1): 34–43.

Parkin, A. J. (1999). *Explorations in Cognitive Neuropsychology.* Psychology Press.

Pech, R. J., and B. W. Slade (2007). "Organisational sociopaths: Rarely challenged, often promoted. Why?" *Society and Business Review* 2(3): 254–269.

Pidd, K., and A. M. Roche (2014). "How effective is drug testing as a workplace safety strategy? A systematic review of the evidence." *Accident Analysis and Prevention* 71: 154–165.

Pincus, A. L., and M. R. Lukowitsky (2010). Pathological narcissism and narcisstic personality disorder. *Annual Review of Clinical Psychology,* 6, 421–446.

Pitman, R. K. (1984). "Janet's obsessions and psychasthenia: A synopsis." *Psychiatric Quarterly* 56(4): 291–314.

Raine, A. (2006). "Schizotypal personality: Neurodevelopmental and psychosocial trajectories." *Annual Review of Clinical Psychology* 2: 291–326.

Rastegar, D., and M. Fingerhood (2015). *The American Society of Addiction Medicine Handbook of Addiction Medicine.* Oxford University Press.

Ray, J., and J. Ray (1982). "Some apparent advantages of subclinical psychopathy." *Journal of Social Psychology* 117(1): 135–142.

Resnick, P. J., and O. Kausch (1995). "Violence in the workplace: Role of the consultant." *Consulting Psychology Journal: Practice and Research* 47(4): 213.

Richards, J. (2012). "Examining the exclusion of employees with Asperger syndrome from the workplace." *Personnel Review* 41(5): 630–646.

Ripoll, L. H., J. Zaki, et al. (2013). "Empathic accuracy and cognition in schizotypal personality disorder." *Psychiatry Research* 210(1): 232–241.

Roberts, S., and L. F. Fallon Jr (2001). "Administrative issues related to addiction in the workplace." *Occupational Medicine* 16(3): 509.

Robertson, D., P. Kirkpatrick, et al. (2015). "Sustaining adults with dementia or mild cognitive impairment in employment: A systematic review protocol of qualitative evidence." *JBI Database of Systematic Reviews and Implementation Reports* 13(3): 124–136.

Robertson, J., and D. Evans (2015). "Evaluation of a workplace engagement project for people with younger onset dementia." *Journal of Clinical Nursing* 24(15–16): 2331–2339.

Ronningstam, E. and I. Weinberg (2013). Narcissistic personality disorder: Progress in recognition and treatment. *Focus,* 11(2). 167–177.

Rosell, D. R., S. E. Futterman, et al. (2014). "Schizotypal personality disorder: A current review." *Current Psychiatry Reports* 16(7): 1–12.

Rosenstein, A. H. (2002). "Nurse-physician relationships: Impact on nurse satisfaction and retention." *AJN: The American Journal of Nursing* 102(6): 26–34.

Rosenstein, A. H., and M. O'Daniel (2005). "Original research: Disruptive behavior and clinical outcomes: Perceptions of nurses and physicians: Nurses, physicians, and administrators say that clinicians' disruptive behavior has negative effects on clinical outcomes." *AJN: The American Journal of Nursing* 105(1): 54–64.

Rosenthal, S. A., and T. L. Pittinsky. (2006). Narcisstic leadership. *The Leadership Quarterly,* 17(6), 617–633.

Sadock, B. J. (2000). *Kaplan and Sadock's Comprehensive Textbook of Psychiatry.* Lippincott, Williams, and Wilkins.

Schall, C. M. (2010). "Positive behavior support: Supporting adults with autism spectrum disorders in the workplace." *Journal of Vocational Rehabilitation* 32(2): 109–115.

Schifano, F. (2005). *Addiction at Work: Tackling Drug Use and Misuse in the Workplace.* Gowes.

Scott, A., and M. S. De Barona (2007). "History of Autism." *The Praeger Handbook of Special Education* 6. Praeger.

Secnik, K., A. Swensen, et al. (2005). "Comorbidities and costs of adult patients diagnosed with attention-deficit hyperactivity disorder." *Pharmacoeconomics* 23(1): 93–102.

Seidler, A., A. Nienhaus, et al. (2004). "Psychosocial work factors and dementia." *Occupational and Environmental Medicine* 61(12): 962–971.

Shaffer, H. J., D. A. LaPlante, et al. (2012). *APA Addiction Syndrome Handbook, Vol. 1: Foundations, Influences, and Expressions of Addiction.* American Psychological Association.

Silverman, K., A. DeFulio, et al. (2012). "Maintenance of reinforcement to address the chronic nature of drug addiction." *Preventive Medicine* 55: S46–S53.

Silverman, K., C. J. Wong, et al. (2005). "A Web-based therapeutic workplace for the treatment of drug addiction and chronic unemployment." *Behavior Modification* 29(2): 417–463.

Simone, R., and T. Grandin (2010). *Asperger's on the job: Must-have advice for people with Asperger's or High Functioning Autism, and their employers, educators, and advocates.* Future Horizons.

Sisti, D., M. Young, et al. (2013). "Defining mental illnesses: Can values and objectivity get along?" *BMC Psychiatry* 13(1): 1–4.

Skodol, A. E., J. G. Gunderson, et al. (2002). "Functional impairment in patients with Schizotypal, Borderline, Avoidant, and Obsessive-Compulsive Personality Disorder." *American Journal of Psychiatry* 159(2): 276–283.

Slavit, W. I., A. Reagin, et al. (2009). "An employer's guide to workplace substance abuse: Strategies and treatment recommendations." Center for Prevention and Health Services.

Solanto, M. V., D. J. Marks, et al. (2008). "Development of a new psychosocial treatment for adult ADHD." *Journal of Attention Disorders* 11(6): 728–736.

Sperry, L. (1997). "Leadership dynamics: Character and character structure in executives." *Consulting Psychology Journal: Practice and Research* 49(4): 268.

Stern, A. (1938). "Psychoanalytic investigation and therapy in the borderline group of neuroses." *Psychoanal Q* 7: 467–489.

Stern, T. A., J. F. Rosenbaum, et al. (2008). *Massachusetts General Hospital Comprehensive Clinical Psychiatry.* Elsevier Health Sciences.

Stone, M. H. (1993). *Abnormalities of Personality: Within and Beyond the Realm of Treatment.* W. W. Norton.

Sunstein, C. R., and A. Vermeule (2009). "Conspiracy theories: Causes and cures." *Journal of Political Philosophy* 17(2): 202–227.

Swami, V., T. Chamorro-Premuzic, et al. (2010). "Unanswered questions: A preliminary investigation of personality and individual difference predictors of 9/11 conspiracist beliefs." *Applied Cognitive Psychology* 24(6): 749–761.

Taylor, C. Z. (2002). "Religious addiction: Obsession with spirituality." *Pastoral Psychology* 50(4): 291–315.

Wang, J.-M., and B. H. Kleiner (2004). "Effective employment screening practices." *Management Research News* 27(4/5): 99–107.

Watson, H., C. Godfrey, et al. (2015). "Screening and brief intervention delivery in the workplace to reduce alcohol-related harm: A pilot randomized controlled trial." *International Journal of Nursing Studies* 52(1): 39–48.

Wei, X., M. Wagner, et al. (2014). "Transition to adulthood employment, education, and disengagement in individuals with autism spectrum disorders." *Emerging Adulthood.* Springer.

Weisner, C., Y. Lu, et al. (2009). "Substance use, symptom, and employment outcomes of persons with a workplace mandate for chemical dependency treatment." *Psychiatric Services* 60(5):646–654.

Wenzl, R. (2014). "Dennis Rader cooperating on book about his 10 BTK murders." *Wichita Eagle.*

White, S. W., K. Keonig, et al. (2007). "Social skills development in children with autism spectrum disorders: A review of the intervention research." *Journal of Autism and Developmental Disorders* 37(10): 1858–1868.

White, W. "Significant Events in the History of Addiction Treatment and Recovery in America." http://www.williamwhitepapers.com/pr/Addiction Treatment%26RecoveryInAmerica.pdf.

Wolde, H. T. "SAP looks to recruit people with autism as programmers." http://www.reuters.com/article/2013/05/22/us-sap-autism-idUSB RE94L0ZN20130522.

Woo, S. M., and C. Keatinge (2008). *Diagnosis and Treatment of Mental Disorders Across the Lifespan.* John Wiley and Sons.

Young, K. S., and C. J. Case (2004). "Internet abuse in the workplace: New trends in risk management." *CyberPsychology and Behavior* 7(1): 105–111.

Zanarini, M. C., F. R. Frankenburg, et al. (2003). "The longitudinal course of borderline psychopathology: 6-year prospective follow-up of the phenomenology of borderline personality disorder." *American Journal of Psychiatry* 160(2): 274–283.

Zanarini, M. C., F. R. Frankenburg, et al. (2010). "Time-to-attainment of recovery from borderline personality disorder and its stability: A 10-year prospective follow-up study." *American Journal of Psychiatry* 167(6): 663.

Zlotnick, C., L. Rothschild, et al. (2002). "The role of gender in the clinical presentation of patients with borderline personality disorder." *Journal of Personality Disorders* 16(3): 277–282.